*If you want to combine your unique talents and pc ... irial
world, read* Creativities *to learn an origi ... und.*
Dorie Clark, *Wall Street Journal* bestselling author ... utive
education faculty, Duke U... ... iness

*Whether you're an entrepreneur, a business person, an artist, or working in the community, it's
your creativity that helps you and others make positive change.* Creativities *is revolutionary in
showing how* <u>everybody</u> *has a creative spark that can be developed, and it provides the focus and
the tools to help you make the most of your distinctive gifts.*
Dr. E. LaBrent Chrite, President, Bentley University

Good leaders provide people space to develop their creative talents. Creativities *provides a great
way for leaders and teams to surface individualized approaches to creativity.*
Frances Frei, Harvard Professor, Ted Talker, Thinkers50, Clubhouse Host, bestselling Author of
Unleashed and *Uncommon Service*

*Creativity is the soul of entrepreneurship, the engine of growth, and one of the greatest joys any of
us can experience. And now, finally,* Creativities *comprehensively and luxuriously pulls back the
curtain to enable anyone to change their life by living creatively. One part rigorous analysis, one
part entertainment, and one part inspirational journey, this is the one book on creativity you have
to read.*
Sydney Finkelstein, Dartmouth College Professor, bestselling author of *Superbosses*, and host of
the podcast, *The Sydcast*

Creativities *provides a fascinating journey through international creativity stories, analyzing the ingredients of their success in an entertaining and structured way. A must read for global executives
who struggle to match their need to inspire creativity with the logic of the what, how, where, who
and why of the creative process that the authors so usefully outline in this book.*
Johann Goettler, President & CEO Siemens S.A., Greece

Creativities *is a book for the ages. It provides substantial recommendations for how a wide variety
of people can develop their creative talent: entrepreneurs, those working in creative industries,
those working in creative functions in large and small organizations – in fact, any individual who
just wants to become more creative.* Creativities' *ideas are grounded in a broad base of literatures
and brought to life through brilliant examples, making it an important treatise for scholars in creativity, innovation, and entrepreneurship. Moreover, because of their need to be increasingly more
innovative to enhance their competitiveness and better satisfy their stakeholder's needs, it should
be read by employees in all organizations.*
Michael A. Hitt is a University Distinguished Professor Emeritus, Texas A&M University. Author
of *Strategic Management: State of the Field and Its Future*

*Creativity is becoming more and more important in the digital world. By exploring the what, how,
where, who, and why of creative process,* Creativities *shows us all how we can be more innovative,
making it an exceptional resource for learning and teaching creativity and innovation.*
Hao Jiao, Distinguished Professor in Strategy, Innovation & Entrepreneurship, Beijing Normal
University, P.R.China

*Creativity is the rootstock of the anatomy of creative endeavors. Bilton, Cummings, and ogilvie
brilliantly deconstruct these endeavors, and in doing so have produced a work with the power to
teach us all to appreciate our own creativity as well as that of others. The structure the authors
place around creative occurrences enables the book to read like a collection of short stories,
making* Creativities *a truly enjoyable read wherever you open it. Seldom have I been more invigo-
rated by a book of nonfiction;* Creativities *helped me to see and understand parts of my world I've
spent decades overlooking. Don't make the mistake of assuming that* Creativities *is solely a book
for entrepreneurs, anyone with a genuine interest in how the world is built will be drawn to this,
a creative work in itself.*
Tom Kolditz, Founding Director, Doerr Institute for New Leaders, Rice University; Brigadier
General, US Army (retired); Professor Emeritus, US Military Academy, West Point; and author of
Leadership Reckoning: Can Higher Education Develop the Leaders We Need?

In order to face the real social, environmental and economic challenges we now face, business and community organizations must encourage people's creative thinking rather than stifle it. Creativities shows us how we can harness our unique approaches to creative thinking for the greater good.
Bernard J. Milano, President, KPMG Foundation (1992-2019) and President, The PhD Project (1994-2019)

Finally, with this book, we're seeing creativity democratised, and excellent approaches like jua kali from Kenya and jugaad from India getting recognised. By also focusing on the why of creativity, the authors confirm that necessity should indeed be the mother of invention.
Vincent Ogutu, Vice Chancellor, Strathmore University, Kenya and inventor of *The Innovation Algorithm*

Creativities *offers an incisive and inspiring examination of an elusive subject. If you're seeking to understand the what, how, where, who, and why of creativity, this book is an essential read.*
Daniel H. Pink, #1 *New York Times* bestselling author of *The Power of Regret, A Whole New Mind,* and *Drive*

If you suspected that there must be more than one type of face, place or case of where creativity comes from then this book is for you. Creativities *contains amazing creative approaches from around the world and a cool 'Creativities Canvas' for thinking through what kind of creator you want to be.*
Jeffrey A. Robinson, Prudential Chair in Business, Rutgers University and author of *Black Faces in High Places*

Creativities *shows there is no 'one way' to be creative and that we can all find our own creative approach. It then provides processes, frameworks and ways of thinking to help readers do just that. The 30 inspirational illustrative 'recipes' are the highlight, and the whole package an ideal manual for courses in creativity and innovation in business schools and beyond. One suspects that a certain amount of fun was had in the writing of the book. Certainly, there's a promise of fun and enlightenment in its use!*
Ed Snape, Dean & Chair Professor in Management, School of Business, Hong Kong Baptist University

By addressing the 'what', the 'how', the 'where', the 'who' and the 'why' of creative processes, Creativities *informs, expands and inspires. The book applies a wealth of relevant cases from popular culture that are smoothly engrained within different models and frameworks of creative practices. An accessible and essential read for students and practitioners within the field of creative industries.* Creativities *is stimulating, enjoyable, and most importantly, creative!*
Bjarki Valtysson, Associate Professor, Department of Arts and Cultural Studies, University of Copenhagen

Leaders today are tasked with navigating their organizations through many novel and complex challenges. Success in this environment requires getting the most out of our people. Creativities *provides insightful and practical tools leaders can use to unlock the creative potential of their people, which in turn will support the development of innovative services, products and practices.*
Ian O. Williamson, Dean, Paul Merage School of Business, University of California, Irvine

Creativity drives individual development and is the driving force of society today. In the digital economy era, social production is a creative production and social consumption is an imaginative consumption. Creativity is the thinking tool and action path to solve complex global affairs and create a better life for Human Beings. The three authors of Creativities, through cooperation across the gap of different time zones and the barriers of the COVID-19 epidemic, with extraordinary academic insights and the use of 4W1H (who, what, where, when, and how) logical clues, have sorted out the secret of Creativity. They open a door to a new world of creativity for each of us.
Yong Xiang (Hardy), Professor and Dean of Institute for Cultural Industries, Peking University, P.R.China, and author of *Introduction to Creative Management*

CREATIVITIES

To Kay, Alex, Steve, Anna, Noelle, Kate,
Caithi, Rob, Laurie and Oisín

CREATIVITIES

THE WHAT, HOW, WHERE, WHO AND WHY OF THE CREATIVE PROCESS

CHRIS BILTON

Reader in Creative Industries, Centre for Cultural & Media Policy Studies, University of Warwick, UK

STEPHEN CUMMINGS

Professor of Strategy and Co-Director of The Atom Innovation Space, Victoria University of Wellington, New Zealand

dt ogilvie

Professor of Urban Entrepreneurship & Economic Development, Saunders College of Business, Rochester Institute of Technology, USA

Edward Elgar
PUBLISHING

Cheltenham, UK • Northampton, MA, USA

Published by
Edward Elgar Publishing Limited
The Lypiatts
15 Lansdown Road
Cheltenham
Glos GL50 2JA
UK

Edward Elgar Publishing, Inc.
William Pratt House
9 Dewey Court
Northampton
Massachusetts 01060
USA

A catalogue record for this book
is available from the British Library

Library of Congress Control Number: 2022934696

This book is available electronically in the **Elgar**online
Business subject collection
http://dx.doi.org/10.4337/9781788979481

ISBN 978 1 78897 947 4 (cased)
ISBN 978 1 78897 949 8 (paperback)
ISBN 978 1 78897 948 1 (eBook)

Printed and bound by CPI Group (UK) Ltd, Croydon, CR0 4YY

CONTENTS

PART III   THE WHERE – THE CREATIVE SET-UP

PART IV   THE WHO – ENGAGING CREATIVE USERS AND COMMUNITIES

PART V   THE WHY – CREATIVE PURPOSES

ACKNOWLEDGEMENTS

Thanks first of all to the folks at Edward Elgar: Fran O'Sullivan, for believing in this project and for regular injections of insight and encouragement; to Sabrina Lynott-May, for her patience and diligence in preparing the manuscript for publication; to Natasha Rozenberg for managing the production and design process; to our proofreader Annabel Maunder; and to the marketing team for all their support. Special thanks to Andy Driver and Natasha for our delicious cover, and to Pranesh Das Purandaradoss for his help in developing the initial cover design concept. We are grateful also to Brendon Palmer for the animated 'swinging donuts' *Creativities* video.

Several people helped us preparing recipes – thanks to Tim Wright for insight on #suchtweetsorrow, Marcela Mora y Araujo for advising on South American football, Vicky Heywood and Michael Boyd for sharing their experiences at the RSC, Sholeh Johnston for introducing us to the Young Vic 'Classics For A New Climate' and Vincent Ogutu for sparking our interest in *jua kali* in 2015. Also, many thanks to Deb Cumming and Nina Weaver for allowing us to share their story of the development of the Operational Hijab as the concluding case recipe in the book.

Chris would like to thank his colleagues at Warwick University for ideas and inspiration, especially Ruth Leary and Jo Garde-Hansen. Students on the BA in Media and Creative Industries and the MA in Media and Creative Enterprises were the first readers for many of the ideas and 'recipes' in the book – special thanks to Qianyi Qiu for advising on Papi Jiang. Thank you to my supportive family for sitting through food and sports documentaries during lockdown, and to Rob Bilton for championing the South Park YouTube documentary.

Steve would like to thank friends and colleagues who have listened to and provided feedback on many of the ideas that came to be in this book: Noelle Donnelly, Jesse Pirini, Christina Lubinski, Ben Walker, Sally Davenport, Ian Williamson, Rachael Thacker, Jacquie Harper, Anita Ravji, Colin Kennedy, Lingy Au, Leon Gurevitch, Tui Te Hau, Rachel Taulelei, and all the creative young entrepreneurs who use The Atom/Te Kahu o Te Ao Innovation Space as a base: https://www.wgtn.ac.nz/innovation/the-atom/entrepreneurs

dt would like to thank the students in her creativity classes at Rutgers-Newark, Rutgers Executive MBA Program in Beijing and Shanghai, Sciences Économiques et Gestion à l'Université de REIMS, Centrum Graduate Business School Pontifica Universidad Católica del Peru, and Facultad de Ingeniería en la Universidad del Pacífico, and the executives who have taken her creativity workshops.

Special thanks to Rosemary Nixon and Zoe Morris, formerly both at Emerald Books, for shaping our ideas on this project in the formative stages, more than five years ago. Thank you to all of the participants in our Academy of Management creativity workshops. Thanks to Professor David Wilson, long-time guru on creativity in business, for his influence and advice over the past 20 years. And thank you to all of the creative people, the celebrated and the obscure, who have helped inspire us in writing this book.

NIGELLA, JAMIE AND THE PROCESS OF ENCOURAGING CREATIVITIES

Recipes are useful… Even great abstract painters have first to learn figure drawing. But I want to make it clear, here and now, that you need to acquire your own individual sense of what food is about, rather than just a vast collection of recipes.

Nigella Lawson, *How to Eat*, 1998

A cookbook is a good metaphor for describing the aims and philosophy of this book. But the metaphor needs to be applied with a 'Nigella' attitude. It's 25 years since Lawson's book, *How to Eat*, was published. It marked a creative sea change.

Until that point, cookbooks were written by two types of people: professional chefs or home cooks of renown. Their books captured their recipes like exhibits. Professional chefs exhibited recipes to dazzle and amaze; virtuoso displays that an intrepid few might attempt but the vast majority wouldn't dare. Home cooks presented recipes that took out the guess work and instructed the humble reader how to use their tools and golden rules in order to rescue their dismal previous efforts in the kitchen. Both of these formats also included lots on theoretical principles and proper technique. Inspiring the reader to develop their own particular love of food or approach to creativity was not on the list of selling points of these books.

Lawson, and her creative contemporary, Jamie Oliver, were different. Oliver was an uncouth youth inspired and excited by what he had observed and been given licence to experiment with in the River Café, and he was keen to share the love. Lawson was an avowed non-chef: a food critic who observed hundreds of chefs and loved to eat. Both were well placed to encourage readers to respect cooking and nurture their own passion for it, while breaking free from what Lawson described as 'the tyranny of the recipe'. Nigella, Jamie, and many who followed in their wake, wrote cookbooks not to preserve and force-feed recipes or a particular style of cooking, but to inspire and give confidence to anyone who wanted to develop their own individual sense of creativity with food.

Lawson was not a professional chef and we are not professional creatives. We have backgrounds in theatre, design, business, media, culture, entrepreneurship and managing innovation spaces. We are paid to work in universities. But we've observed a lot of creatives and we've taught creativity to a lot of so-called 'non-creative' types. We've learned a lot, but four things about creativity stand out:

- First, following a prescribed recipe to the letter is not creativity. It's following. Using a recipe or method to learn and gain confidence to do something different, though: that is creative.
- Second, there is no one best way to create: no universal best recipe or style in which to be creative. Subsequently, creativity should be thought of as plural: in terms of *many creativities* rather than just one approach to creativity.
- Third, anyone, with some inspiration and encouragement (which recipes can provide), can be more creative and can develop their own creative approach or 'individual sense', as Nigella put it, along the way.

- Fourth, there are some simple processes, frameworks and ways of thinking that can help people become more creative, and outlining these, to encourage readers to develop their individual sense of creativity, is what this book is about.

This change in cookbooks led by the likes of Jamie and Nigella is one of the contributing factors to the rise in sales of books in this category while most of the market for printed books has declined. In the past few years, cookbooks have experienced double-digit growth, enhanced in 2020 and beyond with Covid-19 a contributing factor. To us, this illustrates that humans crave creative outlets. Preparing food is something that most of us do, largely out of necessity, partly because it is social, partly because it is comforting, partly because it is challenging, and partly because it is a creative outlet. It's all the things that we might wish our work lives, and indeed our lives in general, might be. Being more 'house-bound' during the pandemic encouraged many to seek to create closer to home: and being creative in the kitchen boomed.

While people buy cookbooks for many reasons, perhaps the most intrinsic relates to our desire to be creative beings. It is the ambition to learn to cook creatively – not by copying the recipe faithfully, but by finding inspiration, understanding principles and learning techniques. Consequently, the first rule of *Creativities* is that there are no rules, and each user must develop or cook up their own version of creativity.

There is, of course, a paradox in this: a paradox at the heart of creativity that was recognized by the first to philosophize about it. The paradox is embodied in the statement that the first rule of creativity is that there are no rules; or in the idea that we are, in this book, providing many case examples (i.e., recipes) while bemoaning the tyranny of the recipe.

Philosopher Arthur Koestler, who published the seminal book *The Act of Creation* in 1970, dealt with this paradox through a term he coined as 'bi-sociation'. In the arts, this bi-sociation resulted in a number of creative acts through the combining of a playful *bathos* with a more serious, systematic, and sympathetic *pathos* (illustrations of creative outputs are shown in the middle column of Koestler's illustration shown as Figure 0.1).

Cosmic Simile →	*Hidden Analogy*	← Poetic Image
Witticism →	*Epigram*	← Trouvaille
Satire →	*Social Analysis*	← Allegory
Impersonation →	*Empathy*	← Illusion
Caricature →	*Schematization*	← Stylization
Pun →	*Word Puzzle*	← Rhyme
Riddle →	*Problem*	← Allusion
Debunking →	*Discovering*	← Revealing
Coincidence →	*'Trigger'*	← Fate

bathos ————————→ **SHORTCUT** ←———————— *pathos*

Figure 0.1   Koestler's (1970) concept of bi-sociation leading to creative outputs

Koestler went on to argue that any creativity that adds value requires a shuttling between opposing poles: between understanding and respecting traditions or systems, and then circumventing them; between a classic formula and a new perspective; between a conventional recipe and a distinctive new spin on it (Jamie and Nigella, for example, often created recipes that seemed comfortingly familiar, but 'with a twist').

This key theme of bi-sociation in creativity – the notion that creativity requires shuttling or 'flow' between opposing approaches or poles, one following a pre-determined trail, the other going 'off-piste' – is one that others have explored in different ways before and since Koestler. And you can see a summary of variations on this theme in Figure 0.2.

Poles to bi-sociate between		Key Authors/Ideas
Bathos	Pathos	Koestler (1970)
Right brain	Left brain	Broca (1860s) 'hemispheric' theories of the brain
Madness, neurosis, degeneracy	Sanity, reason, civilization	Lombroso (1880s) Freud (1900s) R D Laing (1960s) Jamieson (1980s)
Divergent (lateral) thinking Incubation, illumination – focus on innovation, risk, change	Convergent (vertical) thinking Preparation, verification – focus on problem-solving, fit-for-purpose, continuity	Creativity authors, e.g. Poincare (1890s) Wallas (1920s) Guilford (1950s) De Bono (1980s)
Intuitive, emotional	Rational, cognitive	Sternberg, Weisberg (1980s) Gardner's 'multiple intelligences' (1980s)
Loose, decentralized autonomy and exploration	Tight structures, narrow focus and strong leadership	'Pop Management' authors, e.g. Tom Peters (c. 1980s – present day)
Discovery	Creation	Entrepreneurship experts (c. 2000–2020)
Out-of-house Divergence	In-house Convergence	Creativities (2022) 5. The Why
1.The What 4.The Who	2.The How 3.The Where	

Figure 0.2   Bi-sociative approaches to creativity

This bi-sociative spirit informs the structure of this book, *Creativities*. But that structure is divided into five parts that span what we call 'In-House Convergence' and 'Out-of-House Divergence': the What, the How, the Where, the Who, and finally, the Why of creativity. These elements and their relationship to one another can be better understood by extending the cooking analogy.

THE WHAT: WHAT INGREDIENTS WILL YOU CREATE WITH?

Creative individuals and approaches are only the beginning of the creative process. They are often the spark where that process begins, but in order for the creative process to catch fire, other ingredients must be sought out – the art of creative cooking is to scan what's available and what's needed, go out to the market (or the pantry, or both) and seek out different ingredients. Choosing the 'right' ingredients means considering which flavours work together, and understanding that too much of some ingredients might be bland or even distasteful. So, in Part I of the book we explore the What of creativity and invite the reader to identify their own creative sparks, and consider what other ingredients might need to be brought to the table to complement them.

THE HOW: HOW WILL YOU COMBINE THE INGREDIENTS?

The How is where we bring what we have got from the market 'in house' and start to think about how we are going to put things together. In Part II of the book, we explain how creative individuals combine together in creative teams and organizations. Psychological models of the creative individual have been largely superseded by sociological or systems models of the creative process which use collective creativity as the unit of analysis, not the individual 'genius'. But aside from the necessity of combining different ingredients, what factors allow creative teams to thrive? Cooks use a range of methods to mix ingredients – kneading, beating and stirring – as well as additional ingredients to bind them together (egg whites, corn starch, flour). Part II of *Creativities* considers the 'how-tos': the techniques used to blend creative ingredients, as well as the hidden catalysts needed to draw out their flavours in interesting ways.

THE WHERE: THE SET-UP OF THE OPERATION IN WHICH YOU WILL CREATE

How you mix the ingredients is important, but you can't consistently create good outcomes without a good framework that fits with, supports and further inspires your creativity. Part III examines where you might look to locate your creative endeavour. The aim, as with any good cook, is to think about how to build an environment, or 'kitchen', where creativity can be nurtured now and for the future – a space, or set of spaces and systems, from which you (and those around you) can deliver your own approach to creativity. So here, in the third part of *Creativities*, we examine the history of creative work processes and places where creativity can happen: from the earliest attempts to formalize organizations to the most avant-garde workspace trends, and the ways in which these forms can enable or hinder your creativity.

THE WHO: WHO ARE YOUR COMMUNITY AND YOUR 'USERS'?

Having worked through the stages in creative production, models of creativity or innovation often draw a line under the completed product. Just as a meal is not only about food, creativity is not only about the product – the value chain extends on through processes of consumption, adaptation and co-creation: on through to other people, in other words. So, what stakeholders and/or community members should you be looking to bring into the fold to work and co-create with? Part IV examines creativity from the other end of the creative process, in the context of delivery and the user experience. At this point, thinking about who your stakeholders (consumers, governments, intermediaries, etc.) are or could be, and involving them in the creative process, can wrap additional value around the original act of creation.

Our first four elements of the creative process line up with the classic models of the creative process outlined in Figure 0.2, as the more divergent What and Who phases seek new inspiration, which is then brought back into focus by the convergent need to articulate the How and the Where. However, the final part of *Creativities* pushes further beyond these classic models of creativity. Our final creative process part envelops the other four. This is the Why of the creative process. The all-important and overlooked or forgotten question of why do you (the individual, the group, or the organization) want to be creative? And, relatedly, what do you want to get out of the process?

THE WHY: WHY DO YOU WANT TO BE CREATIVE?

This final element in the *Creativities* process is one that circles back to consider the whole package together – and then ask the most important question of all: *why*? Why are you creating? Or, what do you want out of this? This is something that may evolve over time, but it is crucial that we continue to pay attention to it throughout. Focusing on the why enables us to consider and be honest about choices like:

- Do you want to build bigger by looking to scale up?
- Expand upon your creative product through adding and diversifying, or focus and scale back?
- Do you want to take away the learnings, divest and move on to something new? Share it with others who can take it further or achieve some social benefits from your creativity or sell to the highest bidder?
- Are you doing it for love or the money, the craft or the fame?

In a music setting, this last contemplation is often called 'the big question'. Band members may provide different answers to that question, which can result in a group splitting (often citing 'artistic differences'). One of the recipes in this final part of *Creativities* will look at this in a very real way, reflecting on the last days of The Beatles. And it turns out that in order to get what you want creatively, love may not be all you need (or it might be).

Each of our five parts of the book will be illustrated with a modicum of theoretical principles (hopefully enough, but not too much to slow you down), a simple and easy-to-remember framework, and a selection of creative 'recipes' from around the world. These are examples of how others in a wide range of creative endeavours have applied different principles. But, in keeping with Nigella's philosophy, these are recipes to inspire, not copy. They are designed to encourage readers to build their own creative style and increase their confidence in putting together their own creative recipes.

In order to encourage this and help you gather and work on your thoughts through these five parts of creativity, we have developed a simple 'Creativities Canvas' (Figure 0.3). It is a good way to build up a picture of your own distinctive creative process or individual style as you move through the book, and a useful way to think about creative approaches with others as you discuss your ideas. And, as with the five elements of our creativities process and the five parts of this book, you can start jotting down ideas anywhere and see how things unfold – the process can and should be iterative: thinking about the How, for example, can lead you to new ideas about the What and trigger ideas about the Who. But, within the systemic linearity of a book, we start on the next few pages by exploring 'the What' of creativity.

SOURCES AND FURTHER READING

The overarching framework for the whole *Creativities* book is inspired by Koestler's theory of 'bi-sociation'. This argues that creative acts come from an unexpected connection between two conventionally disconnected frames of reference. The opposition between 'divergent' and 'convergent' thinking dates back to J. P. Guilford's speech to the American Psychological Association in 1950, often regarded as the beginning of academic creativity research. Howard Gardner (multiple intelligences), Frank Barron ('tolerance for contradictions') and Robert Sternberg (among many others) have all built on this cognitive approach to highlight the duality of the creative process. More recently, the focus of creativity research has shifted from psychology to sociology – we include Sawyer's work as an exemplar of this approach. His interest in 'focus switching' capabilities in teams mirrors psychological theories of switching between divergent and convergent thinking styles.

Barron, F. (1958), 'The Psychology of Imagination', *Scientific American*, **199**, 255–61.
De Bono, E. (1995), *Serious Creativity*, London: HarperCollins Business.
Gardner, H. (1984), *Frames of Mind: The theory of multiple intelligences*, London: Heinemann.
Guilford, J.P. (1950), 'Creativity', American Psychologist, **5**(9), 444–54.
Hoppe, K.D. (1994), 'Affect, Hemispheric Specialisation and Creativity', in M.P. Shaw and M.A. Runco (eds), *Creativity and Affect*, Norwood, NJ: Ablex, 213–24.
Jamison, K.R. (1996), *Touched with Fire: Manic depressive illness and the artistic temperament*, New York: Free Press.

Koestler, A. (1976), *The Act of Creation*, London: Hutchinson [1964].

Mumford, M.D. and S.B. Gustafson (1988), 'Creativity Syndrome: Integration, Application, and Innovation', *Psychological Bulletin*, **103**, 27–43.

Sawyer, R.K. (2006), *Explaining Creativity*, Oxford: Oxford University Press.

Sternberg, R.J. (1988), 'A Three-Facet Model of Creativity', in R.J. Sternberg (ed.), *The Nature of Creativity: Contemporary psychological perspectives*, Cambridge: Cambridge University Press (repr. 1997), 125–47.

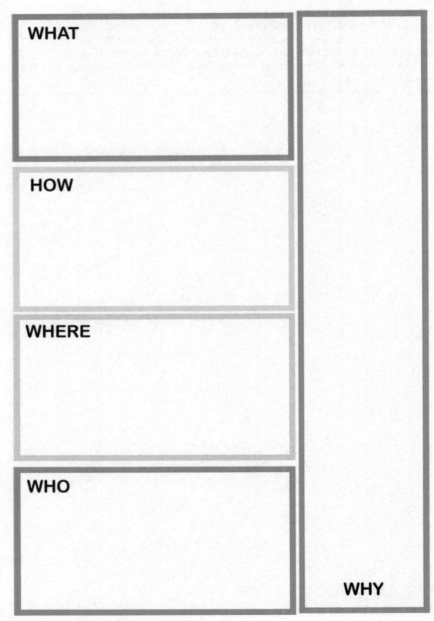

Figure 0.3   The Creativities Canvas

PART I
THE WHAT – CREATIVE ELEMENTS

So, you want to be creative? And you've got some idea of what kind of creator you are and why you want to create (if not, you might want to start by looking at Part V, the Why of creativity).

Let's get started where a chef might begin: at the market. But imagine a different kind of market from the one the chef might be in, though: not full of fresh food, but fresh ingredients with which to create. Before combining these ingredients – people and processes, ideas and traditions, materials and stories – we must first go out and acquire them. Here are four guiding strategies that we've found to be particularly helpful in the 'What should we bring to the table?' stage of the creative process:

- First, if we want to come up with a new recipe, product, service or idea, we may need to seek to bring in new and different elements from those used conventionally.
- Second, if some elements are abundant, be they a particular type of material or an awareness and energy for things like sustainability or social media, we can think about using that 'excess' as a creative spark for an innovative approach.
- Third, can we explore local traditions and approaches and consider new ways of working with them to develop something authentic, but with a novel twist?
- Fourth, if some ingredients that we think we need are in short supply, can we use that scarcity to trigger ideas about new ways to create or new creative offerings?

Seek out the different, don't overlook the abundant, use scarcity as a trigger, think about twisting a tradition – can we create a framework with these four strategies?

One of the clichés of creativity is the instruction to 'think outside the box' – it's the go-to line when somebody asks a sensible question like, 'but what do you mean when you tell us, "be more creative?"' This notion is usually taken to have something to do with 'divergent thinking' or 'thinking different'. But the instruction is not very helpful:

- Where is the outside of the box?
- Where is the box?
- How can we think outside it if we and our subject matter are inside it?
- Can we bring what is outside back to the inside?

'Think outside the box' raises more questions than answers.

In fact, one of the pioneers of creativity research, Margaret Boden, preferred to describe creativity happening *inside* a box – pushing at the edges and stretching its limits in order to transform it. This seems to us to be a more dynamic and also a more realistic way of describing the effort and discipline needed for creativity. People used to use another phrase about creativity a lot more: 'pushing the envelope'. It was a more grounded metaphor, about pushing the limits of what's possible or desirable, that, like Boden, spoke more to the struggles and constraints and effort needed to generate creativity. Maybe there was something in that – so we're bringing it back. The framework we outline for thinking about the six recipes or case examples in this part of the book, and for developing your own individual approaches to creativity, is a variation on the 'pushing the envelope' theme.

The 'What' framework: the market crate

Imagine being in that market of creative ingredients again. Let's think about how to gather up what your creative project needs. Because we don't want to encourage you to think outside any boxes, we will refer instead to a 'crate' that you might carry – a crate to carry our ingredients. To achieve Margaret Boden's creative transformation, we need to push against the boundaries of what we might fill our crate with if we were following the status quo, and extend its edges and your possibilities. Pushing at the sides of the creativity crate can inspire us in four directions:

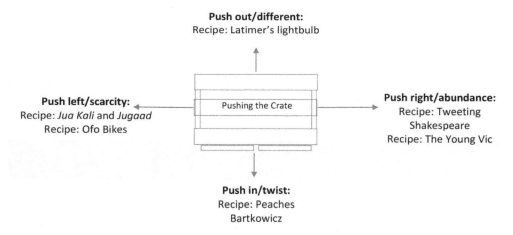

Figure 1.1   Creativities framework 1: the creative market crate

1. Outwards: incorporating different ingredients; ingredient sourcing for change; looking to do different with diversity.
2. Rightwards: gathering additional or excessive ingredients; going beyond what is expected.
3. Inwards: exploring traditional/authentic approaches but in new ways; reinventing traditions, with a twist.
4. Leftwards: embracing frugality and using fewer ingredients; using less to do different.

We'll explore what it means to push things creatively in each of these directions below, and provide six recipes to inspire you to think differently about how you might go to the market to gather your ingredients for creativity.

1.1   PUSHING OUT: GATHERING DIFFERENT

As described in our introduction to *Creativities*, creativity bridges between different, apparently contradictory frames of reference and thinking. In order to make these creative connections, we need a broad enough range of ideas and thinking styles in the first place. In an organization or team, this variety also requires including different types of people with different experiences and perspectives.

Browsing the market of ideas requires curiosity and tolerance. The creative cook's curiosity is piqued by ideas or individuals which challenge expectations and stereotypes. Not only are these unexpected and unfamiliar flavours tolerated; they are sought out and relished.

Creativity thrives on contradictions: the logical, incremental thinker and the intuitive lateral thinker; the solution that perfectly fits the problem like the final piece in a jigsaw, and the solution that breaks the pattern and opens a whole new set of questions; an immersion in craft, skill and tradition and a willingness to experiment; a moment's inspiration and 10,000 hours of perspiration.

Many creative processes and creatives fail because they lack this variety. Perhaps they have not devoted enough time and attention to gather a range of different elements in the first place. Perhaps they have forgotten how to use the variety they have, or allowed one set of ingredients to swamp the rest. Our first recipe illustrates the importance of bringing a variety of ingredients and creative forces to the table at the start of the creative process, rather than relying on just one individual or perspective and hoping for a single lightning strike.

RECIPE 1. LEWIS LATIMER: LOOKING BEYOND THE 'LIGHT BULB MOMENT' (MENLO PARK)

INGREDIENTS:

- One celebrity inventor–entrepreneur (Thomas Edison)
- One African-American draughtsman
- A carbonized bamboo light bulb filament which burns out after a few days
- An interest in how inventions are used, not just how they are discovered

> All of Latimer's inventions, patented and unpatented, relate to improving the quality of life.
>
> Bayla Singer, *The Edison Papers*

On 8 July 2020, former West Indian cricketer and commentator Michael Holding asked British TV viewers, 'Who invented the light bulb?' Most people know that the inventor of the light bulb was Thomas Edison. But Holding explained that the carbon filament in the light bulb, essential to the successful development of the light bulb, was the invention of a black American, Lewis Latimer. Latimer worked for Edison's rival, Hiram Maxim, at the US Electric Light Company. Latimer patented his invention in 1881. In 1885 he left Maxim to work for Edison.

Holding's argument was that most of us make assumptions about what an inventor looks like – and that mental image does not include a black man, the son of runaway slaves, who had taught himself technical drawing and risen through the ranks.

More broadly, though, he was also pointing out that we assume that creativity involves a single moment of breakthrough thinking by a single person or unit – like Edison, or Watson and Crick discovering DNA – when in fact Edison was one of several individuals and corporations working in competition and together racing towards the goal of harnessing electrical power. The focus on a single, particular type of person is linked to the focus on a particular stage in the creative process, the moment of discovery. Metaphorically this is often represented as a spark, a flash, an instant: the 'light bulb' or eureka moment.

Much like Watson and Crick with their 'discovery' of DNA (which probably would not have happened but for the often overlooked Rosalind Franklin – look her up), Edison gets the creative credit for a collective effort with many elements. But without the successful adaptation of his invention by Latimer, Edison's light bulb would have remained a practical and commercial failure. Without Latimer, Edison's creative legacy may have been quite different.

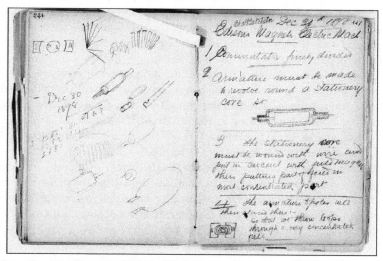

Figure 1.2   Excerpt from the Edison/Batchelor notebooks (Edison's notes on the left, Batchelor's on the right)

Edison himself realized his own creative limitations and built research teams containing ingredients and personnel that complemented his strengths and weaknesses. For example, much is made of the competition between Edison and Nikola Tesla. But it was Edison who gave the Serbian his first break in America, hiring him to work at his Menlo Park research lab. Edison learned much from Tesla's brilliance and ingenuity. And Edison's own divergent inventiveness was complemented by more structured convergent thinkers like Englishman Charles Batchelor, whose task was often to try and make sense of Edison's scattershot combinations of ideas. The two often used the same notebook, with Edison scribbling his thoughts on one page and Batchelor seeking to work them out on the opposing leaf. Such collaborative bi-sociation proved enormously effective.

Latimer was content to help improve others' inventions rather than take the limelight for himself – for example, he contributed to Alexander Graham Bell's patent for the telephone (another invention which is credited to one man rather than to the several innovations which preceded it). There is a generosity and a modesty to Latimer's approach, as well as a focus on practical outcomes rather than conceptual breakthroughs. He not only invented things; he was interested in how they would be used (later he would play a pioneering role in the installation of street lighting systems in cities like New York, Philadelphia, Montreal and London). Yet these contributions – the adaptation of an idea, the technical drawings which make an idea understandable (and subject to a legal patent) – are surely no less important.

The bias towards a singular type of thinking and a particular type of creative person or group underpins the 'myth of genius' in the arts and creative industries too. Picasso denied the influence of African art during his 'African period', notably in his 1909 painting, *Les Demoiselles d'Avignon* – maintaining the apparent purity of European modernist painting and his own role as a visionary artist. In our own times, black artists (actors, directors and writers) have been similarly marginalized, perhaps because, like Lewis Latimer, they don't conform to the conventional notion of what a successful creator in those fields looks like.

Illumination of the genius individual and the light bulb moment of discovery casts a long shadow. Hidden from view, outside the spotlight, it is possible to identify a range of roles, people and contributions waiting in the wings, all playing their part in the creative process. The problem identified by Michael Holding is that by occluding these other people and other types of thinking from our mental picture of creativity, we not only blank out the multiple stages in the creative process; we also discourage other people like Latimer from coming forward. Latimer was himself a victim of this selective focus, both in his own lifetime, forced by his colour to accept a secondary, supporting role in the biographies of Edison and Bell, and in his legacy, depriving other black inventors, technicians and scientists of a potential role model for the future.

Creativities argues for a diversity of thought in the creative process – recognizing its multiplicity, sometimes even its apparent contradictions (like Batchelor's combination with Edison). Diversity of thought is not necessarily correlated to diversity of personnel – but it is surely made more likely. Recognizing the diversity of contributions – by the likes of Latimer, or Tesla or Batchelor or Rosalind Franklin – challenges our perceptions of creativity as the preserve of a particular type of person or people, or one type of thinking.

It should also encourage you to consider whether you have the ingredients necessary on your own to achieve your creative goals; or if you should be looking to push up and out and seek to bring other elements to your creative table, as did Edison the creative force (rather than Edison the celebrity/myth).

RESOURCES

Bilton, C. and S. Cummings (2010), *Creative Strategy: Reconnecting business and innovation*, Wiley.

'Lewis H. Latimer, Electrical Pioneer and Pioneer, a Seldom-Told Story' (video): www .lewislatimerhouse.org/about

Singer, B. (2005), *Inventing a Better Life: Latimer's technical career 1880–1928* (The Edison Papers): https://edison.rutgers.edu/latimer/invtlife.htm

1.2   PUSHING RIGHT: USING ABUNDANCE

As with any recipe, too much of a good thing results in one flavour drowning out the rest. As we will discuss in the next part of the book, once we start blending ingredients together, excess can be the enemy of creativity – excessive reliance on one person or type of thinking can result in over-elaboration and overproduction. Abundance can be useful; the trick is not to produce more, but to produce better. Excess means repeating and amassing more of the same; abundance means using what we have to change expectations and perceptions of what we think we need or want.

The Covid-19 outbreak of 2020 provided many people with an excess of that precious commodity, time. Given that many of us complain about deadlines and not having enough time and space to be truly creative, this might have seemed like a rare silver lining amid the outbreak. But for most of us, promises to write novels, learn languages and take up yoga collapsed in the vacuum of an excess of time and too little structure. For professional artists, abundance of time combined with scarcity of paid work. Rather than using that additional time to produce more (with limited possibility for selling or disseminating the resulting content), many experimented with doing things differently (new modes of online collaboration, developing new skills).

When IKEA's Chief Sustainability Officer spoke of reaching 'peak stuff', he described another form of excess. The generation of novel ideas and products without apparent purpose or value is not creativity; it amounts to what Boden calls 'mere novelty'. In the context of global sustainability, this proliferation is not just unnecessary; it becomes an existential threat. How many more updates for our mobile phone do we actually want or need? How many new devices can we use? How much media content can we absorb? The generation of new ideas without apparent uses or audiences produces the intellectual equivalent of landfill when we should be recycling.

Abundance requires a different mindset, using our resources to create value, not change for change's sake. Instead of exceeding people's needs, abundance exceeds their expectations and perceptions, providing them with what they did not know they needed. We will say more about excess later. But in this part of *Creativities* we want to make a positive case for abundance. Using what we have in abundance allows us to stretch and challenge expectations, boundaries and perceptions.

The problems confronting arts professionals in 2020 were accompanied by an accumulation of amateur, everyday creativity – ordinary people exercising their creative abilities, sometimes for the first time. The destruction of the economy and livelihoods at the same time released an abundance of amateur, home-grown creative content. Poems and photographs appeared on social media timelines. Memes and videos were exchanged on WhatsApp.

Digital technology has made possible a new sharing economy. Clay Shirky has described the 'cognitive surplus' resulting from individuals creating new forms of content online. He suggests that this is exemplified by YouTube and Wikipedia, where an individual 'gift economy' driven by a desire to create and share content online, accumulates into a massive online resource available to all. We will revisit this hi-tech gift economy in Part IV when we consider the expanding circles of creative participation and amateur creativity, especially online.

The longer history of this everyday creative abundance can be found in the participatory arts movement, known in the 1970s and 1980s as 'community arts' in the UK and US, or 'socioculture' in Europe. Participatory arts uses the abundance of creative possibilities, skills and impulses among a large group of participants and weaves these together into an artefact – a festival, a community performance or exhibition, a quilt or mural.

Everyday participation needs to be channelled or curated. With a collective focus, individual creative acts accumulate into something larger and more meaningful. During the 1980s, this was the job of the community arts worker or 'sociocultural animateur' – to stimulate and guide the creative efforts of communities, using professional expertise and experience to build and connect their creativities, not to suffocate their enthusiasms under professional expectations and standards. This requires, in turn, a certain kind of transformational leadership, 'leading from below' without ego or agenda. This is not easy, and there have been plenty of participatory arts projects which have simply served the vision and will of the supervising artist, or conversely, where the self-effacing light touch of leadership has resulted in chaos and confusion. But at its best, participatory arts, like the 'cognitive surplus' described by Shirky, makes possible something extraordinary – using the abundance of everyday imaginations not just to do more but to produce something different from professional creative practice.

The affordances of digital technologies open up new possibilities for participatory arts, allowing multiple stories and ideas to be integrated across platforms and enabling new forms of interactivity. This 'transmedia' approach to storytelling has been deployed to mobilize previously unheard stories, from immigrant communities to elderly people in care homes and children. Not only are different voices amplified, the participants take over the story, taking it in unexpected directions. Our next recipe illustrates the cumulative effect of utilizing an abundance of participatory storytelling.

RECIPE 2. ROYAL SHAKESPEARE COMPANY I: SUCH TWEET SORROW (STRATFORD-UPON-AVON)

INGREDIENTS:

- Six actors, two writers, a network of fans
- A classical play
- An unfamiliar tech platform
- 140 characters per tweet

In 2010, the Royal Shakespeare Company collaborated with Mudlark and Channel 4's digital investment division in an experimental reimagining of *Romeo and Juliet* told through the medium of Twitter, using the hashtag #suchtweet or 'Such Tweet Sorrow'.

Spread over three weeks (the duration of the play), a group of six actors improvised around a framework devised by writers Tim Wright and Bethany Marlow. Each day the actors were given certain actions or plot points they needed to cover – crucially they were also briefed on information they should not say or know until later in the story. Otherwise, they were free to improvise within the limits of Twitter's 140-character limit. The actors were in effect co-opted as co-writers.

With each character tweeting throughout the day, it was difficult for audiences to keep across all of the material being produced. Many would choose to follow one or two characters. Indeed, one of the pleasures of the project was seeing the drama through the eyes of one character, with imperfect knowledge of the wider context; this was something the RSC would pick up in a follow-up project telling the story of *Midsummer Night's Dream* from the perspective of minor characters (Rude Mechanicals, Fairies) rather than protagonists. Some committed #suchtweet fans would gather at the end of the day to compare notes from different parts of the story. Much of the plot played out as rumours and hearsay – nobody seemed quite sure what was happening. Some of the more improbable elements in Shakespeare's story (inexplicable delays to crucial letters, thinking somebody is dead when they are still alive) were well suited to this social media web of gossip and intrigue.

As the story unfolded, audiences started to become more involved. They began to create memes and pictures, even writing themselves into the story in supporting roles. One group of mostly female fans began tweeting under the hashtag #SaveMercutio, following the fight with Tybalt. As Tim Wright notes, their involvement in the story superseded their knowledge of the plot. Wright's own background in digital storytelling helped him to orchestrate this co-creativity – he began to write in new characters on other platforms to weave together some of the threads – Mrs Capulet mysteriously emerged on a Tumblr account; another character, Jago (loosely based on *Othello*'s Iago), also began to provide a misanthropic commentary on the action. Meanwhile, Romeo spent the first week playing an immersive roleplay game 'Medal of Honour' and some audience members had the serendipitous pleasure of discovering him and chatting with him 'offstage' on Xbox Live before he made his entrance to the main action in week 2.

At the same time, Wright acted as a showrunner for the beleaguered actors. Alongside the daily call sheets, a back-channel 'Campfire' was established through which Wright briefed actors having to deal with excited or hostile audience members. A decision was made not to block users, but sometimes silence was the best policy. The actors themselves, like the audience, began to run away with the story. Tybalt became increasingly fiery, and Wright had to occasionally intervene to moderate offensive language in consideration of younger audience members. Romeo, perhaps reacting to negative critical reviews of the lack of 'poetry', became increasingly flowery in his language. Actors had to be reminded of individual and collective timelines, briefed on latest audience behaviour and supported through key plot points (the first meeting of Romeo and Juliet, the knife fight).

Critical responses to #suchtweet were almost entirely negative, even outright hostile. This was not Shakespeare. There was no poetry in the language. The characters were not Shakespeare's. The story didn't make sense. There was too much material. Actors were overtelling the story. The independent theatre community was similarly negative – the money could have been better spent doing something else. This was not a promising direction for digital theatre. Negative blog posts proliferated, many using the #suchtweet hashtag to drive up traffic on their own accounts. The RSC itself seemed ill-prepared to deal with the interactive elements of the story, unsure whether to rein in Twitter users or let the user-generated content take centre stage. One ill-judged piece of product placement by the sponsorship and fundraising department (a branded mobile phone) provoked an audience backlash, highlighting the importance of trust and transparency in a collaborative project. The RSC Education department was perhaps the main beneficiary of the project – for all its faults, #suchtweet did provide a useful way into the play (a set text in English schools at the time) for young people.

And yet, in other ways, as an experiment in transmedia storytelling, fandom and user-generated content, Such Tweet Sorrow was a pioneering project. At the time, Twitter was in its infancy – indeed one negative criticism was the unimaginable absurdity of young people sharing teenage gossip on a platform populated by geeks and journalists. The RSC, under the tutelage of the head of digital development Sarah Ellis, continued to push the digital envelope. Three years later, *A Midsummer Night's Dreaming* was a collaboration with Google Creative Lab, playing out over three nights on a variety of platforms with a focus on user-generated content. The attempt to open out the minor characters and subplots behind the main action built on #suchtweet's model, but this time with closer attention to Shakespeare's original play. Again 'education' was not only directed to schools and young people but to the RSC itself, learning the strengths and limitations of diverse digital platforms and tools.

As a rendition of a Shakespeare play then, Such Tweet Sorrow can be considered a failure. But as an example of cumulative creativity – providing a framework for collective storytelling by a diverse audience – it was undoubtedly successful. The enormous volume of material, which from a conventional storytelling perspective was bewildering and overwhelming, allowed users to interact as both readers and writers in unexpected ways.

Tim Wright, one of the two writers initially commissioned and subsequently involved in project-managing the production, reflects on the shift from analogue culture to 'stream culture'. Audiences dip into the stream, they encounter one piece of content, they miss thousands of others. FOMO, 'fear of missing out', is part of this experience, but there is also an opportunity to immerse oneself in the stream, to interact, to swim with or against the current, encountering unexpected and unique discoveries along the way. Such abundance is unfamiliar to the professional creative artist (or indeed a traditional theatre audience), disciplined to structure, contain and edit rather than to release and tolerate random connections.

Above all, as with the 'cognitive surplus' of any participatory project, #suchtweet offers an abundance of everyday creativity, user-generated content and co-creation. Creativity extends beyond the creative professional to a groundswell of abundant, excessive, collective creativity. The traditional position of the professional artist is displaced but not erased. One final lesson of #suchtweet is that collective creativity needs to be not only released but also orchestrated, channelled and sustained – and this requires a new type of creative facilitation by a new generation of digitally savvy, open-minded, collaborative storytellers.

How might you bring to the table a new abundance of energy or another new ingredient to add to your, or your team's, creativity?

RESOURCES

https://twitter.com/such_tweet
www.hannahnicklin.com/2010/04/such-tweet-sorrow-a-blog-post-in-two-acts/
www.theguardian.com/culture/2010/apr/12/shakespeare-twitter-such-tweet-sorrow

The Such Tweet Sorrow recipe shows how abundance can lead to unexpected creative outcomes by enabling user participation – a theme we will revisit in Part IV. In a stream culture, abundance accumulates multiple options and experiences, which can expand creative possibilities. Recipe 3 demonstrates how abundance can be utilized in a more deliberate, purposeful way: not opening out to a wider world but drawing together creative contributions around a single goal. We call this networked creativity.

Whereas *cumulative creativity*, of the kind we saw in Such Tweet Sorrow, works through volume, *networked creativity* works through concentration: the different participants may spread outwards, but the shared purpose draws them together. The approach has some similarities with crowdsourcing, where idea generation is outsourced to the 'wisdom of the crowd'. But crowdsourcing is usually selective. By casting the net widely, an organization initiates a broad, randomized search, hoping to find the one transformative idea which will then be adopted and applied. Networked creativity is not aiming to identify one good idea, but to connect together multiple good ideas in order to achieve a common goal.

RECIPE 3. THE YOUNG VIC: NETWORKING CREATIVITY (LONDON)

INGREDIENTS:

- A global emergency
- A national theatre
- A local network
- Wooden tickets, a pile of sand, a can of beer

Climate change and environmental protection require creative solutions. One set of solutions involves technological innovation, for example changing the materials used in construction, or finding alternative energy sources. Yet some of these technological innovations carry an environmental cost, either at the point of production (use of resources, rare minerals) or consumption (passing on the environmental costs to individual consumers at home, increased carbon emissions). Measuring environmental impacts requires a wide-angle view as well as a long-term vision; one-off technological innovations ripple outwards into a wider set of changes in production and consumption.

Accordingly, the biggest challenge posed by climate change is not technological but behavioural: how can consumers be encouraged to consume less? Can creative thinking be applied to reduce the carbon footprint of consumption as well as production? A secondary challenge is to change the way we evaluate innovation and change, looking beyond the immediate solution to its secondary impacts.

In 2012, the Young Vic Theatre in London set out to reduce the carbon footprint of its productions by 60%. The initiative was supported by Julie's Bicycle, a non-profit organization which promotes environmental sustainability in the creative industries. The initiative was applied to a series of shows called 'Classics for a New Climate', beginning with *After Miss Julie* (adapted from Strindberg's play) and followed by *La Musica*.

The company began by changing its production processes, for example by bringing forward rehearsal times to make better use of daylight hours. Other innovations included relaxing the 'optimum' temperature for the venue from a fixed 22 degrees to a range of 18–24 degrees. The theatre introduced reusable wooden tokens instead of tickets. The marketing team moved towards a paperless publicity campaign; with the exception of some posters at the front of the venue, all publicity materials were issued electronically, resulting in a 99% reduction in emissions from paper use for *After Miss Julie*. Actors and other staff, and audiences, were encouraged to use public transport or bicycles; transport emissions for *After Miss Julie* were reduced by 68%.

All of these innovations contributed to the overall target of reducing emissions. Yet each was a self-contained initiative; some may have carried a deferred environmental cost (for example, users choosing to print off electronic publicity materials, the emissions from public transport).

The most far-reaching and wide-ranging innovations came through the production design. Here the show's designer deliberately chose to work with recycled materials, giving a broad specification. A stage manager was engaged for an additional three weeks to help source props and costumes locally. This reduced the production costs of the play (which typically account for 5% of a theatre's total carbon footprint). It also helped to create a network of local resources and partners, all of whom were made aware of the Young Vic's initiative. The second play in the series, *La Musica*, directly benefited from this legacy, with 35% of its costumes, props and set coming from within a 0.4-mile radius of the venue, significantly reducing transport costs. *La Musica* went a step further by recycling part of its set from another Young Vic production. Some of the set materials were recycled within the theatre, turned into furniture for audiences; others were recycled through Scenery Salvage and Set Exchange, joining the Young Vic into a network of environmentally conscious theatres across the country.

These innovations had a network effect beyond a single production or series, and beyond the theatre itself. The restaurant and bar cooperated with local suppliers; one local brewery supplied beer in cans which could be taken into the venue, avoiding the ban on glasses and bottles which in return required drinks to be poured into plastic cups. Playscripts were recycled to local secondary schools. Local schools and clubs were given free tickets, meaning that 10% of audiences were within walking distance of the venue. The sand used in one production was donated to a local nursery's play area.

As well as networking with other neighbourhood organizations and community groups, the Young Vic worked with its audiences. The wooden tickets were cumbersome to use, but this difficulty may well have made audiences more aware of the theatre's environmental sustainability project. Audiences for *After Miss Julie* could hire a programme instead of buying it; the programme itself was peppered with information on the show's environmental initiatives, and the actors' biographies mentioned the biggest environmental challenges they had faced during the production. *La Musica* took this a stage further and painted the production information on the wall, negating the need for programmes. At the end of the show, audiences exited through a 'green walkway' featuring a mural describing the production's environmental actions.

As with the scientific discoveries featured in Recipe 1, creativity is often associated with singular inventions – a one-off piece of breakthrough thinking, often by a single individual. However, the value component in creativity depends on a wider perspective – what have been the consequences of the creative act, beyond the moment and place of action? This broader perspective is particularly resonant in the context of sustainability – measuring environmental impacts requires a longitudinal, big-picture approach which accounts for multiple users and multiple stages.

The impact of 'Classics for a New Climate' spread beyond one set of initiatives by one venue. Local partners joined in to support the project, leaving a legacy of relationships with local suppliers which could provide resources and partners for future sustainability work. Audiences took the principles of sustainability home with them. One of the surprising metrics in the Julie's Bicycle audit of the project revealed audience individual energy consumption to be lower in the theatre than at home; any changes in behaviour resulting from the show could accordingly have an even greater impact in the aftermath.

Rippling outwards from the Young Vic Theatre, these secondary impacts reflect a systems model of creativity in which individual creative acts are embedded in a field (the network of local businesses around the theatre) and a domain (the various stakeholders involved beyond the cast and crew, in particular the audience). The approach of opening up the project through local partnerships and audience engagement to tap into a surplus of energy in the community for sustainability and give people something tangible to put their energies towards in this regard also describes a democratizing approach to creativity. Here the creative work is shared and collective action continues to stoke a cognitive surplus beyond one individual attacking a problem alone.

As an approach to sustainability in the creative industries, Classics for a New Climate broke new ground – it also introduced a distinctive type of creativity, based on participation, networks and collective value creation. Perhaps it can inspire others to tap into an abundance of passion for other causes in their communities.

RESOURCES

www.juliesbicycle.com/latest/case-studies/3410-after-miss-julie-at-the-young-vic/
www.juliesbicycle.com/latest/case-studies/11381-youngvicla-musica/
www.juliesbicycle.com/resources/sustainable-production-guide

1.3   PUSHING IN: TRADITION WITH A TWIST AND EVOLVING AUTHENTICITY

We began Part I of *Creativities* by pushing out, seeking out difference and diversity in order to challenge conventional definitions and assumptions regarding creativity. Now we consider the bi-sociative opposite move: pushing in, in pursuit of authenticity and integrity.

The pursuit of difference is equated with 'mere novelty' – and novelty without value is not creativity. The counterbalance to novelty in theories of creativity is value. What is valuable is sometimes reduced to 'fitness for purpose', or, more crudely, 'what works'. Here we argue that 'pushing in' also requires a certain integrity to our own intrinsic values and beliefs, rather than chasing after the unfamiliar and exotic.

While 'pushing out' is important to engage with new and unfamiliar ideas, these novel ideas need to be integrated with the familiar. 'Pushing in' encourages us to embed new discoveries with our pre-existing experiences, traditions and resources. In culinary terms, this is the difference between attempting to replicate a recipe from a different culture, and trying to adapt that recipe to fit with some of our own ingredients, methods and tastes.

Definitions and 'recipes' for creativity are themselves highly variable, based on different cultures, politics, philosophies, religions or anthropological traditions. Importing a recipe from another creative culture requires some 'pushing in' to connect with our own creative resources and needs.

The Western recipe for creativity has its roots in 16th-century humanism, when European philosophers rebuilt their worldview around human endeavour instead of an all-powerful God. But the word 'creativity' only became popularized in the 19th century with the rise of

Romanticism, which amplified an individual vision capable of transcending everyday collective norms and tradition. Eastern cultures, including Buddhism and Confucianism, have placed much greater emphasis on those collective traditions. Some Eastern religious traditions view the artist as a shaman, a vessel through which a greater creative power flows. To this day, many indigenous cultural traditions (for example, Aboriginal Australians or African tribes) eschew the idea of individual authorship, relying instead on traditional knowledge and wisdom which are shared by the tribe. When these other traditions confront the Western recipe for creativity, the ingredients do not mix. For example, Western intellectual property law is framed by the concept of the individual author or inventor who originates a new idea. Tribal artefacts do not conform to this model, leaving them with little protection against predatory Western entrepreneurs and importers. Confucianism emphasizes imitation over originality, and China too has struggled to conform with Western conventions on copyright in the creative industries. When we mix up the different regional traditions, recipes have to be adapted or even abandoned altogether.

Pushing in requires us to adapt, based on an understanding of our own values and traditions. Recipes from other cultures can provide inspiration, but will need to be adapted to incorporate locally available ingredients. This is the essence of regional flavours or 'terroir'. Just as Chinese food will taste different in London or San Francisco from Guangzhou, and a pizza in Brooklyn will taste different from one in Naples, so Wallas' recipe for creativity (preparation, incubation, illumination, verification) will need to be remixed – not only for different geographical territories, but for different organizational cultures, even for different individuals.

Good examples of this can be seen in television series like David Chang's *Ugly Delicious*, which explores the delicate balance required to at once honour and tweak or twist food classics with long traditions like tacos, fried rice or fried chicken; or Frank Pinello's *The Pizza Show*, which similarly looks at the respect, knowledge and love required to take that most basic and revered fast food and continue to serve it up in creative ways.

Pushing in recognizes that 'authentic' creativity is rooted in a shared ethos or culture. Grabbing ingredients off the shelf in pursuit of a magical formula might be a way of shaking up our creative practice, but it is unlikely to be sustainable unless it can be connected into existing skills, ideas and traditions. The market's cornucopia of ideas and practices can dazzle and seduce us away from what we really need. We should be especially wary of attempting to replicate 'authentic' ideas and methods from other cultures which we don't fully understand. Authenticity requires us to remake the foreign and the exotic in our own image: repetition with a twist.

Sometimes creative ideas come not from pushing out to the unfamiliar, but pushing in to discover our own capabilities or even our limitations. A tennis backhand may not be the most exciting recipe for creativity. But the way most people hit that shot today is completely different from the way it was played just a few decades ago. The creative twist that gave rise to the modern backhand came from two teenage girls: Chrissie Evert and Peaches Bartkowicz. And rather than trying to copy somebody else, it started with doing what came naturally.

RECIPE 4. PEACHES BARTKOWICZ: THE TWIST BEHIND THE MODERN BACKHAND (LOUISVILLE)

INGREDIENTS:

- 1 Peaches
- 1 concrete wall
- Mentors who backed a unique individual to keep doing it her way
- A ground-breaking professional league (mixed with an atmosphere of women's liberation)
- Two hands (not one)

One of the most breath-taking aspects of Roger Federer's tennis is his backhand: modern observers stand in awe of it, often marvelling that he only uses one hand!

While this shot may seem remarkable in a world where only two of the top-100 women pros and a dozen of the men hit the shot with one hand (down from 28 in 2010 and 43 in 2000), it was only 50 years ago that everybody hit the backhand this way. Even Federer thinks kids should learn the two-handed version now. Why? 'It's easier', he says (www .atptour.com/en/news/federer-tsitsipas-future-one-handed-backhand-2019). But it is also because it enables a shot that traditionally was largely a defensive one to become, for many players, an attacking weapon hit with greater spin and at greater angles.

So, where did the modern two-handed backhand come from? Did it coincide with advances in sports science? The application of ergonomics? Or the use of computer-aided design and simulations? No. It came from a girl named Peaches who shouldn't even have been playing tennis and her competitor Chrissie Evert.

The United States was the world's tennis mecca in the late 1960s (another historical fact that seems hard to fathom now), but it was a sport generally enjoyed by the well-to-do men and their wives in the traditional country-club set.

In the mid-1960s, Jean (known as Peaches) Bartkowicz from the little town of Hamtramack, Michigan, was not particularly well-to-do. One summer, late in the 1950s, she found an old, discarded racquet in the bushes behind the tennis courts. With little to entertain herself, she mended the racquet, started hitting a ball against a concrete back-board and kept at it. The racquet was so heavy that she hit a backhand with it the only way she could as it accelerated off the concrete wall: with two hands.

Today's two-handed players were fortunate that Hamtramack was also the home of dynamic husband and wife tennis coaching duo Jean and Jerry Hoxie. The couple ran a unique public camp for kids at the same municipal courts where Peaches found her racquet. Jean in particular – the first woman in Michigan to coach a boy's high school tennis team – was something of a local personality. Peaches saw the Hoxies' camp and joined in.

Peaches, not knowing that she shouldn't, put everything – both hands – into her double-handed backhand. And it was consistent. She could hit 1,000 in a row against the wall. But that wasn't how tennis was played: one hand was the proper, proven, and most efficient way. But the Hoxies, unlike any other coach of the time, didn't seek to change Peaches' approach. Instead, admiring her moxie, they helped her make it better. And while their relationship became complicated as Jean became more overbearing, when

Peaches began to rise through the ranks the Hoxies gave her cover when people questioned or made fun of Peaches' swing.

The Hoxies were mavericks too and the kind that you didn't mess with. And Jean in particular knew that tennis conventions were based on the way men traditionally played, not women. If a girl's physique led her to find that playing a backhand with two hands was more suited, then so long as that girl could win, she saw no good reason why that shouldn't trump tradition.

While she may not be that well known now, Peaches was a phenomenon in the 1960s, with a US junior record that has never been beaten to this day. She reached the pinnacle of junior tennis, winning the junior Wimbledon title in 1964 and the junior US title in 1965 before joining the world circuit.

Peaches' rise coincided with that of women's tennis. A tight-knit group of trailblazers demanded that their game should be taken more seriously by the mainstream and the traditionalists. It is an era depicted well in the movie *Battle of the Sexes*, about Billie Jean King's match with self-described 'male chauvinist pig' Bobby Riggs.

King was one of nine members who joined the new ground-breaking Virginia Slims Circuit in 1970 when it split from the established circuit. Peaches was another. The VS Circuit wanted and promoted engaging personalities and interesting stories to drive sponsorship and television ratings. Peaches was a key member of that original group (and is played by Martha MacIsaac in *Battle of the Sexes*).

But the big breakthrough in terms of public awareness that a backhand could be hit with two hands on the racquet came a few years later when the trail blazed by King, Bartkowicz and Company was followed by Chris Evert. Evert, described by the press as 'America's Darling', became one of the most popular and most watched celebrities in the world. She also hit the backhand with more than one hand.

Just one generation later, the centuries-old approach that Bartkowicz and Evert challenged is in danger of becoming extinct, put to the sword by an approach so natural to young women left to their own devices, but one that almost nobody involved in the game 50 years ago could have imagined.

It's a story that should make us all think twice about telling a young talent that the way they are doing it is too overwrought, too much, or just plain wrong. And, it might cause us to think about working differently with what we've got – instead of adding new ingredients to our creativities crate, looking inside for ingredients that we might serve up at new angles.

RESOURCES

fivethirtyeight.com/features/how-two-grade-schoolers-set-off-a-tennis-revolution/
www.wtatennis.com/news/1652333/in-the-moment-peaches-bartkowicz

1.4   PUSHING LEFT: EMBRACING SCARCITY

While the market can offer unexpected bounty, more often we return to our kitchen with some ingredients missing. These absences force us to improvise, substituting other ingredients, changing the recipe or making do with what we have. Scarcity necessitates changes, and these changes challenge best practice models and expectations. 'Pushing in', working with what we have, takes us towards the next stage in our creative journey, working with what we don't have.

Earlier we considered how abundance of one kind of creative ingredient (human capital, time) is often used to compensate for scarcity of another (economic capital, technology or equipment), sparking creative solutions. Our final stop in the market of creative ideas takes us to somewhere far removed from the indulgences and excesses of Western societies, to less developed parts of the world where a lack of resources is the mother of invention. It's time to push the envelope left.

In commercial settings we all know that creativity is constrained by resources, deadlines and market effects. Even when these external constraints are removed, for example in the creative practice of some artists and writers, personal circumstances (family, income, social situation) still frame creative possibilities, and many artists supplement these limitations by self-imposed routines and structures of their own. More broadly, creative work is funnelled through a range of constraints – domain-specific expertise, ethics, critique, confidence, motivation. Blocks and frustration help trigger creativity; resource constraints help to shape it.

Biographical studies of Shakespeare or Charles Dickens remind us of the extent to which their work was shaped by external constraints, from the context of Elizabethan staging and audiences to 19th-century serial publication. At the internal level, Jonah Lehrer's now-discredited discussion of Bob Dylan's song-writing makes a convincing case for the importance of 'blocks' in the creative process; when one neural pathway is blocked, the brain activates another, and Dylan's period of peak productivity was preceded by a period of desperate inability to produce anything. That experience has been borne out by our own interviews with writers, as well as prominent novelists like Jonathan Franzen speaking in praise of writer's block, frustration and despair as necessary components in the creative process.

Sometimes these absences and barriers are characterized as 'uncreative'. 'Uncreativity' describes the ballast within the creative process. It also describes a lack of apparently essential ingredients in the creative process – lack of confidence, freedom, time, or self-belief. These limitations can manifest as apparently uncreative behaviours which nevertheless underpin the creative process – diligent, laborious practice, expertise within a discipline, an understanding and respect for traditions. And in a creative team, these behaviours are sometimes personified as the 'uncreative' person – the one who gets in the way and slows us down.

The 'person from Porlock', who famously interrupted Coleridge in his composition of *Kubla Khan*, is perhaps the best-known example of this 'uncreative person'. Yet we know now that Coleridge was not really interrupted, or rather that he had already written and rewritten his poem several times over. The person from Porlock can better be seen as representing a part of the poet's consciousness, the wakeful self commenting on a poetic (and perhaps opium-infected) dream. The knocks on the door are the interruptions we all need to transform mere novelty into something substantial and valuable.

When scarcity (e.g., deficit of imagination, loss of a budget, lack of time) is projected onto a supposedly uncreative individual, we are reminded again of the need for diversity and tolerance in the creative process – whether we are the poet or the person knocking on the poet's door. And what appears to 'block' our creativity may in fact be the trigger for a new creative approach.

RECIPE 5. *JUA KALI* AND *JUGAAD*: EXTRAORDINARY WITH LESS (NAIROBI AND MUMBAI)

INGREDIENTS*:

- Wood and nails (left over from another job)
- A pressing local need
- Lack of resources, a pinch of frugality, a dash of improvisation
- *If you don't have all the ingredients, just use whatever you can find

In June 2020, a nine-year-old Kenyan boy was awarded a Presidential Order of Service for his invention of a hand-washing machine. Stephen Wamukota had learned about the dangers of Covid-19 on TV. His machine allowed users to pour water and soap using a foot pedal in order to avoid touching surfaces with their hands. Stephen's father James explained that while he was out at work, his son had constructed the machine from some wood obtained to make a window frame, some nails and a plastic container. The machine was a little unsteady, so James tightened up the construction. He also posted pictures of the machine on Facebook, where it was picked up by news agencies including CNN and the BBC.

Stephen may be continuing a Kenyan tradition of improvised innovation called *jua kali*. *Jua kali* ('hot sun') refers to the fixers and repairmen who work by roadsides in some of the poor districts of Nairobi in the open (hence 'hot sun'). Using whatever materials are to hand, they provide quick, cheap solutions to everyday problems – an empty petrol can pressed into an oil lamp, a cocoa tin used to repair a car exhaust. Since their emergence in the 1960s, *jua kali* associations have become part of Kenya's entrepreneurial economy, registered and supported by the government. Much of their work recycles old material, especially scrap metal, and patches up or customizes existing products.

Jua kali is part of a global movement towards 'frugal innovation', making use of available resources to solve immediate problems, especially among people who cannot afford to buy ready-made solutions. In India, *jugaad* is a Hindu word which can be translated as 'an improvised fix using simple means' or, more colloquially, 'a hack'. In their book *Jugaad Innovation*, Radjou and Prabhu give the example of the 'Mitticool', a fridge made of clay which uses the condensation and evaporation of water in the upper chamber to cool the contents of the lower chamber. The 'fridge' is in essence a clay pot, inspired by a newspaper caption describing a broken clay pot as a 'poor man's fridge'.

Jugaad starts at the point of use, taking into account practical applications, resource constraints and local needs. This is a reversal of the Western innovation model, which starts with ideation before moving on to application. *Jugaad* also places a higher premium on 'value' over 'novelty' than in many Western models of creativity – *jugaad* innovations are typically reworkings or reinventions of existing technologies, not radically new 'breakthroughs'. Finally, *jugaad* pursues a 'good enough' solution to a pressing problem – there is a 'making do' attitude which focuses on an immediate social context and need.

These three principles of *jugaad* can be summarized as:

- Frugality: user-driven not producer-driven, working within constraints of locally

available resources and technologies;
- Flexibility: adaptive innovation, not radical innovation;
- Inclusivity: value-based innovation which measures quality locally not globally.

Jugaad and *jua kali* challenge many of the principles of Western creativity and innovation. Western approaches typically value people over processes (producer-led, 'genius' thinking), seek radical or 'breakthrough' solutions by 'thinking outside the box', and see value in terms of transformative potential for the wider sector or market, not local needs.

The Hindu word *jugaad* contains an implication of criminality, bypassing rules and conventions in pursuit of a quick fix. In Kenya too, *jua kali* has some negative connotations – the improvised repair may not last long, and the term is often synonymous with low quality and unreliability. Stephen's machine had to be 'tightened' by his father. There may be cases where *jugaad* is not fit for purpose – we might not expect or desire ad hoc improvisation to feature in aeronautical engineering or pharmaceuticals.

Global companies like Procter & Gamble in the US and Tata in India have attempted to apply *jugaad* thinking to product development and manufacturing respectively. Western business media (*Business Insider, Harvard Business Review, Financial Times*) and think tanks (the UK's innovation agency NESTA) have explored its implications. Applying *jugaad* in a Western cultural context might require some decentralization and distribution of innovation processes away from specialized innovation units or R&D departments into frontline operational teams. There are similarities here with 'lean' or 'agile' processes in software development – but these tend to work best with small creative teams, not corporate mass production.

Jugaad and *jua kali* shift creative power downwards towards local and operational activities, subverting the conventional producer-driven model of Western innovation and creativity. In a global context where creativity is often wasteful, reinventing or 'updating' products we do not really need and using up scarce resources, *jugaad* and *jua kali* may offer more sustainable alternatives. Perhaps your creativity might be similarly enhanced by taking ingredients out of your crate, and seeking to do more with less.

RESOURCES

Radjou, N. and J. Prabhy (2012), *Jugaad Innovation: Think frugal, be flexible, generate breakthrough growth*, San Francisco, CA: Jossey-Bass.
www.bbc.co.uk/news/world-africa-52898797

One of the principles of the approach referred to as design thinking, which has become increasingly popular in business in recent years, is to 'embrace constraints' and have them inspire rather than frustrate the creative process. This thinking regarding scarcity as a creative spur can be seen in stories like:

- The increasing number of cookbooks with titles like *Perfect Plates in 5 Ingredients* or *Hugh's Three Good Things*. As the author of the former explains, 'I'm stepping back from the [overly] complicated to let the ingredients do the talking.'
- The team marketing the BMW-owned MINI reboot in the UK in the 1990s, finding their budget slashed, had to engage in guerrilla marketing that proved far more effective than a conventional campaign.

- IKEA's requirement for furniture that had to be flat-packed (leaving with furniture in the boot of one's car diminishes the likelihood of changing one's mind when compared with waiting for it to be delivered at a later date) led to many design innovations.
- How the first place in the world to roll out electronic payments is not where we might expect it to be – Japan, China, Germany, the US, or Europe – but in East Africa, where the technical and financial constraints encouraged breakthrough risk-taking and creativity (check out the story of M-Pesa in Kenya and Tanzinia). *Jua kali!*
- The tale about Coco Chanel's fashion advice: before you leave home you should remove one item of clothing.
- Or in the words of the author of *The Little Prince*, Antoine de Saint-Exupéry, 'It seems that perfection is attained not when there is nothing more to add, but when there is nothing more to remove.'

So, what if a group of university students in China tried to solve the problem they and their fellow students had of being late to class with a very traditional Chinese form of transport, developing a business model constrained by the smallest amount of capital possible? It might lead to one of the world's fastest-growing new industries.

RECIPE 6. OFO BIKES: CHEAP OLD BIKES, WITH A HIGH-TECH TWIST (BEIJING)

INGREDIENTS:

- Five friends always late for class
- Bikes left behind
- Everyone on WeChat
- Walled, flat campuses

Recently, a *Harvard Business Review* article titled 'Why Can't China Innovate?' explored the perception that China 'doesn't do innovation':

'The Chinese invented gunpowder, the compass, the waterwheel, paper money, long-distance banking, the civil service, and merit promotion', it began, and, 'Until the early 19th century, China's economy was more open and market driven than the economies of Europe.' But, the authors explained, today most 'believe that the West is home to creative business thinkers and innovators, and that China is largely a land of rule-bound rote learners—a place where R&D is diligently pursued but breakthroughs are rare'.

The article outlined a number of reasons provided for this:

- Most Chinese start-ups are founded by engineers, not designers or artists;
- The scale of government, its influence on business activity and its failure to protect intellectual property rights;
- The Chinese education system, with its brutal regime of exams and focus on rewarding high test scores rather than creative thinking.

But despite these reasons (or perhaps because of them), China's governments, universities and businesses are embarking on a major innovation drive, determined to become a world leader in what they describe as mass innovation and mass entrepreneurship. Massive incubators are being built and subsidized and new policies implemented: such as that announced in 2016 that will allow students to break their university studies at any point in their degree programme and start a business, with the understanding that their university must take them back at the point where they left – either if the venture has failed or has been so successful that the entrepreneur has sold it and wants to return to their studies.

Certainly there is no lack of confidence among young Chinese people that they can lead the world in innovation. A couple of years ago, we asked an audience made up of academics from all over the world to fill in a questionnaire, including the question: what is the world's most creative country? Over 50% wrote the United States. Nobody wrote China. When we asked the same question in Beijing, nearly 80% of Chinese students answered 'China'.

Unquestionably if you spend time in China, you see innovative start-ups popping up everywhere. One such is Ofo Bikes, which has been labelled China's Uber for bicycles, but this is a label that likely undersells what Ofo does.

Ofo was started at Peking University in Beijing by a group of that university's students and graduates that belonged to the university bicycle club. The idea was to enable students to use a WeChat app to rent a bike to race across their typically massive campuses between their classes or social engagements in an environment where the sheer scale of people made it hard to park and then find your own bike quickly.

Ofo had a ready supply of low-tech bikes to recycle as they began to roll out their business model. Every year Chinese students leave their bikes behind them, as they are cheap and difficult to take on public transport. These are then gathered into university bicycle graveyards, where they will eventually become landfill.

Refurbing such bikes and then spraying them the distinctive Ofo yellow, the company amped up the low-tech. Short rides over generally flat Chinese university campuses mean no need for gears or comfy seats. You could hear the distinctive rattle of an Ofo bike as they came up behind you on PKU's shared pedestrian and cycle pathways.

Much of the cost of running a rental bike service used to come in maintaining the docks the earlier sharing bikes were slotted into – so Ofo reduced the tech further and did without docks, favouring instead simple combination locks. Send the code of the bike you want to rent and a Qcode key is sent back immediately. Your Ofo account on WeChat is then deducted a few yuan and away you go.

Another major cost of rental bikes is gathering up and returning bikes back to key locations. Because Ofo bikes can only be used on the campus they are designated to, the bikes don't go wandering and can be redistributed and otherwise maintained by Ofo's little three-wheeler motorcycles. Keeping the bikes on campus is helped by the fact that China's large urban universities are mini walled cities with only a few gates manned by security guards who ask for ID – anybody seeking to make a break on a canary yellow bike is going to stand out! And while campuses are walled and flat, they are massive (PKU has over 50,000 students; Tsinghua University next door has 75,000), university timetables are tight, and the time between classes short – being able to grab a bike directly outside a lecture (no docks remember) and ride it to the next lecture theatre on your schedule is well worth the few yuan and a bone-shaking ride.

Ofo had other competitors, higher-tech, sleeker bikes like Mobike, but Ofo's rattlers were by far the cheapest – and, subsequently, the most popular. But Ofo has been taken under the wing of Chinese ride-sharing giant Didi (which has recently defeated

Uber to dominate the Chinese car-sharing industry). Didi saw the potential in the Ofo model, and investment and expansion plans were quickly developed. The first targeted overseas beachhead for Ofo is the British university and science-park-dominated city of Cambridge, and then some of Australia's major cities. Some of the West's most creative minds are now travelling via an innovative business model developed by some of the East's, and the growth in bike and e-scooter providers in the last ten years can be traced back to those students at the PKU bicycle club.

Source: Photo by Stephen Cummings

Figure 1.3   Dump at Peking University for bikes left behind by students going home for summer

NB. We finish this first part of *Creativities* by reproducing the key What elements of the Ofo case on a Creativity Canvas in Figure 1.4 on page 24 (we do likewise with the last recipe from each of the subsequent parts of the book).

RESOURCES

https://hbr.org/2014/03/why-china-cant-innovate

In this part of the book we have illustrated some of the choices available to you as you assemble the ingredients you need to fashion your own creativities. You might need to discover a more diverse range of possibilities and people (push out), or you might need to reconnect with your own authentic values (push in). You might find yourself dealing with an abundance of people, time or resources allowing you to 'use more to create differently' (push right), or you might prefer to strip down and simplify, using scarcity to improvise a solution which matches the present need (push left). Whichever direction you choose, it's worth remembering that no single direction is inherently superior to the others, and in many cases they overlap. And whatever ingredients you assemble, these are only the start of the creative journey – as we will discuss in Part II, the next step is deciding how to combine them.

SOURCES AND FURTHER READING FOR PART I

The framework for Part I draws upon Boden's definition of creativity as taking place within a 'bounded conceptual space' (Boden 1994, 79–84). The discussion of 'pushing out' suggests a correlation between diversity of personnel and diversity of thought. The lack of cultural diversity in the creative industries workforce and the consequences for creative output have been the ongoing subject of excellent research by Dave O'Brien, among others. 'Pushing right' or 'abundance' relates to Shirky's model of 'cognitive surplus' – it also draws upon the idea of 'affordances', the resources available which shape creative options. The latter is relevant also to 'pushing out' and scarcity. Here 'jugaad' and 'frugal innovation' have attracted much interest in the management literature.

Ajith, P. and A. Goyal (2016), 'Jugaad Innovation in Indian Rural Marketing: Meaning and Role', *SCMS Journal of Indian Management* **13**(1), 5–18.

Boden, M. (1992), *The Creative Mind: Myths and mechanisms*, London: Abacus.

Boden, M. (1994), 'What is Creativity?' in M. Boden (ed.), *Dimensions of Creativity*, Cambridge, MA/London: MIT Press/Bradford Books, 75–117.

Bound, K. and I. Thornton (2012), *Our Frugal Future: Lessons from India's innovation system*, London: NESTA.

Brook, O., D. O'Brien and M. Taylor (2019), *Culture is Bad for You: Inequality in the cultural and creative industries*, Manchester: Manchester University Press.

Conor, B., R. Gill and S. Taylor (eds) (2015), *Gender and Creative Labour*, Chichester: Wiley/The Sociological Review.

Culpepper, M.K. (2018), '"Yeah, That's What I am Now": Affordances, Action and Creative Identity' in L. Martin and N. Wilson (eds), *The Palgrave Handbook of Creativity at Work*, Cham, Switzerland: Palgrave Macmillan, 107–124.

Glăveanu, V.P. (2012), 'What Can be Done with an Egg? Creativity, Material Objects and the Theory of Affordances', *The Journal of Creative Behavior* **46**, 192–208.

Prabhu, J. and S. Jain (2015), 'Innovation and Entrepreneurship in India: Understanding Jugaad', *Asia Pacific Journal of Management* **32**(4), 843–868.

Prahalad, C. and R. Mashelkar (2010), 'Innovation's Holy Grail', *Harvard Business Review* **88**(7/8) (July/August), 132–141.

Radjou, N. and J. Prabhy (2012), *Jugaad Innovation: Think frugal, be flexible, generate break-through growth*, San Francisco, CA: Jossey-Bass.

Shirky, C. (2010), *Cognitive Surplus: Creativity and generosity in a connected age*, London: Allen Lane.

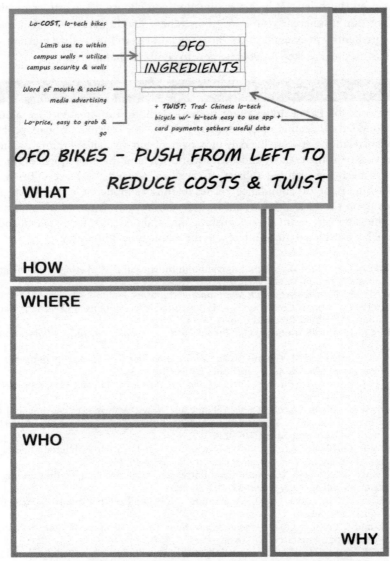

Lo-COST, lo-tech bikes

Limit use to within campus walls = utilize campus security & walls

Word of mouth & social-media advertising

Lo-price, easy to grab & go

OFO INGREDIENTS

+ TWIST: Trad· Chinese lo-tech bicycle w/- hi-tech easy to use app + card payments gathers useful data

OFO BIKES - PUSH FROM LEFT TO REDUCE COSTS & TWIST

WHAT

HOW

WHERE

WHO

WHY

Figure 1.4   Creativities canvas example 1: Ofo and the What of creativity

PART II
THE HOW – CREATIVE BLENDS

After assembling the ingredients for a creative enterprise, we need to step back and start thinking about how to blend these elements into effective teams and combinations.

Making connections between ideas and people in order to figure out 'how' creativity is going to get done requires some deep thinking – this second part of the creative process accordingly sits on the in-house side of the creative bi-sociation we are encouraging in *Creativities*. But there are strategies which can help you make the magic happen and help the creative whole be greater than the sum of its elements. We've tried various ways of expressing these strategies, but have come to the conclusion that we cannot do it better than Daniel Patterson and Mandy Aftel and their four rules of creative combinations in their book *The Art of Flavour*. So, if you'll excuse a continuation of the cookbook analogy at this point, we'll borrow and expand on them here:

- First, similar ingredients need a contrasting flavour (so, for example, if your creative elements are all quite alike, you may need to introduce some seasoning to lift things).
- Second, contrasting ingredients need a unifying flavour (for example, if your creative elements are very diverse, you may need to develop a clear purpose or values for them to rally around).
- Third, heavy flavours need a lifting note (a technically oriented or serious creative enterprise may require the introduction of some fun or levity).
- Fourth, light flavours need to be grounded (a more light-hearted enterprise may need to be given more gravity to have impact).

Creative teams and networks have been framed by social theories rather than by individual psychology. As with any recipe, the individual ingredients in the creative team need to be assembled collectively in the right proportions and in the right order. Properly aligned, a creative team will be more than the sum of its parts in the same way as a great dish will be more than the sum of the ingredients if we apply some of the creative mixing strategies advocated by Patterson and Aftel. Part I, the What, highlighted the diversity of thought within creative teams. Part II, the How, addresses the diversity of approaches to leading that creative team.

Blending creativity therefore refers not only to combining different members of the team, but also blending different approaches to creative leadership. We look to capture this in Part II's framework for identifying how best to align your blend.

The 'How' framework: blending creative teams using creative leadership

Achieving that ideal blend of the creative elements that you are bringing to the table requires a combination of different approaches to leading the creative team, which we summarize as a framework with four angles:

- **Sifting**: aligning the different ingredients which make up the team and mapping their relationships to each other is an analytical, deliberate process. In a large organization, this might involve HR departments, organizational psychologists and project managers; in a smaller enterprise this may just come down to you.
- **Mixing**: once the team is in place, it needs some energy to animate it, to put one ingredient against another, adding some drive and commitment and disrupting complacent, settled relationships. This is a dynamic process associated with charismatic leadership and entrepreneurship (and 'intrapreneurship').
- **Balancing**: as with Patterson and Aftel's creative mixing strategies, the balance between contrasting flavours is crucial. Sifting and mixing might look like a winning formula, but these different tendencies need to play off each other. This means not placing excessive trust in any one model or individual leader.
- **Remixing**: teams and the people in them are not static, and their environment is continually evolving. This requires a different kind of leadership; a more reflective, vulnerable leader who can see when the old patterns are failing and can persuade the team of the need to change from the bottom-up – often against their instincts – and start the process again.

Taken in isolation, none of these models can be considered ideal. Too much sifting results in a static, introverted model with no sense of dynamism or urgency. Mixing injects energy and purpose, but taken to excess places too much power in the hands of dynamic individuals (the mixer) while squeezing the energy and initiative out of everybody else. Balancing might seem to offer the best of both worlds, but disrupting or recalibrating the creative team can itself become formulaic and predictable. And remixing, while it is a necessary bridge between the other tendencies, can again distort into something less creative, endlessly tinkering with the team and breaking down its momentum.

The resulting four approaches of leading a successful creative team – sifting, mixing, balancing, remixing – are accordingly best seen as complementary, counterbalancing tendencies rather than self-contained approaches. They can be seen as stages in a process rather than alternatives, and most creative teams will need to find a balance or 'blend' between them. These different tendencies can also be seen as stages in the team's development, with time's arrow running from left to right as the creative team and its leadership evolve, as illustrated in Figure 2.1.

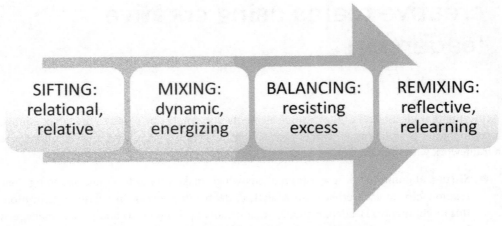

Figure 2.1   Creativities framework 2: the creative blend continuum

Different approaches to blending the team will need different approaches to leadership. Like a sound engineer or lighting designer using the board to adjust levels, we may need to dial up or down different leadership capabilities depending on the team's situation and needs. Starting at the left of the figure, we can fade up or down the analytical, deliberate models of visionary leadership, focusing on psychological insight and individual competences to 'sift' the creative team. Mixing will require a more dynamic, charismatic approach to leadership, focusing on animating the collective energy and dynamics of the team. Balancing these tendencies might mean scaling up either the sifting or mixing tendencies in order to challenge leadership certainties and complacent formulae – here the leader will need to be more detached, perhaps even somebody from outside or new to the organization. Remixing requires more reflective, vulnerable leadership which can learn from past failures and rebuild the team around a new consensus – and lead from the bottom-up rather than the top-down. Finally, we should recognize that leading a creative team can be a collective act, not an individual role, so some small creative teams will self-manage rather than answering to a nominal leader.

These different ways of leading and blending a creative team will be detailed further in the following sections. We will include one 'recipe for failure' to illustrate the dangers of following one tendency in isolation or to excess. The other recipes are arranged to highlight different elements, but in all cases it remains important to see these approaches in combination rather than in isolation, overlapping and evolving over time. Finding the right proportion of sifting, mixing, balancing and blending will depend upon the team, the task and the setting.

2.1   CREATIVE SIFTING: PUTTING TOGETHER THE CREATIVE TEAM

There are numerous tools for 'sifting' a team, used by HR professionals to identify individual abilities: Belbin's team roles, Myers–Briggs personality types, even simple person specifications in a job advertisement. The key difference in a creative team is that these capabilities are always relative and relational. The criteria for creativity – novelty and value – are relative to a context and must be balanced against each other. Individual creative competences must accordingly be assessed against others in the team. This point is well made in Kirton's Adapter-Innovator inventory, showing that the successful team requires a mix of different personalities and abilities. Similar to Patterson and Aftel's rule that similar ingredients need a contrasting flavour, Kirton argues that teams need oppositional balance. A team of mostly innovators will need to recruit adapters to apply and connect their disparate innovations into a valuable outcome. A team of mostly adapters will need some innovators to inject energy and disruption into a pragmatic consensus.

Sifting aims not only to identify the right ingredients but to position them in relation to each other. Some team members may be apparently unproductive in themselves, but draw out the creative potential of others – like the 'lifting' or 'grounding' notes used by Patterson and Aftel to act upon the other ingredients in a recipe. Alongside the analytical process noted earlier, this aspect of sifting requires an emotional intelligence, able to recognize relationships and connections between people as well as their individual qualities.

All of this might take some time and a willingness to experiment, to make mistakes and try again with a different combination. Like leaving a dough to rise or a sauce to thicken, the sifting process is slow, reflective and patient – the collective equivalent of what Wallas called 'incubation' in the mind of the creative individual. Enough time must be allowed for connections to percolate through the team, but not too much time for these connections to turn stale and overfamiliar. The person coordinating the creative team must read the signals of changing group dynamics, knowing when to accelerate and when to slow down. Ultimately too, 'sifting' must be balanced by the next stage in the process: mixing.

In the recipe that follows, sifting a creative team did not immediately produce the desired results. Football is a sport where highly rated players can fail, where the collective dynamic is often difficult to decipher from the outside. Players take time to adjust to each other and to a new coach. Short-run success is not always sustained and a long-term development may require some short-term failure. But for all the potential setbacks, 'Bielsa Ball' is a good example of 'sifting' the creative team, with an apparently unpromising set of players galvanized to achieve by an overarching purpose as they are relocated into a new system.

RECIPE 7. LEEDS UNITED AGAIN: BIELSA BALL (SANTIAGO, BILBAO, MARSEILLE, LILLE AND LEEDS)

INGREDIENTS:

- 1 obsessive, visionary leader
- 11 players from the second tier of English football
- Trust in the team process, not the product
- A generous dollop of self-belief, a sprinkling of beauty and a dash of brittleness
- Pinch of pragmatism (if available)

Football coaches ('soccer' if you're reading this in the United States) are charged with getting a group of players to perform better than the sum of their parts. Marcelo Bielsa is the coaches' coach, revered by younger disciples like Mauricio Pochettino (who played for Bielsa in Argentina) and Pep Guardiola (who describes Bielsa as the best coach in the world). Bielsa managed the national sides of Argentina and Chile before moving to Europe and coaching Atletico Bilbao in La Liga and Marseille and Lille in Ligue 1. On 15 June 2018 he arrived at Leeds United, a club with a distinguished history but which had spent the last 14 years in the lower tiers of English football.

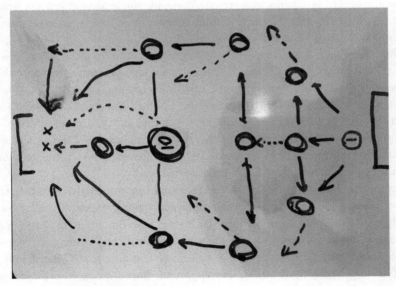

Source: Drawing by Chris Bilton

Figure 2.2   Sketch of Bielsa Ball formation in action

Bielsa's signature formation is a flexible 3–3–1–3: three banks of players with a no. 10 playmaker linking with the front three, and runs from defenders into the midfield, runners from midfield to support the attack. The aim is to allow rapid transitions between attack and defence, with each player drilled in their own position, but coached to switch positions, especially between the attacking trio and the midfield. His teams hold on to possession with rapid, close passing, exhausting the opposition before cutting them open. When out of possession, they press hard and high up the pitch to win the ball back quickly (the dotted arrows indicate this high press). His system allows players to express themselves as equal 'protagonists' but also to switch roles when needed. As they become more familiar with the coaching style, they improve individually and collectively.

The formation requires commitment and discipline from both players and coach. Bielsa is notorious for his detailed tactical analyses of opponents (sometimes crossing the line with allegations of 'spying') and lengthy team talks, often keeping the players in the dressing room for hours after a game. In his first season at Leeds there was a concern that players were not fit enough to play 'Bielsa Ball' for an entire season; having dominated the league for the first six months, the team fell away in the run-in, eventually losing their playoff semi-final with a number of players out injured. In Bielsa's second season, the team became inconsistent as the season progressed. The enforced interruption of Covid-19 towards the end of the 2019/20 season may have been timely, and Leeds finally qualified to return to the English Premier League as champions of the second-tier Championship division. Bielsa's third season saw the club back in the top flight, where they eventually finished ninth in the Premier League – a significant achievement for a newly promoted side. They also won over many new fans with their dynamic, unpredictable style of play.

Despite his stellar reputation, Bielsa is by no means the most successful manager in terms of results and trophies. Argentinian football writer Marcela Mora Y Araujo draws a connection with other Argentine coaches, inspired by a love for the aesthetics of the game, not just by results. These include Jorge Valdana, who went on to initiate the 'galacticos' era of superstar players at Real Madrid and who likened the coach to the conductor of an orchestra – and the best-known Argentinian of all, Diego Maradona. Maradona the player (possibly the greatest player) is the subject of another recipe, in Part V, the Why. But during the 2010 World Cup, in what seemed like a desperate move, Maradona was appointed manager of the Argentina national team. After scraping through the qualification tournament, Maradona won over many of his critics in the opening round of the World Cup, with Argentina scoring freely and playing some of their best football, despite some surprising team selections. The star player, Lionel Messi, failed to score a single goal in the tournament, but was instrumental in setting up his teammates. Then in the quarter-final Argentina were taken apart by a ruthless counterattacking Germany team, losing the game 4–0. Maradona's ebullient joy in attacking football only served to expose his team's brittle defence.

Bielsa's teams too have a certain brittleness – his players have been coached to play in a certain way, his teams continue to pass and press even when the odds are against them. Perhaps this is why Bielsa is nicknamed 'El Loco' – the madman. He is uncompromising, unbending, obsessive. But from a purely aesthetic perspective, Leeds United are a great team to watch – a far cry from the brutal, ugly football when the club was winning trophies under Don Revie in the 1970s. From a creative team perspective too, there are no real superstars – instead, average players become good players, good players become very good. The players understand their roles, they play for each other, and they develop collectively and individually. They are all 'protagonists'. Their trust in each other and in the system allows them to exchange positions, cover for each other, find each other. Kalvin Phillips, a product of the Leeds academy, showed how Bielsa Ball could empower both the team and the individual to grow, with Phillips transformed from journeyman pro to a pivotal member of England's national team.

Like creative teams, football teams need convergence to provide structure. They also need flexibility – and while Bielsa's teams are designed to be flexible (the famous 3–3–1–3 formation morphing into 4–1–4–1, the fluidity of players interchanging positions), the system itself is not. A creative team must not only be oriented internally, calibrating the strengths of one player to another; they need to be oriented externally – what should the team do against a rampant, counterattacking German side, or when losing a playoff semi-final? There are perhaps moments when a carefully conceived structure needs to be discarded, when strong principles need to be replaced by pragmatism.

For these reasons, Bielsa may never win as many trophies as Jose Mourinho or his protégé Pep Guardiola. Indeed, as we were going to press in February 2022, Bielsa was sacked as manager following a disappointing run of results (once again, injuries to key players were a factor). Yet his players continued to express their gratitude and love, and the Leeds fans continued to sing Bielsa's name. It's a reminder that Bielsa and his supporters cared more about a style of football than about winning. By steering his players to be the best they could be, Bielsa was delivering a different measure of success – not just a winning team but a creative team, which other coaches are now seeking to emulate and which could inspire creative orientations beyond football. How might different formations, styles or mixing roles help to realize new creativities in your team?

RESOURCES

'Bielsa: El Loco and Leeds', Sky Sports documentary, July 2020: https://youtu.be/y4idhEak09E
'Bielsa: The Manager Behind the Myths', BBC World Service documentary: www.bbc.co.uk/sounds/play/p08qvw3g

The search for the perfect formation in a sports team must be tempered by other tendencies – a willingness to change an apparently winning formula, something we will return to when discussing 'balancing' and 'remixing'. But teams also require animation and energy. That collective energy is the theme of our next section, as we consider 'mixing' the creative team.

2.2   CREATIVE MIXING: STIRRING THINGS UP

'Mixing' the creative ingredients is the flipside of sifting. If sifting requires a meticulous, analytical attention to individual behaviour, mixing is more emotional and all-embracing. Creative teams need energy and purpose. The much-overused term applied in the creative industries is 'passion'. Of course, an energized team which has not been correctly aligned (sifting) will self-destruct in a colourful explosion of wild ideas and overcommitment. But a correctly aligned team will be inert without some energy to drive it forward. In cookery terms, a cook who 'mixes' is less concerned with careful measurement, more open to improvisation, less bound by the recipe. Above all, mixing is an active movement requiring energy.

Where does this energy come from? Leadership? Urgency and the pressure to deliver? Self-belief and intrinsic motivation? 'Deadline magic'? Or from darker places – ambition, fear, rivalry? Of course it could come from all of these. The trick, in the words of a writer we interviewed, is to find 'the right amount of fire'. Too much self-belief and urgency will lead to a race to the bottom, cutting corners and brushing aside critical questions. Too little and nothing gets done.

Sometimes in a creative team, the entrepreneurial mantra of 'ready, fire, aim' is necessary. Such an approach describes the 'agile' approach to project management which emerged in the software industry – setting deadlines with a preference for short timescales, then trusting the team to self-organize and get the job done, defining a clear process and letting the objectives take care of themselves. The ad hoc, self-organizing agile team is the antithesis of the cautious and meticulous 'sifting' process described earlier. In an agile team, objectives can be reconfigured or discarded, formations altered, systems broken. Structure is replaced by process. In place of the more deliberate, steady approach of sifting, mixing implies movement, energy and speed.

'Agile' teams are driven by a collective energy. It is common, for example, for clients or users to be included in regular 'scrum' meetings which drive the process forward. The scrum is a short meeting (preferably standing rather than seated) focusing on actions, not discussion, and designed to kick-start the day's activities. Work is organized in 'sprints' – short bursts of concentrated activity with a clear end date (in the case of software development, this would be the 'shipping' or delivery date).

'Agile' procedures aim to include everybody on the team. Often, though, the source of energy in a creative team comes from one person – usually, but not always, the nominal leader. This creative leader must cajole, encourage, inspire and bully the team to keep moving forward, even if they are not sure where they are going. This too can be effective, especially in small entrepreneurial organizations. The problem is that this dynamic leadership style is less inclusive. Not everybody on the team will be affected positively by the leader's energy. And over-reliance on one dynamic individual locks in patterns of hierarchy and control which in the long run might sap the energy of the team, making it harder to adapt and less agile – we will return to this when we consider the need for 'balance' in the creative blend. First, we consider an example of energetic 'mixing' in an entrepreneurial creative team.

In the previous recipe, it was necessary to balance 'beautiful football' with results on the pitch. In theatre it is necessary to balance the endlessly fascinating journey of rehearsal with the pragmatic need to put the show in front of an audience. Too much tinkering in the rehearsal room results in an introverted performance where the performers are watching each other's interactions rather than responding to an audience. Too much emphasis on 'the show' results in a slick, shallow professionalism which has not matured through the multiple drafts and reworkings of a rehearsal process. Sometimes the careful planning needed in 'sifting' the creative team needs to be offset by a rough and ready energy, a desire to perform. This energy can be achieved through 'mixing'.

The mystery ingredient here is speed. Rather than carefully calibrating and analysing the team, mixing uses 'deadline magic' to accelerate decision-making and force the issue. In the following recipe, a tight deadline drives out uncertainty and introverted self-analysis, forcing the team to focus on the immediate requirements of the task. In this case, it helps that the team is relatively small (revolving around just two individuals) and the task is relatively contained (a 22-minute animation). But it is noticeable, too, how the focus on product can benefit the process. It is also worth pointing out that the decision to accelerate the process was not imposed by the network; it was a decision taken by the creative team themselves. In our conversations with artists, writers and musicians, self-imposed constraints are generally found to be constructive, whereas externally imposed deadlines are typically resented. This highlights another variant in the creative leadership models being discussed in the How part of *Creativities*. For many creative teams, collective leadership from below is more effective than leadership imposed from above or outside.

RECIPE 8. SOUTH PARK: ANIMATION ON SPEED (CULVER CITY)

INGREDIENTS:

- Two college friends who share a love of Monty Python
- A DIY aesthetic
- An immovable weekly deadline
- Liberal sprinkling of fart jokes
- Speed (not the drug)

Since its debut in 1997, *South Park* has consistently been one of the most popular comedy shows on US cable TV, especially among the lucrative 18–34 market of younger viewers. It has won Emmy awards and helped to establish the reputation and financial future of its host network, Comedy Central. From June 2020, HBO Max acquired the streaming rights, with streaming already adding significantly to the viewing figures on linear TV.

The show is crudely animated and reliably offensive, combining scatological toilet humour with irreverence bordering on contempt for celebrities, politicians of every stripe and the media world of which it is a part. The animation today is done using computers, but looks identical to the early hand-drawn stop-animation of the 'Spirit of Christmas', a prototype video circulated anonymously which brought the show's creators to the attention of studio executives, first at Fox, then at Comedy Central. The cast of characters (with the exception of Chef) have not changed through 25 seasons and counting. The humour and style still seem like the spontaneous outpourings of a group of fourth-graders, fascinated by toilet humour, battling with parents, curious but strangely innocent as they engage with an adult world of celebrity, religion, politics and money. The four kids, Stan, Kyle, Kenny and Cartman, have not aged, apart from one transition from third to fourth grade. The same might be said of the show's producers.

Remarkably, the show is still produced by Trey Parker and Matt Stone. The pair brainstorm ideas in a writers' room with other producers and writers, but Parker is responsible for delivering the final script. A team of animators translates the ideas and sketches from the writers' room into finished animation, and music is dubbed in as required. Parker and Stone still voice all of the main characters, apart from a few (mostly female) roles. Speed in writing is matched by speed in performance, with many scenes recorded in a single take, capturing the jeopardy and energy of live performance.

Even more remarkably, Parker and Stone make one episode of *South Park* every week – in between series they have worked on other projects like feature-length movies or the Broadway hit musical *The Book of Mormon*. The six-day production cycle compares with around six months for an episode of *The Simpsons* or ten months for shows like *Family*

Guy or *Rick and Morty*. Parker and Stone write, produce, direct and perform. The rest of the team also multitasks, doing character animation, backgrounds and effects at the same time, not in linear stages. Producers and studio staff are roped into the voice recording as necessary.

The speed of production is of course helped by the use of computer animation instead of hand drawing. But story and content must also be conceived from scratch every week, starting on a Thursday. This means that each episode is produced in sequence rather than multiple episodes being produced in parallel (as with *The Simpsons* for example). This allows the show to react to actual events and news in real time.

In the documentary *South Park: Six Days to Air*, Parker explains that every week he starts with a sense of possibilities and ends the week in despair, believing the episode is the worst they have ever done. But he also explains that the brutal schedule allows no time for writer's block. If an idea is not working, there is no time to start again – they must find a way of making it work. If he was working over months instead of days, he estimates they might be able to make the show 'maybe 5% better'. Working fast allows a random, spontaneous approach, especially in the writers' room. One female participant comments that the feel of the writers' room is relaxed and open – ideas are not shut down, and in an unexpected phrase she describes the room as a 'safe space'. There is not much time for ego or power games: the show must go on – every Wednesday.

Far from being stressful, the short schedule ensures an almost carefree approach. While both Stone and Parker have their bad days, these mood swings are absorbed into the weekly cycle – they are predictable and short-lived, framed by the rhythm of the six-day schedule. The schedule also prevents Parker and Stone from taking themselves too seriously, or from basking in their unexpected success. Returning from receiving multiple awards for *Book of Mormon*, they appear in the documentary almost relieved to be back in the frantic race to produce another episode.

The tight schedule results in a creative freedom. The characters blurt out whatever is on their minds – there is no self-censorship. The writers are forced to work in the same way, with no time for second thoughts. They can respond to current events, and this topicality is often the starting point for the story arc. The lack of forethought ensures that character is king – in the writing room, much of the humour comes from thinking how a character would react in a situation, and Stone and Parker will often slip into role when improvising a line.

In the case of *South Park*, the recipe for success is speed. The computers can produce the frames, but the writers have to provide the ideas to fill them. Working fast animates the creative team; the constraint of time removes all other constraints. Parker in particular is prone to self-doubt. Speed is his antidote – the self-imposed deadline means those doubts have no time to gather and fester. But speed also animates the relationships within the team, allowing for a paradoxically relaxed and unconstrained process – anything goes, because everything must go in six days. It also might explain the show's extraordinary consistency – the relationship between Parker and Stone, their shared sense of humour, is at the heart of everything. Despite their success, they still pride themselves on being outsiders, like the indie filmmakers they once aspired to be, like the punk bands who play fast and play live, unrehearsed and uncut. Working fast means that this creative relationship and punk attitude have not grown old – like Stan and Kyle, they are scatological children, saying whatever comes into their mouth rather than using their heads. There are certain limitations of course – the show is perhaps not as sophisticated as *The Simpsons* or as intellectually clever as *Rick and Morty*. But it is perhaps braver, more spontaneous and more intuitive than either – and the team who make *South Park* are enjoying the ride.

If your team is getting bogged down in plans, procedures and hierarchies, could a dash of deadline magic help to animate and concentrate your creative how?

RESOURCES

South Park: Six Days to Air: https://youtu.be/qgkbiVURAlQ
South Park's Missed Deadline (Tom Jenkins, *Medium*, 17 October 2013): https://medium.com/
    sitcom-world/south-parks-missed-deadline-2e4b0a200052

2.3   BALANCING CREATIVITY: RESISTING EXCESS, ACHIEVING AN ARCHITECTURAL BALANCE

Balancing the creative team inevitably contains elements of both sifting and mixing because it aims to achieve a balance between them – between controlling and aligning the team and giving free rein to energetic individualism.

By devoting too much time to 'sifting' the ingredients, we can end up locking people into fixed roles and responsibilities, with no space for change or growth. Stereotyping of 'creative' and 'uncreative' individuals within the team, blocking certain modes of thinking (especially critical thinking which challenges the consensus), reinforcing hierarchies and divisions might give a very clear alignment to the team. Everybody knows and will do what is expected of them. But this team is unlikely to be very creative. What is missing here is the possibility of mixing things up, allowing different individuals or ideas or approaches to be promoted from below, challenging the established pattern.

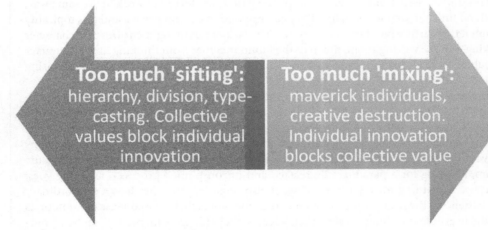

Figure 2.3   Balancing between sifting and mixing

It is also possible to allow too much space to maverick individualism, continually disrupting and challenging the consensus. In such a team, a febrile atmosphere of creative destruction means nothing and nobody can take centre stage. This might be a very exciting and vibrant team, liberating even, especially if coming from the more controlled and coordinated model of 'sifting' plans and tactics. But again, will such a team be creative? Perhaps not. The vaunted desire to move fast and break things leaves little time for any clear-sighted 'sifting' of priorities, abilities and purposes. There are likely to be plenty of ideas and possibilities in this team, but an inability to apply and direct them.

In the film industry, impetuosity co-exists with meticulous planning. While production schedules are typically plotted to the minutest detail, bigger decisions by studio heads about budgets, releases and future production slates are often characterized by an 'act now, plan later' mindset. This combination of extreme uncertainty and the need for control (budgetary, artistic, personal) concentrates decision-making power among a relatively small group of senior executives. Their power is not only institutional; it is personal. In the creative industries, where social life and business overlap, individual power spills outside the world of work into a netherworld of social drinking and 'parties', where charismatic gatekeepers exert their power over the powerless, who are desperate for admission to the inner circle.

Charismatic leadership inspires, but it also oppresses. Charismatic leaders are not good at delegating power, and even if they do, their own dark energy has often squeezed the energy and initiative out of those around them, prompting a leadership crisis as the entrepreneurial business tries to adapt to more complex corporate governance structures. If the organization fails to manage that transition, the power of the charismatic leader grows increasingly inexorable and destructive, until at some point the enterprise implodes. Too much sifting locks the team into fixed roles and behaviours with no space for outsiders to question the underlying assumptions. Too much mixing from the leader, disrupting traditional norms and values, may eventually destroy those it seeks to lead. This is the story told in Recipe 9.

RECIPE 9. THE WEINSTEIN EFFECT: THE DANGERS OF CREATIVE EXCESS (LOS ANGELES)

INGREDIENTS:

- 1 charismatic, influential bully
- An inner circle of powerful, unaccountable men
- An outer circle of women looking for a break in a hyper-competitive market
- 81 Academy Awards, 341 nominations, 1 Best Picture Oscar
- A surfeit of narcissism, excess of power, absence of control

> A big part of a producer's job is getting people to do things they don't want to do.
>
> Lucy Prebble, November 2017

It is easy to forget that before the allegations of sexual assault in 2017 culminated in his conviction and imprisonment in February 2020, Harvey Weinstein was the toast of Hollywood. The same qualities which made him a dangerous sexual predator were also what made him so effective as a producer – brash, charming, domineering, manipulative, never taking no for an answer. At the Oscars, Weinstein's Miramax punched well above its weight, using aggressive advertising and personal contacts to win over the Academy voters. At the 2012 Golden Globes, Oscar winner Meryl Streep described him as a god (she would later distance herself from these remarks).

The number of actresses who had won awards in Weinstein's films, who Weinstein claimed owed him their careers, strengthened his hand with vulnerable young women and their agents.

People working for Weinstein were caught up in an energetic, aggressive culture built on ambition and fear. They worked hard, they denied themselves and repressed their criticisms because they wanted to please their boss, but also because they feared his explosive anger. We know now that the flipside to Weinstein's 'starmaker' myth was the number of careers he destroyed – the actresses who said no, the insiders who dared to stand up to him. We know, too, that the winning culture of Miramax led people in his organization – and many outside his organization, such as agents, reporters and casting agents – to ignore his excesses, even to become complicit in them.

Thorsten Hennig-Thurau has described the 'nobody knows anything' trap in the film industry, based on William Goldman's famous mantra describing the near impossibility of predicting a successful movie. When analysis appears impossible, decisions come to rely on 'instinct'. The decision-maker is no longer accountable for mistakes, because 'nobody knows anything'. This in turn leads to a concentration of power around a very small number of people making very big decisions with little accountability. Weinstein was at the centre of this power structure. In place of 'analysis paralysis', Weinstein provided speed, energy and results.

When Miramax arrived on the scene, it projected an 'outsider' maverick mentality – disrupting and challenging the Hollywood elite. Like many challenger brands, Miramax also inspired a fiercely loyal 'insider' culture, marked at first by strident declarations of loyalty to 'Harvey', which would return to haunt those who uttered them. Later that insider culture hardened into a culture of denial, with senior staff either turning a blind eye to Weinstein's 'indiscretions' or even lining up to denounce his victims.

We now know, too, that the maverick outsider had become the ultimate Hollywood insider, hiding behind the closeted, tight-lipped culture of the old Hollywood (the 'casting couch', the exercise of power). While claiming to disrupt the old order and 'empowering' women, Weinstein was perpetuating ancient hierarchies and privileges. The #MeToo movement revealed that Weinstein was neither a one-off nor an exception, but part of a long-standing industry hierarchy which allows high-profile senior male leaders in the creative industries to exploit young women. Even the undeniable energy which shot through Weinstein's early career turned in on itself. Weinstein's team worked harder and faster than their rivals. The energy and drive he radiated could inspire those closest to him, especially if they were male; but it also squeezed the energy and drive out of many others, especially if they were women, especially if they crossed him.

'Mixing' destabilizes and disrupts creative teams. But it can also destroy and confuse. The cautious 'sifting' of people and ideas provides a necessary counterpart to maverick energy. Without the apparently boring and deadening effect of rules and procedures, creative teams can apparently break through, but they can also break. On the other hand, Miramax and the Weinstein Company were also beset by an extreme form of 'sifting', which filtered out opposition and dissent. Surrounded by insiders who were too frightened or indebted to change course, Weinstein's 'team' became a monoculture in which one personality dominated everybody else.

The destruction and chaos wreaked by Weinstein on others, on his own company and on himself, is a cautionary reminder of what happens when charismatic leadership is given a free rein, without morality or accountability. It also highlights the importance of checks and balances within a creative team. And while Weinstein was an extreme example of a maverick, charismatic leader, there has been a steady ripple of #MeToo revelations in other 'creative cultures', from Disney Pixar in the US to theatre, television, music and games companies around the world.

To return to the beginning, Weinstein's failures are closely related to his successes. Rhetoric and emotion can light a fire under a creative team, but less showy structural changes in the way teams interact and operate will be needed to keep the flames burning. Creative people like to place themselves outside the establishment, as maverick rule-breakers – this was Weinstein's pose. Actually, creative teams cannot survive on raw energy; they need structures and rules. Energy is necessary in a creative team, but so is direction. Taken to its extreme, the virtues of mixing – stirring things up, making waves, building excitement and commitment – can shade into vices. Balancing the team, sifting as well as mixing, can provide a necessary brake on these excesses. In the aftermath of #MeToo, female producers and directors have begun to establish their own production companies and develop their own projects (see Part IV, the Who, for two of the pioneers in this field). Perhaps Hollywood is finally attempting to address long-standing inequalities which continue to hold back women and people of colour. Balance remains a long way off in the film industry, as in most branches of the creative and media industries. But recognizing the dangers of excess (excessive control and power vested in one individual) may be a first step.

Are there excesses of power and control in your workplace? Is your creative team dominated by a charismatic 'mixer' or a bureaucratic 'sifter'? How might these inequalities look if exposed to outsiders? Who could act as a whistleblower, and how would they be viewed by those on the inside? How could you build a better balance between leaders and followers, sifting and mixing, control and creative release?

RESOURCES

Prebble, L. (2017), 'Harvey Weinstein', *London Review of Books*, 2 November.
The Catch and Kill Podcast with Ronan Farrow: https://podcasts.apple.com/us/podcast/the-catch
-and-kill-podcast-with-ronan-farrow/id1487730212

The Weinstein case is essentially a recipe for leadership failure. Mixing for Miramax and for *South Park* was the job of a 'mixer' – somebody controlling the team's creative process – and that somebody is either the leader or the entrepreneur who drives the team forward. But mixing can also be something done by the team itself, an active self-directed mixing which relies on an architecture or system to achieve energy and interaction rather than on organizational leadership.

Finding the right architecture for these serendipities and interactions to emerge in turn requires a different leadership approach, a more bottom-up, less individualized model which sets boundaries and channels within which mixing can spontaneously evolve. This approach to leadership takes us closer to the more deliberate 'sifting' model from earlier in terms of design

– but is premised on a dynamic, unplanned 'mixing' model in its desired outcome. Rather than the top-down, bullying leadership of Weinstein, designing a system in which others can mix on their own terms takes us into the territory of organizational design (which we will consider in more detail in Part III, the Where).

This also takes us into the territory of 'ambidextrous' organizations and dual leadership. If sifting and mixing are two halves of an equation which needs to be balanced, a creative team will require a blended approach to leadership. Sifting the team places the players in the right positions to get the best out of each of them. Mixing the team gets them playing together and bouncing ideas off each other. This combination of deliberate structure and dynamic energy requires an approach described as 'leading from the middle'. Leading from the middle means combining *vision* (sifting the team in relation to internal strengths and external environments) with *action* (mixing the team to energize internal relationships and external networks).

Some of the 'sifting' models considered earlier incorporate this element of improvisatory, dynamic process. For example, De Bono's Six Thinking Hats defines different roles in a creative team but allows teams to reassign and exchange these roles depending on the needs of the project and the interactions within the team. Educational approaches to creativity are premised on drawing out the multiple capabilities of individuals rather than boxing them into predefined competences and personality types – here too we can see a more dynamic, evolving model of organization which is deliberately designed but dynamically driven.

To summarize, creative teams will require a balance between sifting and mixing approaches. This in turn requires a blend of competences, both within the team and within the team's leadership. And that leadership may also require a blend of top-down interventionist leadership and bottom-up facilitating leadership. If this sounds simple and self-evident, achieving such a balance is more difficult in practice, as Recipe 10 illustrates.

RECIPE 10. MIT BUILDING 20: THE MAGICAL INCUBATOR (BOSTON)

INGREDIENTS:

- Plywood, concrete, asbestos
- An assortment of scientists, geeks and hackers
- A temporary structure which is continually evolving
- A spoonful of discomfort, a sprinkle of office numbers, a corridor of uncertainty

By indirections find directions out…

Hamlet, Act 2, scene 1

During the Covid-19 lockdown of 2020–21, as we attended yet another Zoom conference call, many of us were nostalgic for the old days of face-to-face meetings. Bumping into people in the street, in the foyer, in the pub, creates space for unexpected ideas and opportunities. Some of us may even have an 'elevator pitch' ready for such an occasion. In lockdown, such chance encounters were notably lacking.

Businesses have previously attempted to capture the serendipity of the unplanned physical encounter in their architecture. Steve Jobs designed the central atrium at Pixar as a crossroads between offices. When that didn't work, he relocated the toilets in the atrium – to the annoyance of many employees. The advertising agency Bartle Bogle Hegarty used to require its creative teams to trudge to the print room at the far end of the building to collect their completed artwork – in the hope that they might bump into some-body else along the way. Neighbourhood planners refer to 'inclusive bumping spaces' and 'bumps into per square metre' (BIPSM) as desirable features of a socially connected neighbourhood.

In 2004, Frank Gehry designed the Stata Building at MIT with these principles in mind. The spectacular building was arranged around a curving two-lane 'student street' with offices, cafeteria and social spaces arranged around it, to encourage professors and students to cross paths as often as possible. While the principles were sound, the structure was not – in 2007, MIT sued Gehry for a variety of problems in the building, including cracks in the masonry, leaks, and patches of mould. Meanwhile some of the occupants complained that the building was difficult to work in, requiring them to wear ear plugs.

Gehry's building was constructed on the site of an older MIT creative hub, known simply as Building 20. This was a ramshackle wooden structure, hastily thrown together in 1943 to house scientists working on microwave physics and electromagnetics as part of the US military science endeavour. After the war, the temporary building became home to a variety of small research teams and projects. The 'plywood palace' of the 1950s and 1960s was the building of last resort for MIT scientists with nowhere else to go, accumu-lating a motley crew of semi-detached people and disciplines – from particle accelerators to piano repairers to hackers. It also provided space for untried and experimental projects – Noam Chomsky developed his work on linguistics here, and Amar Bose conducted the research which would eventually result in the Bose speaker system.

Because the building was 'temporary', occupants could modify it at will. New sections were added to the structure, wires were poked through the wall into the lab next door. In his book and TV series *How Buildings Learn*, Internet pioneer Stewart Brand described Building 20 as a 'low road' building – cheap, accessible and easy to modify – in contrast with the kind of landmark architecture which would eventually replace it.

Building 20 was only three storeys high. Its sprawling, horizontal design, extending along Cambridge's Vassar Street, contrasted with the taller vertical buildings around it, where different floors reinforced departmental divisions and hierarchies, and where the horizontal space for interaction was more restricted.

The room numbering system in Building 20 was said to be confusing, unlike the rest of the MIT campus. Offices were allocated ad hoc as different people and teams moved into the building. There are similarities here with the 'chrono-chaotically numbered' offices at CERN in Geneva – another site of unexpected discoveries, where the visitor is liable to become lost without a map. When we lose our way, we are more likely to find something we were not looking for.

Frank Gehry and Steve Jobs both aimed to achieve something like the serendipitous open architecture of Building 20, but using an artfully constructed plan which imposed itself on the workforce. Brand argues that the success of Building 20 was that it reversed this logic – people imposed their own personalities and needs on the building, moulding it around their behaviour rather than having their behaviour shaped by the building. The fact that this building was cheap and 'temporary' gave its occupants licence to adapt it by knocking down partitions or changing the fixtures. The chaos and disorientation were the product of people, not planning.

Building 20 was demolished in 1998. While it can be seen as the predecessor for today's open-plan offices and sprawling campuses with their communal gyms, canteens and social spaces, it is also their antithesis. Companies like Google and Facebook attempt to corral the unplanned space and time of their employees and contain them within the corporate structure. Yet most of our vital encounters still take place outside the formal workplace in unplanned, transitional spaces – the kitchen, the photocopier, the hallway, the smokers' area. Mostly these are spaces we pass through, not places we go to. In the corridor we greet familiar faces and meet strangers – it is this mix of planned and unplanned encounters which allows creativity to thrive.

The word corridor is derived from the Latin *'currere'* – to run – later used by the Italians to describe the passage between or within buildings. Corridors are kinetic. They encourage activity and momentary contact, not the structured interactions of a meeting room. They lie halfway between the open office and the office cubicle – literally so in some cases – allowing the transitions between different spaces – structured and unstructured, seen and unseen – which can facilitate the mental 'field-switching' of creative thinking. In English the phrase 'corridors of power' reflects our understanding that true power resides not in a single office, but in the unseen connections between them. These might appear impenetrable to those outside the organization, but for those on the inside, 'corridor culture' forms a vital link between cultures, teams and individuals. This combination of disorientation and orientation, strong and weak ties, the familiar and the strange, is at the heart of the creative mix.

Building 20 was undoubtedly a creative space, measured in the discoveries and disciplines which it spawned over 55 years. When blending a creative team, Building 20 and its successor serve as a reminder of the limits of both 'sifting' and 'mixing' when a vision or purpose is imposed by leadership or design from above. The key is to allow the team to evolve its own shape and connections. Whether pursuing the perfect balance in a creative team or in a creative building, sometimes less is more.

Where are your chance encounters and serendipitous conversations taking place? Are these times and places inside or outside your workplace? When was the last time you had a creative 'corridor conversation'? Could you customize or rewire the structure of your office, your day, your team to allow for more unexpected connections to occur?

RESOURCES

Goldberg, S. (2007), 'MIT Says Gehry Building Leaks', *The Guardian*, 6 November: www.theguardian.com/world/2007/nov/06/architecture.internationaleducationnews
'How Buildings Learn', by Stewart Brand – Episode 2 'The Low Road': www.youtube.com/watch?v=09pekAKuXjc

2.4　　CREATIVE REMIXING

Marc De Rond has described the 'remixing' of the Cambridge rowing eight, with the coach repeatedly experimenting with different combinations in the boat before settling on the starting crew for the Boat Race. Unlike a sports crew, creative teams are typically project based, assembling, dispersing and reassembling. At the same time, individual creative talents are continually evolving and emerging, meaning that even a successful combination may start to disintegrate.

Consequently, 'remixing' the creative team can be seen as a bridge between the sifting and mixing processes described earlier. By dialling up different competences within the team, by disrupting or redirecting an apparently successful partnership, it is possible to recalibrate the relationship between coordination (sifting) and mobilization (mixing). Where balancing is inwardly directed, shaping the internal dynamics of the team, remixing also takes into account the external context – changes in the business environment (competitors, customers, culture).

Remixing therefore can be a 'breakthrough' move – if you can feel your team getting a little stale or you want to draw on past success but take it to the next level, remixing can be the way forward. But it involves risk, and it takes dexterity. Breaking up a successful team and starting again will again require empathy from the team leader, but also self-awareness from team members as their own talents and interests evolve.

As with the previous recipes, teams can self-manage this adaptation, or it can be a task for leadership. Knowing when to rein individuals in and when to bring them to the front is something the team manager learns from experience, but also from an intuitive reading of individual behaviour and relationships inside the team, and the changing environment and structure outside.

The two final recipes in the How part of *Creativities* are re-mixing recipes. The Royal Shakespeare Company (RSC) recipe (about a 400-year-old company seeking to remix so as to honour the traditions upon which its reputation is founded while staying relevant in the 21st century) highlights the role of leadership. But we should not underestimate the importance of followers, especially those 'first followers' who connect the leader to the rest of the team. In a team, especially a creative team, leadership is often distributed across team members, not embodied in a singular leader. So if the team is locked into negative patterns of excess or imbalance, it's often up to the team members themselves to make the necessary corrections. We have used 'sifting, mixing, balancing, remixing' as transitive verbs, acting upon a team – the work of a chef in control of their recipe. At the risk of overcooking this metaphor, like those fabulous mixing bowls in fairy tales, sometimes the creative team needs to mix itself. The balance we advocate cannot be the sole responsibility of leadership. In the case of the RSC, this involved 'leading from the middle' to endorse and enable creative behaviours from the bottom-up, rather than imposing a vision from the top-down.

Remixing a creative team is a reflective, relearning process. For the RSC, there was some introspection, reflecting back on the longer history of ensemble in theatre, and relearning from the failed interventions by previous leaders in the more recent past. There was also an outward reflection, considering how audiences and funders saw the organization, in order to effect a wider circle of change. We sketch out some of the key aspects of this 'recipe' in the How box in Figure 2.4 at the end of Part II.

However, remixing also requires some bold reimagining of the creative team, being prepared to break familiar habits, routines and assumptions. Hence, before we get to the RSC recipe (Recipe 12), we present another, titled 'A blend of rivals'. This reflects on Abraham Lincoln's decision, shocking to many at the time, to bring his obstinate opponents in the Republican Party together into his cabinet at a time when he felt America was on the brink of being pulled apart. This time the collective process transcends the individual differences, the remixing is a bold combination of opposites, and the outcome is the kind of unexpected synergy which we argue is the essence of blended creativity.

RECIPE 11. ABRAHAM LINCOLN: A BLEND OF RIVALS (WASHINGTON, DC)

INGREDIENTS:

- One unlikely and unselfish leader
- A wide range of other strong flavours
- A collective desire for the revival and improvement of the enterprise
- A great sense of timing
- A good sense of humour, as required

The 21st century has thus far been an age of the individual. Politics, business, sport and the arts have witnessed a proliferation of individual greatest, or richest, of all time lists. The US presidents ranked from 1st to 45th, the top 10 Supreme Court Justices of all time, the 100 richest entrepreneurs, the greatest movie stars, or directors, of the last 100 years, and so on. Today there is a proliferation of celebrity chefs; until the 1990s people focused more on leading restaurants or kitchens. Popular music follows a similar pattern. According to a UK music industry survey of 2015, solo artists like Ed Sheeran, Adele and Taylor Swift have come to dominate sales, replacing groups like Oasis and Arctic Monkeys from a decade earlier.

While this focus on great men and women makes for good parlour games, or click-bait on a news website, focusing on individuals often misses a truth of creativity. Behind (or more correctly around) almost every good creative individual is a great team. This is something that the individual always rated as the GOAT (greatest of all time) president, Abraham Lincoln, knew in spades. And because he also realized that great teams benefited from diverse points of view, you could say he knew it in clubs, diamonds and hearts as well.

Pulitzer prize-winning historian Doris Kearns Goodwin's book *Team of Rivals: The political genius of Abraham Lincoln* cuts across this current of focusing on individual genius by telling the story of how Lincoln's success was largely based on his ability to pull together and enable a team made up of disparate opponents. It has become famous in recent years as an inspiration to Barack Obama – and the one book, he says, he would choose to have with him if stranded on a desert island – and by being made into a 2012 movie for which Daniel Day Lewis won an Oscar for his role as Lincoln.

Goodwin begins the book with the stories of the four candidates in the running at the hotly contested Republican primary of 1860: New York Senator and former Governor William H. Seward, widely considered the frontrunner; former Missouri Attorney General Edward Bates, preferred by more conservative elements of the party; Ohio Governor Salmon P. Chase; and Abraham Lincoln, former US Representative from Illinois and the least likely candidate.

While Seward was considered the favourite, as he was the most widely recognized political figure and almost had a majority of pledges, detractors thought he was too radical on slavery and too liberal on immigration, meaning that he would not be able to carry all the northern states in the elections, leading to a subsequent Democratic win in the general election. Edward Bates on the other hand was seen as too conservative for liberal Republicans and had never enlisted in the army: problematic at this time for a potential commander in chief. Salmon Chase's candidature was hampered by personal attacks from powerful Ohio politicians, and he was unable to mount a serious challenge. By skilfully making himself the unobjectionable second choice of each of the Republican factions, Lincoln emerged as the one choice a majority could agree upon and surprisingly won the nomination and went on to win the presidency.

Then Lincoln did something even more unexpected. Determined to hold his party and the country together, and revive it at a time of heightened partisanship, Lincoln went back to the past and persuaded each of his former rivals – Seward, Bates and Chase – to join his Cabinet.

Seward, whom Lincoln appointed Secretary of State, came to respect and collaborate closely with Lincoln. Bates was appointed Attorney General and also came to appreciate the President. Chase, however, who had become Secretary of the Treasury, continued to scheme against Lincoln from within the Cabinet, hoping to replace him as the Republican nominee in the next presidential election. But Lincoln kept Chase in the Cabinet until 1864, recognizing his superior skill at financing the war effort. He even doubled down on his faith in Chase's abilities by also recruiting Chase ally Edwin M. Stanton to become Secretary of War, and then appointed Chase as the Chief Justice of the US Supreme Court in 1864, believing him the best man to secure the rights of newly freed black citizens.

In addition to managing the disparate personalities of his Cabinet, Kearns also tells how Lincoln sifts through a series of generals, including George B. McClellan, Henry Halleck and George Meade, until he finds success through the unlikely combination of Ulysses S. Grant and William T. Sherman. While this approach to remixing old foes and rivals into his team seemed odd and risky to many at the time, Lincoln himself explained it this way: 'We need the strongest men of the party in the Cabinet. We needed to hold our own people together. I had looked the party over and concluded that these were the very strongest men. Then I had no right to deprive the country of their services.'

In an interview with Kearns after the movie came out, she was asked about Lincoln's other traits, apart from those associated with Lincoln's ability to mix, sift, balance and remix divergent ingredients into his team. She identified two. Both of which are useful to consider if you are looking to blend creative elements effectively.

The first is maintaining control of the timing of key actions. Kearns relays how Lincoln reflected that

> had the issue of the Emancipation Proclamation come up six months earlier, he would have lost the border states. And if he had waited any longer than he did, he would have lost the morale boost that it provided and the extraordinary contribution that the African American soldiers made in the Army. So it almost was the perfect timing, and I think that came from his own sense of where the country was.

There will be some in a remixed team that will want to act earlier and others who want to wait, and the world is littered with great creative ideas and entities that arrived too early or too late to meet the market. So a key to good creative team leadership is to have good judgement about this.

A second was his ability to keep things light when they get tense, as they often do when you have a team comprising strong but different (and difficult) personalities. Lincoln's office at the White House became both a place to meet, discuss, and make the tough decisions, but also a place where the Cabinet could relax. That was such a huge part of Lincoln's blend, Kearns believes. 'He'd be in the middle of a terrible Cabinet meeting, and he'd tell this funny story and make everyone laugh… There's something about humor and laughter that's so refreshing, that in difficult times if you can remember to look at yourself and laugh from the outside in.'

Could you bring a 'rival' into your own creative team – or agree to sign up to a team of rivals under another's leadership? What kind of social skills (humour, conviviality) have you used to lighten a difficult meeting? How do you control the parameters of a creative team (timing, resources, key decisions) while still allowing space for creative differences? What benefits might a team of rivals bring to your own creativity?

RESOURCES

Cunningham, L. (2012), 'Doris Kearns Goodwin on Life, Death and the Presidency', *Washington Post*, 28 November: www.washingtonpost.com/national/on-leadership/doris-kearns-goodwin -on-life-death-and-the-presidency/2012/11/28/99909950–38bb–11e2–8a97–363b0f9a0ab3 _story.html
Kearns Goodwin, D. (2005), *Team of Rivals*, Simon and Schuster.

RECIPE 12. ROYAL SHAKESPEARE COMPANY II: REMIXING THE ENSEMBLE (STRATFORD-UPON-AVON)

INGREDIENTS:

- Trust, empathy and dynamic difference
- A theatre organization inspired by its own history
- An artistic recipe repurposed for a whole organization
- Equal parts of orientation and animation

During the decade 2003 to 2012, the Royal Shakespeare Company transformed its corporate culture under the joint leadership of artistic director Michael Boyd and executive director Vikki Heywood. When they arrived at the RSC, they found an organization recovering from successive leadership interventions, facing increased competition for audiences and funding, and fractured by a deepening divide between artistic and administrative staff. Boyd and Heywood set out to rebuild the company's identity and purpose around the shared values of 'ensemble'. Ensemble describes a collective approach to theatre which was embedded in the RSC's formative years as a company under Peter Brook and Peter Hall, as well as in the traditions of Shakespeare's own ensemble, The King's Men. Boyd and Heywood set out to transfer the values of ensemble from rehearsal room to boardroom, based on mutual respect, collective communication, openness, trust, and – above all, what Boyd described as 'dynamic difference' – an ability to harness conflict towards change.

Mapping this new direction for the company was an exercise in sifting. It was vital that each company member, from the box office staff and finance team to the actors and stage crew, should understand the values of ensemble and what these meant in relation to their own day-to-day work. Boyd talked individually and collectively to colleagues, board members and stakeholders – he published a kind of manifesto for ensemble in the UK theatre's trade paper, *The Stage*. Boyd disliked corporate rhetoric and preferred to speak of values and shared purpose rather than 'brand'; he also used an emotional, intuitive vocabulary more attuned to an arts organization – the new values of ensemble were peppered with phrases like 'surrender of the self', 'moral imagination' and 'the ability to be appallingly honest'.

But it was also necessary to motivate these values, to turn understanding into actions. Leaders had to actively 'mix' the team, stirring up old habits and relationships, breaking down the barriers between rehearsal room and administrative offices, tolerating dissent and conflict as a means to open debate and rebuild consensus. In discussions with Heywood and Boyd, and in our observations of rehearsals, we noted some of the leadership approaches designed to achieve this 'remix'.

- **Modelling behaviour**: Heywood described to us the need to embody the values of ensemble in her own actions. She refused to exploit her hierarchical privileges, for example business class travel or preferential parking places. When she wanted colleagues to engage with new ideas, she would be seen reading books or engaging with academic consultants. She attempted to 'be the change' not just to describe it. For the organization as a whole, Heywood claims that ensemble 'forced managers to behave in inclusive ways'.
- **Leading from the middle**: As a director, Boyd wanted to encourage his actors to take risks and express their own ideas. In rehearsals, we observed him addressing his actors more like a coach or mentor, helping them to reflect on their actions and ideas and providing a common vocabulary within which these ideas could be shared. This leadership approach is the antithesis to the top-down leadership style of Harvey Weinstein and was consistent with the values of trust and empathy at the heart of ensemble. Heywood, too, was concerned to get people to buy into the new ethos, not to thrust it upon them. Decisions took longer when taken collectively, but they were more robust and meaningful than top-down decisions imposed from above.
- **Opening out**: For Boyd and Heywood, leadership was not only inwardly directed. The RSC started to engage more openly with audiences and other external stakeholders, inviting opinions, even criticisms. They wanted the organization to feel connected to bigger social and ethical arguments, which might challenge internal groupthink, based around values described by Heywood as 'corporate collective communication, self-awareness and responsibility'. In rehearsals, Boyd brought in outside speakers to place the play in a wider political and social context, building up a shared vocabulary and understanding which would frame future conversations about the play, taking the actors beyond their individual personal preference to a wider set of reference points.
- **Tolerating difference**: A keystone of creative teams is the ability to encourage what Boyd called 'dynamic difference'. Differences of opinion were brought to the front, encouraging debate and resolution rather than grudging acceptance. The attitude was not that 'anything goes', but that every idea has value and must be argued for, including the ideas of the director.

By embracing a different set of values and a different approach to leadership, Boyd and

Heywood were able to successfully transform the RSC, building new relationships with audiences, winning round funders and even changing the physical infrastructure of the theatre building. At the same time, the collective process of ensemble also brought artistic success, winning over critics and audiences. As a recipe for remixing creative teams, the ensemble model demonstrates that organizational change is not down to the leader alone, but that leaders play a key role in building energy and commitment from everybody else. Such models of distributed leadership and collective decision-making are not unusual in artistic organizations; the visionary leap of the ensemble at the RSC was to apply this approach to the creativity of the whole organization, the boardroom as well as the rehearsal room.

The dual leadership, between artistic director and executive director, helped to bridge divisions in the organization. Dual leadership is not unusual in arts organizations, but there is often a tacit hierarchy, with either the artist or the administrator calling the shots. Because Boyd and Heywood trusted each other and worked as equals, this inclusive ethos filtered through the organization as a whole. Again, the comparison with Miramax and Weinstein is revealing. If Boyd had played up to the stereotype of maverick artistic visionary rule-breaker, if Heywood had reduced her contribution to bureaucratic control freak, the partnership would not have worked. They both embodied the sifting, analytical mindset needed to plan and coordinate a creative team, as well as the mixing, energizing approach needed to drive through change. Remixing required a joint effort across different capabilities, different people and different divisions to remake the organization.

Are there other disciplines or traditions (artistic, organizational, historical) which you could draw upon to remix your creative team? How does the language and behaviour of the leader influence your team's attitude and trust? How does the leadership of the RSC differ from Lincoln's 'team of rivals'? What values would you want to relearn if remixing your creative team?

RESOURCES

Bilton, C. and S. Cummings (2011), *From Bard to Boardroom: How to Encourage Creative Strategy in Your Organisation*: www.bl.uk/britishlibrary/~/media/bl/global/business-and-management/pdfs/non-secure/f/r/o/from-bard-to-boardroom-how-to-encourage-creative-strategy-in-your-organization.pdf

Hewison, R., J. Holden and S. Jones (2010), *All Together: A Creative Approach to Organisational Change* (NESTA): https://media.nesta.org.uk/documents/royal_shakespeare.pdf

Heywood, V., C. Bilton and S. Cummings (2014), 'Promoting Ensemble: Creative Leadership in Practice at the Royal Shakespeare Company' in C. Bilton and S. Cummings (eds), *Handbook of Management and Creativity*, Edward Elgar Publishing.

In Part II, the How of creativity, we have described 'blending' creativity as a bi-sociative combination of opposites. Sifting a creative team means separating out the elements; mixing describes agitating those elements together. Balancing attempts to orchestrate these different elements against each other, avoiding excessive reliance on one model, approach or leader; remixing pulls in both directions, breaking and remaking connections in order to reinvent new patterns and combinations.

While Part I describes the What of creativity, focused on creative people and capabilities, Part II, the How, has described the combinations of individuals in collective teams and processes.

Our model of sifting, mixing, balancing and remixing draws on Koestler's theory of bi-sociative connections and is inspired by other theories, from Frank Barron's 'tolerance for contradictions' to Keith Sawyer's 'focus switching', all of which describe an ability to move between mental states (divergent and convergent, rational and intuitive). None of these models provides a perfect solution to the How of creativity – rather it is the dynamic movement between them which allows new combinations to emerge. These unexpected combinations between apparently contradictory frameworks are the outcome of Koestler's bi-sociative connections.

If you want creative outcomes, the challenging, unusual combinations of a 'team of rivals' can take us further than the like-minded, comfortable and familiar. Like the first time you tasted balsamic vinegar with strawberries, bacon and banana, or chocolate and potato chips, there is something extremely satisfying in realizing that a combination that at first glance may seem implausible, works. One of the reactions that people often have to finding a new working partnership like this is, 'so if this tastes good, what else might work?' And it is this spirit of bi-sociative creativity that we want you to take away from this part of *Creativities*, and on to the next.

We conclude Part II with a Creativities Canvas for the Royal Shakespeare Company's ensemble, showing 'how' different approaches were used to lead and blend a creative team.

SOURCES AND FURTHER READING FOR PART II

In Part II we consider the blending of creativities in teams. This has been an important topic in creativity research, shifting the focus from creative individuals onto the relationships between them, in order to understand how different team roles, thinking styles and abilities can complement and support each other (Belbin 1996, De Bono 1990, Kirton 2001, Nijstad and Paulus 2003, Sawyer 2003, West 2002). The concept of 'uncreativity' – that certain supposedly 'uncreative' individuals or processes can actually be part of the creative process – is also relevant here (Bilton 2015). We also consider how different types of leadership can support team roles – the perils of 'charismatic' leadership (Nisbett and Walmsley 2016), the possibilities for 'distributed' or 'covert' leadership (Mintzberg 1998), vulnerable leadership (Brown 2015). All of this points towards a 'systems' model of creativity (Csikszentmihalyi 1988, Gruber and Davis 1988, Kanter 1988), in which leadership and organization can themselves be integral to the creative process rather than standing outside it (Basadur 2004, Kanter 1988, Mumford et al. 2002, Zhou and George 2003).

Basadur, M. (2004), 'Leading Others to Think Innovatively Together: Creative leadership', *The Leadership Quarterly* **15**(1), 103–121.

Belbin, R.M. (1996), *Management Teams: Why They Succeed or Fail*, Oxford: Butterworth-Heinemann.

Bilton, C. (2015), 'Uncreativity: The Shadow Side of Creativity', *International Journal of Cultural Policy* **21**(2), 153–167.

Brown, B. (2015), *Daring Greatly*, London: Avery Publishing.

Csikszentmihalyi, M. (1988), 'Society, Culture, and Person: A Systems View of Creativity' in R.J. Sternberg (ed.), *The Nature of Creativity: Contemporary Psychological Perspectives*, New York/Cambridge: Cambridge University Press, 325–339.

De Bono, E. (1990), *Six Thinking Hats*, London: Penguin.

De Rond, M. (2008), *The Last Amateurs: To Hell and Back with the Cambridge Boat Race Crew*, Cambridge: Icon Books.

Gruber, H. and S. Davis (1988), 'Inching Our Way up Mount Olympus: The Evolving-Systems Approach to Creative Thinking' in R.J. Sternberg (ed.), *The Nature of Creativity: Contemporary Psychological Perspectives*, New York/Cambridge: Cambridge University Press, 243–270.

Kanter, R.M. (1988), 'When a Thousand Flowers Bloom', *Research in Organizational Behaviour* **10**, 123–167.

Kirton, M. (2001), 'Adapters and Innovators: Why New Ideas Get Blocked' in J. Henry (ed.), *Creative Management*, 2nd edition, Milton Keynes: Open University Press, 169–180.

Mintzberg, H. (1998), 'Covert Leadership: Notes on Managing Professionals', *Harvard Business Review* **76** (Nov–Dec), 140–147.

Mumford, M.D., G.M. Scott, B. Gaddis and J.M. Strange (2002), 'Leading Creative People: Orchestrating Expertise and Relationships', *Leadership Quarterly* **13**, 705–750.

Nijstad, B. and Paulus, P. (2003), 'Group Creativity: Common Themes and Future Directions' in P. Paulus and B. Nijstad (eds), *Group Creativity*, 1st edition, Oxford: Oxford University Press, 326–340.

Nisbett, M. and B. Walmsley (2016), 'The Romanticisation of Charismatic Leadership in the Arts', *Journal of Arts Management, Law and Society* **46**(1), 2–12.

Sawyer, R.K. (2003) *Group Creativity: Music, Theatre, Collaboration*, Mahwah, NJ: Erlbaum.

West, M.A. (2002), 'Sparkling Fountains or Stagnant Ponds: An Integrative Model of Creativity and Innovation Implementation in Work Groups', *Applied Psychology: An International Review* **51**, 355–387.

Zhou, J. and J.M. George (2003), 'Awakening Employee Creativity: The Role of Leader Emotional Intelligence', *The Leadership Quarterly* **14**(4/5), 545–568.

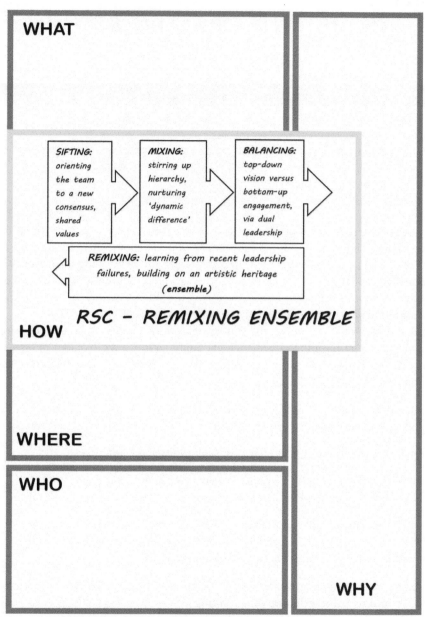

SIFTING: orienting the team to a new consensus, shared values

MIXING: stirring up hierarchy, nurturing 'dynamic difference'

BALANCING: top-down vision versus bottom-up engagement, via dual leadership

REMIXING: learning from recent leadership failures, building on an artistic heritage *(ensemble)*

RSC – REMIXING ENSEMBLE

WHAT

HOW

WHERE

WHO

WHY

Figure 2.4   Creativities canvas example 2: the RSC and the How of creativity

PART III
THE WHERE – THE CREATIVE SET-UP

You've got the ingredients to build your creative endeavour, and you've figured out the blend to start making things happen. But now you need to think about where to put it all together, a means of producing your creative output consistently and developing further creative ideas and products. While the first two parts of *Creativities* were about the What and the How of the creative process, this third part is about developing the Where: the organizational approaches or processes utilized to move your creative endeavours forward.

In Part I, the What of creativity, the simple framework we developed to help think about what to look for in terms of the ingredients that might go into a creative idea or development, was the crate. Two sides of the crate framework, like a box you might take to market, expressed choices on the left and right side about:

- generating more with fewer ingredients than is conventionally the case; or
- creating something better with more or other than conventional ingredients.

While on the top and bottom, there were considerations about whether:

- new and different creative ingredients were being sought; or
- old ones re-thought and utilized in a way to put a 'twist' on an approach or tradition.

The crate became the organizing schema for Part I of *Creativities*.

In Part II, the How, the organizing framework was *sifting*, *mixing*, *balancing* and *remixing*. Here we outlined key blending decisions to be considered:

- between the mix of creative ingredients being directed by a higher or a lower degree of design or directedness that we called 'sifting';
- a higher or lower degree of thrust and enthusiasm that we called 'mixing';
- an ability to combine direction and energy that we described as 'balancing';
- a willingness to combine different, contradictory approaches and to look for new unexpected combinations, which we referred to as 'remixing'.

Sifting indicates a strong focus on method, theory and pre-planning. Mixing indicates a more energetic 'act now, ask questions later' approach. Balancing is more holistic, but it also means challenging norms and hierarchies that may have become habitual. Remixing indicates a more reflective, learning-by-doing approach which embraces new and unexpected outcomes emerging from below.

Here in Part III, the Where, the metaphor we draw upon to build an organizing framework is that of the formation of the benches that we might work around in the kitchen. More precisely, how should you arrange your bench or benches and the activities around them within your kitchen to best suit the processes for advancing your creative endeavour?

As for specific strategies for this part of the process, the Where is a little different from the previous two parts. Here, the overarching strategy is to assess which structures and/or approaches line up with what you are seeking to achieve in your creative enterprise (we'll come back to this 'Why' question in Part V). The Where framework outlines four organizational forms and Part III explores their strengths and weaknesses – it's your task to figure out the Where that's best for you, if you have that choice. Or, if you find yourself having to create within a particular organization already, your task is to develop strategies that creatively exploit your organization's strengths and minimize its weaknesses. Beyond that, the final section of Part III explores how you might seek to refresh your creative approaches and rethink where you create.

The 'Where' framework: the creative bench formation

As with the previous two parts of *Creativities*, the bench formation framework brings together research done around how to best organize for creative development and learning. It focuses creators on two key choices: the degree of control exerted by the originators of the creativity, and the scale of the enterprise.

ORIGINATOR CONTROL: TIGHT VS LOOSE

The first creative process choice relates to the level of control of the organization. Should this be tighter, with decisions directed by the founder, leader or corporate policies and practices at the centre? Or should this be looser, with much more latitude for self-management, collaboration, organic development, and inspiration for new pathways coming from multiple directions?

To illustrate using our kitchen analogy: tight control would be a form of organization or process where everything would be expected to be done according to the head chef's vision and instructions, or the corporate model being consistently 'rolled out' in a particular branch or franchise. An example of loose control, on the other hand, could be a process whereby ideas and decisions emerge as a group of chefs and other stakeholders gather around one bench and share thinking about the ingredients and blend to find the collective best way or a consensus.

CREATIVE SCALE: LARGER VS SMALLER

This second dimension of the bench framework, may be less of a choice. Generally this is more a product of where you are at in terms of the resources at your disposal and how long you've been at it, or 'in business'. This is about the scale of your creative enterprise relative to the rest of the 'industry' or your competitors. Are you seeking to promote creativity in a larger organization or a smaller one? To illustrate again via the food business: are we talking about creativity within a large chain like McDonald's or Jamie Oliver Restaurants; or a single exclusive dining room or a small food truck?

Putting these two axes together results in a 2 × 2 schema with four creative process formations. We label these as follows:

- M-form – larger and tighter (e.g., Toyota);
- X-form – larger and looser (e.g., Disney);
- Star-form – smaller and tighter (e.g., Apple/Tiger King);
- O-form – smaller and looser (e.g., Factory Records).

Next to these labels (in brackets) we have listed the cases or recipes we use to illustrate the strengths and weaknesses of these formats and how they can be managed later in Part III. And in Figure 3.1 we provide a diagram or symbolic representation of their shape. In the sections that follow, we will describe each of the four creative organization types and their strengths and weaknesses. As each type has both strengths and weaknesses (which we will summarize at the end of each section here), there is no one best way. The key is to develop the form, or the hybrid form, that best suits your situation and the outcomes you want to create.

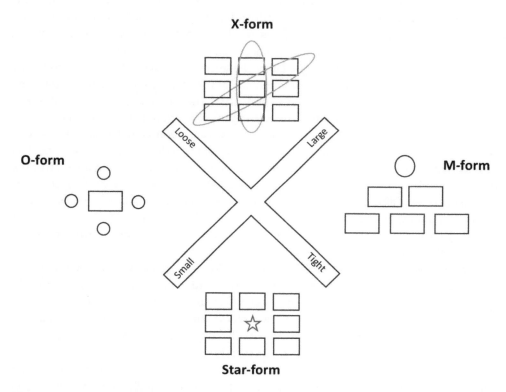

Figure 3.1   Creativities framework 3: the creative bench formation

3.1   THE CREATIVE M-FORM: ELEPHANTS CAN DANCE (SORT OF)

The M-form organization is generally associated with the classic, triangle organization chart that people associate with working in a modern business. In fact, the M-form has become symbolic of the shape of the modern multinational corporation and the uncreative, pigeon-holed nature of office life. But, this is not how the form was envisaged, and, as our recipe about creative practices at Toyota will demonstrate, the M-form can be an extremely powerful creative force.

Over 2 million people each year visit the Uffizi Gallery in Florence. But almost none realize that the building was built to house the first M-form organization. The word 'office' comes from the Latin *officium*, meaning service, duty or function. Later, this became *oficio* in Spanish, and in Italian *officio* or *uffizio*.

Before the Uffizi was a gallery, it was an office – and one with a particular creative purpose. The Medici family presided over Florence's growing power as a city-state in the 16th and 17th centuries and sought to invest in its (and their) further success. This investment had grown an increasing staff of semi-permanent chancellors, lawyers, notaries and accountants and a full-time secretariat, which came to number in the hundreds. This was in stark contrast to the aristocratic or monastic amateurism that governed the rest of the world's city-states. Not long after his ascension to power in 1537, Cosimo I decided he needed to create permanent housing for his administration. The result was the Uffizi, designed by leading architect Giorgio Vasari.

While it functions now as an art gallery and one of Italy's most visited tourist attractions, you can still observe signs of how Cosimo and Vasari (who would have worked with something of a 'blank slate' compared with a commission for a church or palace that would have to confirm to established norms) thought a multifaceted organization should present itself and its processes. It is a three-storey U shape where visitors would be welcomed into the ground floor rooms and divisions (now galleries), some adorned with sculptures, maps and other artworks, others laboratories, arranged to provide a sense of grandeur. Offices and meeting spaces were on the higher floors, affording those who worked there a good view of those who entered the complex without being seen themselves – a way of providing oversight of what was coming, impressing those who observed, and compartmentalizing projects and moving resources efficiently between them.

The Uffizi represents the archetypal organizational M-form with its vertical perspective and its horizontal compartmentalizations. As architecture critic Lewis Mumford notes, it is 'the original cliché of bureaucratic architecture at its best… to be reproduced with minor variations [for centuries] on a monumental scale' in tower blocks with divisions on different floors and organizational charts and their segmentations to this day. The M is wide to enable creative spread, and tall to enable oversight.

The most famous explanation of how the M-form organization, prefigured by the Uffizi, became the norm in the modern world was outlined by Alfred Chandler in his books *Strategy and Scope: Chapters in the History of the Industrial Enterprise* in 1962; and *The Visible Hand: The Managerial Revolution in American Business* in 1977. 'Modern business enterprise is easily defined', Chandler explained; 'it has two specific characteristics: it contains many distinct operating units and it is managed by a hierarchy of salaried executives' (Chandler, 1977: 1). Chandler is describing the format of the hierarchical triangular organizational chart made up of boxes and lines that became such popular ways to describe organizations in the 20th century.

While this organizational form might sound and look both uncreative and boring, certainly when compared with the other three forms we describe here, it has its creative strengths and should not be overlooked – as it often is, which we will illustrate. And, in fact, it hasn't always been understood and depicted in such a generic and non-descript way. Perhaps the first attempts to characterize this form in industrial times were drawn by those American railroad companies whose circumstances Chandler saw (the need to operate across widening territories in a coordinated and consistent way) as driving the spread of the M-form.

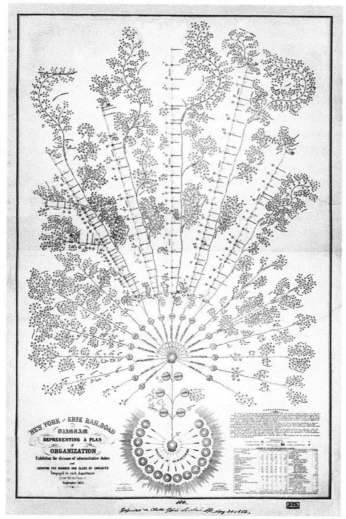

Figure 3.2 McClellan's original organization chart from the New York and Erie Railroad, c. 1860

Moreover, in the early 20th century, examples of the M-form were seen as more creative than their competitors. For example, Alfred P. Sloan used it to enable General Motors to overtake Ford and Chrysler by creating and developing a whole range of different brands, each with their own positioning and personality. In the 1920s and 1930s, Sloan's team developed a creative practice whereby each of GM's arms sought to serve a specific market segment. Despite some shared components, each arm or brand distinguished itself from its stablemates with unique technological applications and styling. The shared components and common corporate management enabled economies of scale and the sharing of resources, while creative freedoms within the arms promoted distinctive flourishes. The result was what Sloan called a 'ladder of success'. An entry-level customer started out with the 'honest hard-worker' Chevrolet, then rose through Pontiac, Oldsmobile, Buick, and ultimately to the sleek and sophisticated Cadillac. The Ford organization, with its founder ruling the roost at the centre of everything, stuck to its Model T, one-size-fits-all philosophy to the point of collapse. It was only the (grudging) acknowledgement that GM was more creative, and subsequently changing its ways, that saved Ford.

This organizational form got a bad reputation for creativity as the 20th century wore on, though, as it came to be associated with bureaucracy, a dull greyness and efficiency over innovation. The view of the M-form and creativity as opposites started to thaw towards the end of the century. And perhaps the most famous document illustrating the change is the bestselling book, *Who Says Elephants Can't Dance?* by Lou Gerstner, CEO of IBM from 1993 to 2002. Gerstner was credited with saving and turning around IBM after it lost its way, as it became more enamoured with maintaining its creative advantage than developing it (much like Ford in the 1920s). Published after he retired in 2002, *Elephants* told the story of how IBM became more agile and flexible.

Relatedly, since the beginning of the 21st century, creative organizations with scale and direct control imposed from the centre have sought to employ more playful metaphors in their visual descriptions of how they work, indicating a recognition that big does not necessarily mean uncreative. The BBC have created an organizational process chart in the shape of a flower; and Homebase have depicted their organization using the metaphor of a three-legged stool, to name a couple of examples.

We could go on, but the strengths and weaknesses of the form are already illustrated in this history and they are summarized below. And in the recipe that follows, the story of creativity at Toyota illustrates how some elements of a big, tightly organized beast can be more creative than a smaller, looser form.

The M-form summary

Strengths
- can create simultaneously in multiple ways;
- scale can provide financial cushions for investment in creativity;
- able to specialize and compartmentalize/'walk and chew gum' at the same time;
- large staff provides an ability to observe creative processes, learn and plan objectively for the future.

Weaknesses
- can be bureaucratic, slow, mechanistic;
- as processes become policies, culture becomes homogeneous, divisions become silos, and creative sparks stop flying;
- can be bland, or lacking in personality.

RECIPE 13. TOYOTA: DYNAMIC CREATIVE CAPABILITIES (TOYOTA CITY, JAPAN)

INGREDIENTS:

- 1 massive automobile manufacturer
- 1 unique national culture of frugal and clever innovation
- Deep reflection on what strengths are driving creativity
- A pinch of wabi-sabi

Perhaps the oldest tool or framework for thinking strategically about how to develop an organization is SWOT analysis. SWOT, which was developed by management consultants over 50 years ago, stands for strengths, weaknesses, opportunities and threats, and this has been the most popular strategy framework applied in organizations all over the world for the past few decades according to surveys by management consultancy firms.

Its popularity may be largely due to its simplicity: you simply list the organization's strengths to focus on and weaknesses to mitigate within the organization; and the opportunities to seize and threats to avoid external to the organization. However, along with being the most popular framework, it's also the framework that most people express frustration with. This is partly because people take off with a hiss and a roar and create a long list of strengths that becomes too lengthy to focus on and target actions in relation to. This lack of focus is for two reasons:

- First, because it would make more sense to outline the external opportunities and threats before moving to look at strengths. This is because something is really only a useful creative strength if it enables you to exploit an opportunity or avoid a threat. So, in the framing of this book, we would say that in the What and How phases, you are looking for opportunities to do something creative, while in this Where phase you are looking for the strengths related to your people, place and configuration that you can deploy to act on these opportunities.
- Second, because some strengths are potentially more creative than others and, if they are not ranked accordingly, they can get lumped in with dozens of lesser-order strengths.

Both of these issues can be dealt with. There is no need to tackle strengths first; you can start anywhere (in fact, in its original incarnation, SWOT analysis was called SOFT analysis – F was for faults – but after this proved unpopular it was retooled into a W and the order of things changed to create the memorable word SWOT). So, we think it is useful to peruse your creative opportunities first before digging into your strengths. And, there are now some great techniques for filtering strengths so that the most important ones rise to the top.

The first is to apply another framework called VRIO to focus on the strengths that can add the most creative value over time. VRIO stands for 'valuable, rare, inimitable and organization' and suggests that the real creative strengths that are focused upon should be those that are:

- Actually **valuable** to the end user, not just valuable to the organization (e.g., a large bank balance is great, but of no direct value to your customers; styling, however,

might be).
- **Rare**, in that the strength is not one widely shared by other providers (and conse-quently something that you can differentiate yourself on).
- **Inimitable**, in that if other providers don't have it and can see the value in acquiring it for themselves, they could not do it (e.g., an old family recipe or access to a scarce resource).
- If a strength gets over these three bars, these are the things that the **organization** must promote (e.g., if 'teamwork' is V, R and I, the organization should reward this rather than individual performance).

The second is to focus on the strengths that are capabilities: or, the things that actively create stuff, rather than the things that are just stuff. So, for example, money that you can use to pay talent is not a capability, but add the ability to scout and see talent and then you have a capability. In other words, capabilities are verbs (e.g., scouting), not nouns (e.g., money).

Some now argue that we should focus even more particularly on 'dynamic capabilities'. These are sometimes referred to as 'second order capabilities', or capabilities that will, if nurtured, create future capabilities. An example might be a particular creative spirit that will continue to promote particular creative solutions (something that will be apparent in each of the first four recipes in Part III) or a connection to a particular *terroir* (which we'll explain later).

This reflection on how to match organizational or process strengths to opportunities is useful for assessing what the key creative capabilities or processes that one of the world's largest organizations, Toyota, deploys.

How does an operation as large and widespread as Toyota stay creative? How does it combine the mass of an elephant's body with the dexterity of a trunk to keep itself nourished? A lot of it comes down to understanding which parts of its process drive real, value-adding creativity, and designing the organization so as to nurture those strengths accordingly.

Figure 3.3 shows three levels, but the most important strengths that have driven the organization's creative evolution for the past 75 years are those at the core. On the surface are the strengths that one might readily associate with Toyota's success: like the global sales network, the brand recognition, the state of the art manufacturing prowess, the research and development departments. But, while what these elements might create for customers may be valuable, and they might even be difficult for newcomers to the auto industry to imitate, they are certainly not rare in the automobile industry. Every auto manufacturer still operating possesses these things.

So, looking deeper, one might pick out Toyota's more unique capabilities: the ability to take and adapt skills and approaches from across its diversified network and beyond (whether these relate to materials or human capabilities) and apply these to the auto business; productivity improvement approaches (Toyota not only applies these things, it develops them: approaches like total quality management with its emphasis on creating higher quality at lower cost as part of a 'quality circle' were invented at Toyota); and a culture of frugality, born out of a context of having limited resources in the decades after the end of the Second World War. These are activities that add value and are dif-ficult to replicate, and they are rarer globally than the surface strengths outlined in the previous paragraph, but they are still not rare among auto manufacturers in Japan and

South-East Asia. There are probably half a dozen competitors that could lay claim to similar capabilities.

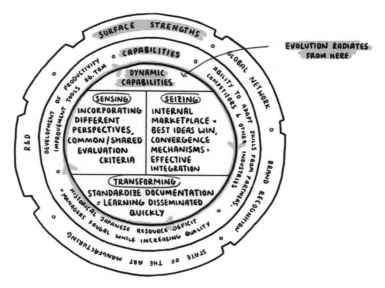

Note: Copyright Stephen Cummings

Figure 3.3   Toyota's strengths, capabilities and dynamic capabilities

But the valuable, rare and inimitable aspects of Toyota's operations that enable it to innovate for the long term and recreate and reconfigure quickly if there is an urgent need, are three other capabilities that Toyota points to as being at the centre of where creativity comes from in the company.

The first relates to policies focused on incorporating a wide range of perspectives and potential ingredients for creativity from a wide range of industries and **sensing**, matching the opportunities seen to the company's manufacturing and marketing strengths.

The second is Toyota's policy and culture around the notion of a market for ideas from anywhere in the company. This means that any person or group can put forward a creative idea and have it assessed. If the company decides to **seize** upon and invest in one of these ideas, they look to quickly integrate it into existing operations rather than it being worked on separately in an incubator or a lab (we'll see a different approach taken in the Skunk Works case later in Part III). This helps ideas, if they fly, to become part of the reality of the organization quicker.

The third is enabling rapid **transformation** through a laser focus on simplifying and standardizing the company's documentation. This means that, unlike many large organizations, time isn't wasted, as different documentation processes or criteria from across the many parts of the whole organization and opportunities for development can be assessed and acted upon quickly. The extreme tidiness of Toyota's documentation system enables other things – like creative ideas – to form from the ground up in a more organic way. And this, in a circular manner, helps facilitate the sensing of opportunities by enabling these to be assessed and documented effectively because everybody in Toyota understands what the criteria for adoption are at any point in time.

What might be the underappreciated dynamic capabilities that help you and your team sense and seize creative opportunities?

RESOURCES

Cummings, S. and D. Angwin (2015), *Strategy Builder: How to Create and Communicate More Effective Strategies*, Wiley.

3.2   THE CREATIVE X-FORM: IN SQUAD WE TRUST

Despite the negative aspects of the classic M-form organization being more associated with bureaucracy today, the large-scale squad approach (or what we might call the X-form, which we will explain shortly), has more affinity with one root of the word 'bureaucracy'. It is like a bureau, but on a grander scale.

The bureau is a fantastic piece of furniture that reached its zenith in the late 19th century – the famous Wooton bureau made in America may be one of the finest examples. The bureau process the X-form promotes enables a skilful administrator to operate like an apothecarist, bringing together or crossing the necessary elements from particular compartments on a case-by-case basis (hence the X in X-form), so as to best address the particular issues at hand.

A well-known modern example of this approach, or a place for this kind of creativity, is Spotify's organizational structure: a matrix of horizontal squads and vertical chapters divided into particular tribes, but from which particular guilds can be quickly assembled to work on new projects and developments (do an image search for 'Spotify's organizational structure' to see it in a diagram). If the M-form encourages people to stay in their lane to ensure the consistency and efficiency of delivering existing products and services that have been created, the X-form encourages people crossing lanes to keep the creative sparks flying and create new ideas and solutions. It's less efficient, more wasteful, but often more fun and serendipitous as well.

If the X-form is where you think you'd like your creativity to happen, or it just happens to be the type of organization you are working in, it will likely be matched with a different kind of architecture. The offices dating from the Medici to the railroads and through to the modern tower blocks will not suit. Fewer boxes, towers, and hard borders are what's called for, and it is no accident that thinking differently about the Where of creativity embodied by the X-form parallels the emergence of open-plan workspaces.

These ideas are also not as recent as you may think. They can be seen in the first open-plan offices sketched up in the social democracies of Europe in the 1960s, where the idea was to get more people involved in the creative process, rather than the vast majority being told to follow orders from the top; or in some of the innovative thinking about the mobile committee structure of the new League of Nations (the forerunner of the UN) in the 1920s and 1930s (see Figure 3.1); or even in Thomas Edison's workspaces in his premises in Menlo Park in the late 19th century.

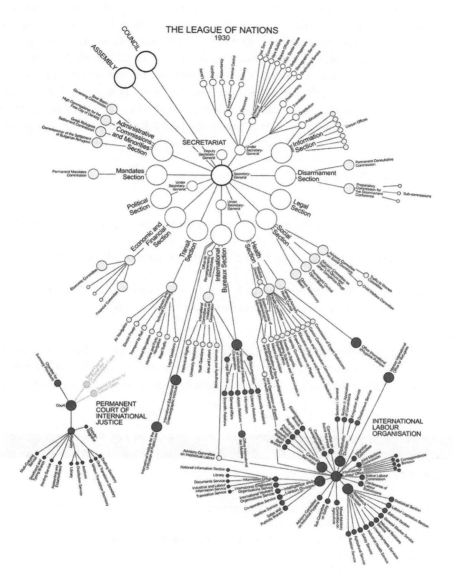

Source: By Martin Grandjean – own work, CC BY-SA 4.0, https://commons.wikimedia .org/w/index.php?curid=63389413

Figure 3.4   A diagram of the League of Nations organization, c. 1930

This notion of matrix or cross-cutting and resetting project teams, with units given the encouragement to band up, change formation, and reform depending on the task at hand, has a number of strengths (as summarized at the end of this section). One of its weaknesses, however, is that there is little holding the whole together. Many successful X-forms mitigate this by having a strong shared belief in a vision, or what has come to be called 'abductive' logic.

In contrast to the more conventional inductive logic (reasoning through observing a number of actual events) and deductive logic (reasoning from established theories), abductive logic seeks to guide discovery not by observation of the past and present, but by imagining what might be possible in the future. A good example would be the way in which NASA engineers rallied around President Kennedy's call to put a man on the moon by the end of the 1960s, even though, at the time, they hadn't yet figured out all the science and technology that would enable them to do it.

The X-form summary

Strengths

- scale creates a financial cushion and enables diverse perspectives to be combined on creative projects;
- a focus on looser cultural control rather than tight policies enables freedom to take risks and create;
- spreading risk may enable current cash cows to fund new creative projects;
- connections across conventional boundaries can spark creativity.

Weaknesses

- things can get messy and inefficient quickly as projects multiply and staff are spread thin;
- can be difficult to coordinate as individuals or groups follow leads and take tangents;
- as collaborative relationships become ingrained, cliques can form, reducing new interactions.

RECIPE 14. WALT DISNEY: DISNEY'S PLUS (LOS ANGELES)

INGREDIENTS:

- A creative entrepreneur who liked to promote and combine other creative talent
- Unique and much-loved characters
- A vision to create things that appealed to both children and adults
- 1 land of opportunity
- A lot of inexpensive land

The Where of creativity was product led for Walt Disney, and Disney's products were his cartoon characters and a novel idea. Prior to Disney there was entertainment for children and entertainment for adults: the only exception was carnival-type parks, which were often of dubious quality and little educational value.

Disney had first conceived of an idea for what he called 'Mickey Mouse Park' in 1948, partly influenced by wondering, as he had done for many years, what to do with his daughters in his limited free time and partly what to say to the hundreds of letters he received from people wanting to visit his Burbank film studio and realizing that, actually, there wasn't really anything very exciting to be seen there.

Disney's idea was to blend these needs together and create something that had not really been done before: multimedia entertainment that families (children *and* adults) could enjoy outdoors together. Disney's cartoon characters were unique for their times in operating at two levels at once – funny and adventurous for kids, soulful and relatable for adults. Disney wanted to take his cartoon characters and other ingredients that celebrated the world around us, and place them in a park-like setting that would appeal to all ages.

As he began to explore the idea, he drew inspiration from World Fairs, 'theme' parks like the Henry Ford Museum and Colonial Williamsburg, and Tivoli Gardens in Copenhagen with its connections to Danish fairy tales. His ideas quickly outgrew the vacant lot next to his studio in Burbank, so he sought advice as to the best place to build it.

The advice he received was good. Los Angeles had the perfect climate. But with a growing middle class made increasingly mobile as car ownership soared, and new inter-state highways being built out from Los Angeles, the land he needed at a price he could afford was only available in Anaheim, Orange County, about 30 miles south-east of LA. And, by working with local government, Disney's team was able to get the road builders to add a couple of extra lanes to Route 101 (now the I5) that was proposed to pass by Anaheim.

While the land in Orange County was relatively cheap, Disney found that turning his dream into reality was fiercely expensive, certainly more expensive than his film studio could afford. So, he had to think about how he could parlay and connect what he had into a way of making the money to fund the enterprise. Banks refused to invest in what they thought was a pipe dream. So Walt's brother Roy came up with another idea. Use Disney content to create a new connection with the fastest growing medium at the time: televi-sion. Disney agreed to produce a weekly television show called *Disneyland* that packaged up existing and new films and was beamed across the United States (and the wider world) for the ABC network. In return, ABC agreed to fund the development of Disney's park, also now named Disneyland.

It was a ratings winner and must-see TV for at least two generations of viewers each Sunday evening. The show, hosted by Walt from 'the office of Walt Disney', acted as a weekly one-hour advance advertisement for Disneyland, where the host invited people to 'take part in the building of Disneyland'. Organizational chart diagrams drawn by Disney in the 1950s and 1960s, explaining the way in which the elements of Disneyland grew outward from the original films and characters and cross-pollinated one another, are nice depictions of what an X-form organization structure can do (see the *Fast Company* article in 'Resources' below to view some of these).

Disneyland, however, was even harder to create than it was to imagine and fund. So much of what it would require had never been done before, and bringing cartoon charac-ters and other worlds to life would require a criss-crossing of landscaping, art, set design, animation, computer programming, animatronics, actors, scripts, live action, film, logis-tics, and supply chain management, among other things. But Disney's great strength as an organizer of creativity was to connect different talents into teams; provide an inspiring vision of what the final result might look like (Disney called this 'Imagineering', design thinkers might call it 'abductive logic'); express confidence that they could figure out how to achieve it; and then get out of the way. The cross-functional project teams for which Disney, according to John Hench (one of the original Imagineers – those who Walt pulled together to work on the Disneyland concept), was 'always scouting for talent', combined old stagers from his studio with new young talents, and they achieved and exceeded expectations. Included in these teams were a number of what are now seen as pioneering female artists and designers, including Mary Blair, Harriet Burns and Alice Davis.

Not wanting to overly manage these teams, Walt resisted the idea that he should have an office in Anaheim, preferring to stay in Burbank and just drop by to visit and ask a challenging question or two from time to time. Comparing this with the conventional organizations of the day, Imagineer Bob Gurr described what Disney created as 'an absolute marvel of super organization without being organized'.

The park was unveiled during a special televised press event broadcast by ABC on 17 July 1955. Attendance was worryingly low to begin with, but as demand picked up, Disney and his team could feel that not only would the park be a success, but it would be a key element in the future development of what the Disney Corporation would grow to become.

Disney passed away in 1966, aged just 65. As newscaster Eric Sevareid put it, Disney knew better than anyone that while there may be very little grown-up in a child, there is a lot of child in every grown-up. He knew that the world appears to a child as if it is gift-wrapped, and the key for Disney was to present that in an uncynical way for adults too. If he could make what he created first and foremost appealing to children, and then layer on characters and human insights that adults could appreciate, he would achieve what he set out to create. And it turned out that Disneyland would become just one piece in that growing puzzle.

Nobody had ever made anything like Disneyland before. When it was made, and after Walt Disney passed away, the people who worked for him reflected on the influence of his creativity. Rolly Crump claimed that after Walt died, he and a group of his fellow Imagineers went out for a few drinks and just looked at each other wondering what they would do next. He recalled that John Hench said, 'Well, I guess we'll find out now how much of our work Walt did for us.'

As it happened, Walt's creative ingredients, vision and organization, had done a lot. But Walt didn't actually need to be there in the room for the creativity he imagined to continue. He wasn't actually in the room before he passed away, even though it felt like he was. And that spirit would continue after he died. Walt probably always wanted to do more than just a Disneyland, said his Director of Operations Dick Nunis, 'He was trying to leave us with a vision for the future.'

That's why the day after he died, the flags were flown at half mast, but Disneyland remained open. Dick Nunis explained, 'That's what Walt would have wanted. He would have said "The show must go on".'

As Bob Gurr put it, 'Walt was gone but we knew that there was a next chapter waiting for us.' We all have creative 'spirits' or predecessors that we can draw upon to inspire us to greater creativity. It can be a useful exercise for you and your team to name and share yours.

RESOURCES

Budds, D. (2015), 'The Secret to Walt Disney's Corporate Strategy', *Fast Company*, 1 July: www .fastcompany.com/3048046/the-secret-to-walt-disneys-corporate-strategy
The Imagineers, Episode 1 (Disney+ or other streaming platforms)

3.3   THE STAR-FORM: A SINGULAR FOCUS

In many ways, the best way to think about how to organize for creativity is a function of scale. The last 100 years' advances in information technology and financial systems have afforded increasing opportunities to create on a large scale: for elephants like Toyota and the BBC to have creativity within core elements of their processes, and other large 'beasts' like Lockheed to have a creative out-rigger, side-car (or side-hustle) established alongside them – as we'll see later in Recipe 17. For others like Spotify, Disney and the United Nations, creativity is engendered through utilizing the scale of their diversity and encouraging cross-pollination.

The M- and X-forms of organizing we have explored thus far, however, have their weaknesses. Primary among these is an inability to have a clear, single-minded vision and be able to act quickly to pursue it. Both the Star-form and the O-form organization processes we look at next seek to capture and exploit the nature of a small, nimble organization (although many of these 'entrepreneurial' endeavours become very big too).

As they grow, though, they seek to retain a uniqueness about the way they do things. They are like snowflakes, or DNA chains, compared with the generic triangles and grids that we associate with M- and X-forms. Their uniqueness makes their creativity desirable and difficult to copy, but also delicate and fragile: their complex, tailored systems can fall apart incredibly quickly. They can get caught on tangents, and fly too close to the sun. They are also highly dependent upon their creative leaders or leadership groups. Whereas M-forms are led by policies from the top and X-forms shepherded from the side or behind, Stars and Os are directed much more personally.

All organizations used to be a bit more like these snowflakes, before the generic bureaucracies and matrix organizations and the charts that represented them became the norm in the 20th century. If you look at early management author Clinton Edgar Woods' drawings of organizations, you can still see the resemblance to real organizations' process flows rather than just departmental boxes and lines (see Figure 3.5 for an example).

By their creative nature, the Star- and O-forms are idiosyncratic. For the Star-forms, these idiosyncrasies tend to reflect those of one star founder and/or leader. This is why the lists of the greatest or richest entrepreneurs published in fora like *Forbes* magazine tend to be populated by people with large egos (and this ego-orientation may be related to the fact that these lists have been dominated by white men – something which is now widely critiqued).

For the O-forms, the process idiosyncrasies are a reflection of a group and often their connection to a particular place or places, something that we'll define and explain as *terroir*. But first, having outlined the creative strengths and weaknesses of the Star-form, we'll look at two variations on a Star recipe with two very different outcomes.

The Star-form summary

Strengths
- clarity of vision/purpose;
- homogeneous culture increases speed of decision-making, ability to act on instinct;
- a clear identity/personality/brand of creativity can emerge and be promoted.

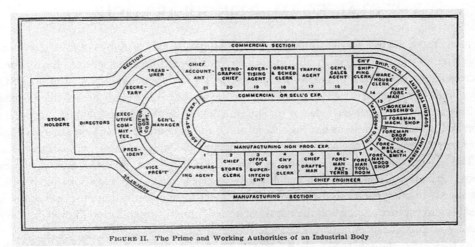

FIGURE II. The Prime and Working Authorities of an Industrial Body

Source: https://commons.wikimedia.org/wiki/File:Prime_and_Working_Authorities_of__an_Industrial_Body.jpg

Figure 3.5   Clinton Edgar Woods: the organizational body, c. 1902

Weaknesses

- dependent on the continued brightness/relevance of the star – the vision fades if the central star fades;
- prone to tangents/flights of fancy;
- lack of self-reflection, critical questioning as people defer to the all-powerful creative centre/culture.

RECIPE 15. STEVE JOBS AND THE TIGER KING: STAR-CENTRED* (SAN FRANCISCO AND OKLAHOMA)

INGREDIENTS:

- 1 extremely charismatic leader with guru potential
- A truly original creative spark
- An appeal to a group of underappreciated others
- An untapped market for something exotic

Everyone knows something about Steve Jobs: the star around which Apple (perhaps the most well-known organization we might categorize as a Star-form) was built. Apple rose with Jobs at the helm, then it fell, then Jobs was forced out, then it fell even further, then he was enticed back, and it rose again. Then he passed away and nobody is sure yet what the future holds for the company that he built around his own, unique design sense and intuitive grasp about how users wanted to interface with technology.

Jobs channelled the anything-is-possible, technology-can-be-beautiful ethic of Palo

Alto and Silicon Valley, the home of Stanford University and an incubator for dozens of well-known tech start-ups. Many of the world's most talented individuals were drawn to and gathered around him, buying into and following his vision of what a technology company could be.

The best way to understand Jobs' creative strengths and weaknesses may be to explore the contrast that his biographer Walter Isaacson draws between him and his contemporary and rival Bill Gates, who built Microsoft into one of the last century's finest M-form organizations.

He and Gates collaborated for a time, but then fell out after Jobs felt that Gates had stolen many of his ideas and incorporated them into Microsoft Windows.

Jobs thought those ideas were his. Gates claimed they both took them from Xerox, saying that it was as if he had broken into the Xerox lab to steal a TV only to find that Jobs had already stolen it. Jobs saw himself as the author of his creativity, Gates as the discoverer, combiner and curator of new ideas. It was Jobs' ego in this respect that enabled him to leap way ahead of what his competitors were doing: he just knew his ideas were that much better than anyone else's and he wasn't going to wait for the laggards to catch up.

Gates didn't rate Jobs' understanding of the technological details, but respected Jobs' knack for design, 'He really never knew much about technology, but he had an amazing instinct for what works.'

When Apple introduced iTunes after Jobs returned to the company in the late 1990s, Gates sent an internal email to Microsoft that said, 'Steve Jobs' ability to focus in on a few things that count, get people who get user interface right, and market things as revolutionary are amazing things.'

But Gates thought Apple's reliance on Jobs was a weakness, and claimed that much of Apple's post-iPhone success came from Jobs' genius, and not from Apple's processes. 'The integrated approach works well when Steve is at the helm. But it doesn't mean it will win many rounds in the future', Gates predicted.

Jobs had fewer good things to say about Gates. In a backhanded compliment, Jobs once said, 'I admire him for the company he built — it's impressive.' But he was more direct about Gates' creative ability: as Gates transitioned away from Microsoft and into his philanthropic interests, Jobs claimed that 'Bill is basically unimaginative and has never invented anything, which is why I think he's more comfortable now in philanthropy than technology.'

And, he thought that Microsoft reflected what he saw as Gates' weaknesses. In 1996, Jobs appeared in a PBS documentary called *Triumph of the Nerds*, which charted the rise of companies like Microsoft and argued that Microsoft made 'third-rate products'. 'The only problem with Microsoft', he continued, 'is they just have no taste. They have absolutely no taste. And I don't mean that in a small way, I mean that in a big way, in the sense that they don't think of original ideas, and they don't bring much culture into their products.'

It is certainly true that Jobs' design sense and cultural sensibility is at the core of the Apple brand, the company's major strength, and the reason for Apple's success. He has an uncanny knack for seeing technological development through the eye of the user or consumer. But, his unrelenting drive for what he thinks (or knows) is right also alienates good people and can lead to flights of fancy and overstretch.

Seeing a parallel with the most watched entrepreneur of 2020 at the start of the Covid-19 pandemic may seem unusual, and for some perhaps sacrilegious. However, Jobs (and other prominent innovators at the centre of creative organizations, like Jeff Bezos and Elon Musk) shares a number of creative characteristics with Tiger King Joe Exotic, the star of the Netflix television documentary that traced the rise and fall of the tiger breeder and zoo proprietor.

Both were seen by their employees, who would go well above and beyond for their leader, as visionary; both were at the top of their respective fields (even though tiger breeding may not be seen as a legitimate field by many); both took big risks; both believed that they were ahead of the game and were dismissive of many of their competitors; both had outsized egos; both were like gurus who provided meaning and purpose to social outcasts and misfits and made them feel that they were a part of something bigger and better than their peers (tech nerds; people down on their luck).

And Jobs and Exotic had similar weaknesses: they both went too far out on a limb on occasion; both seemed unnecessarily arrogant at times; both lost sight of organizational details; both made enemies.

While we are not seriously suggesting that Exotic's achievements are in any way close to Jobs', we draw the comparison between their creative styles to make a point: that the type of creator and creative organization most highlighted by the media and most admired by the public have weaknesses that should be considered as well as strengths.

The Star-form model is the heroic version of organizing for creativity. But while this may be the preferred approach for heroes like Jobs, it – like all of the four types outlined here – has down sides. Creators like Jobs and Exotic may be no better or worse creatively than those who take a more measured and structured approach, like Gates. They all just do it differently. So, if you want to be leading from the front and at the centre of a creative enterprise, a Star-form may be the way to go. If not, you can be creative in a more structured environment, or in our final more collaborative format: the O-form.

* Note: this case was written during 2020's Covid-19 lockdown. We apologize if Tiger King no longer seems particularly interesting or relevant.

RESOURCES

Isaacson, W. (2011), *Steve Jobs: The Exclusive Biography*, Simon and Schuster.
Tiger King: Murder, Mayhem and Madness (Netflix, 2020).

3.4   THE O-FORM: GATHER ROUND

When John Favreau took on the task of show-running Disney's first development of the Star Wars franchise with the Mandalorian series, he did something unusual. Rather than running with the ball, he passed it five ways to five other directors, and then stepped back and let them create. These directors – Dave Filoni, Rick Famuyiwa, Deborah Chow, Bryce Dallas Howard, and Taika Waititi – came from very different backgrounds. But Favreau bet that their diverse and innovative takes, combined with their deep love and respect for the elements and mythology of Star Wars, the universe in which it sits, and that universe's creator George Lucas, would take the franchise forward in ways that he could not on his own, while at the same time maintaining the integrity of the iconic series' beloved story-telling and sci-fi technology aesthetic.

Favreau's criteria for selecting the five are illustrative of what he wanted to achieve creatively:

You didn't have to be the most experienced. You didn't have to have worked on Star Wars before. You didn't even have to have ever directed live-action before… The thing was that you had to be willing to collaborate, you had to love Star Wars, and you had to want to do something great and help invent this new thing.

The resulting creative process? As Favreau explains it:

You're gonna see a lot of people that are working in this incubator of story and technology, come together 'cause they love Star Wars with an enthusiasm that seems to be very contagious. There's a real enthusiasm that's very organic, as we're telling the stories. It's a very collaborative environment… that takes on its own life and own personality. (*Making of Mandalorian series: The Directors* [video]: https://collider.com/the-mandalorian-jon -favreau-dave-filoni-interview/)

In this respect, Favreau channels Walt Disney's desire to grow creative collaborations and bring others into the spotlight (which we saw in the Disney recipe earlier), but in a more small-scale way: working on a particular project or artefact rather than for a multinational corporation. Favreau also shares much with the protagonist of Recipe 16, Tony Wilson of Factory Records.

Creative entrepreneurs like Favreau and Wilson are in it, first and foremost, to cultivate the collective vibe of the creative product that emerges over time through unique creative connections. They are not in it for the money – although that may follow. Their view is that creativity is best served by a group of collaborators in a particular place rather than one man or woman's universal vision and intensity.

What they appreciate can be best summed up in the French word *terroir*. It's a hard concept to express in English, the word has no real equivalent in that language. Even when English tries to capture what *terroir* means, it comes up short. The Complete Oxford English Dictionary lists the word in the briefest terms, describing it as 'rare' and claiming it has two meanings: 'a. Territory. b. Soil'. 'Regional variation' is a good example of a typical attempt in the vernacular that uses two English words to not even capture the half of it.

The French mostly, but not exclusively, use *terroir* in relation to food and wine. In wine, *terroir* is the reason why, for example, a bottle of Romanée-Conti, grown in the Burgundy village of Vosne, can retail for $15,000, and one from the field down the road can sell for $150. Partly it's rarity, partly it's history, partly it's mythology, but it is also related to the unique processes used and, at root, the peculiarly distinctive make-up of the soil and the vines that grow from it. In food, *terroir* is the reason that a region's cuisine is unique, why Normandy's cuisine is different from Provence's, or Northern Thai cuisine is different from Cambodian. It's a combination of geography, history, the atmosphere, the culture of the people and their lifestyle, prominent individuals and leaders, mythology and more.

Using it in the French sense, we can say that *terroir* is the reason why Favreau gathered his creative forces in Los Angeles to draw from the vibe that inspired George Lucas' creation of a galaxy far, far away. By the same token, Factory Records could only have grown in Manchester in the soil of Thatcher's Britain.

In management-speak, the word 'culture' has become a popular way to try and capture this idea. But, we would argue that culture has become a somewhat banal and less effective signifier to indicate how the interaction of people *and* place, social *and* environmental conditions, can influence the creative process than *terroir*. The modern use of culture puts its emphasis on people and their interactions and seems less resonant of the way in which people and place can connect into one creative being.

The O-form summary

Strengths
- the whole can become more than the sum of the parts as people's close relationships enable creativities to build;
- lack of scale enables a focus on and attention to a particular niche;
- can dig deep into and reflect a particular *terroir* that is difficult to imitate.

Weaknesses
- can easily just go around in circles, without gaining traction;
- can become self-indulgent/inefficient/lose sight of customer/user;
- limited cash flow makes it hard to develop new ideas/take new risks;
- very hard to franchise/grow as creativity is associated with the original team.

A smaller, looser O-form organization can see and feel and explore the local *terroir* and see it as an integral part of a particular brand of creativity to be nurtured and developed. The low-ego entrepreneur-aesthetes in this category, like Favreau and Tony Wilson in Recipe 16 below, may not be as high-flying as the single-minded entrepreneurs like Jobs or Elon Musk – they are, by definition, closer to the ground – but they offer a model that is just as inspirational and may be better suited to your creative endeavours.

RECIPE 16. FACTORY RECORDS: COFFEE TABLE CREATIVITY (MANCHESTER, UK)

INGREDIENTS:

- A collection of fiercely independent boys with particular strengths
- One slightly bigger boy with a mission to share
- A collective love of a maligned 'second city'
- One iconic band surrounded by a great supporting cast of others
- A cinematic perspective

Manchester's Factory Records was founded in 1978 by television presenter Tony Wilson, his friend Alan Erasmus (with whom he had launched a club and venue called The Factory), and Rob Gretton, manager of a soon-to-be-iconic band. Inspired by Gretton's band Joy Division, Wilson took the £12,000 bequeathed to him by his mother and started an independent (i.e., unconnected to a major label and their distribution network) record label.

Wilson, described as an 'aesthetic entrepreneur' and 'civic chauvinist for Manchester', quickly brought mercurial producer Martin Hannett, visionary graphic designer Peter Saville and industry insider Jon Savage on board to expand the number of different perspectives that could be applied to one idea: a record label that treated its artists as equals and was about much more than music.

Each partner loved Manchester with a passion and the label was named in a nod to both The Factory club and Manchester's hard-working, industrial heritage. But each partner also brought something different to the table. Gretton brought an uncompromising toughness (and Joy Division). Savage a knowledge of (and a healthy disregard for) London's music scene, which dwarfed everything else in the UK at that time, and how Rough Trade Records – the UK's first independent record label – did things. Saville wanted to apply cutting-edge art, philosophy and technology to the design of record sleeves and flyers. Erasmus understood the media and promotion. Hannett brought a distinctive production style that utilized technology and unorthodox approaches to creating music that sounded modern and industrial.

They were brought together by Wilson's missionary zeal and what one critic called a 'cinematic vision' of what a music label could be: a state of mind, a body of work, an expression of a culture, a statement of a city's intent. They worked together bouncing ideas in what became the confrontational conversation pit around the coffee table in the living room of Erasmus' dilapidated flat, which remained the company's head office for many years.

The first signing was Joy Division (whose remaining members, after singer Ian Curtis's death, later went on to form New Order). They and Gretton were holding out on signing with other labels due to a fear that the contractual conditions meant they would lose artistic control. Wilson offered them a 50/50 split of profits for a one-album deal when other labels would typically offer 10–20% and seek to shackle them to multiple-album deals. As a gesture to show how serious Wilson was about doing right by the band, he signed the contract in his own blood.

Factory was not the first independent label, but it was probably the most innovative and had the broadest creative ambitions. Their landmarks included:

- a distinctive aesthetic that meant fans often bought Factory records without knowing the music (handy given that radio playlists were controlled by the major labels);
- Saville's covers were artworks in their own right and often didn't reveal the names of the artists or a track listing;
- lavish marketing, such as the die-cut 'floppy disk' sleeve for New Order's Blue Monday (the release became the best-selling 12-inch record of all time, but the sleeve was so costly they lost money on every sale);
- the creation of the Haçienda Club (in Manchester!), perhaps the world's first super club and for a time the world's most iconic club (it lost money – New Order's Peter Hook wrote a book about it titled *How Not to Run a Club*);
- giving everything a number (Joy Division's Closer was FACT25, the Haçienda was FAC51, FAC61 was a legal writ prepared by Martin Hannett).

No surprise, given the list above, that Factory was ultimately a financial failure. But it was an unprecedented cultural success. The partners sought nothing less than elevating their home from a pitied city to a place with a musical pedigree rivalling neighbouring Liverpool and more edge and swagger than London. And they did it.

With the glow of hindsight, start-up guides now praise Factory's achievements, drawing lists of lessons that can be taken from them: a collaborative DIY ethic can drive innovation; believe that you can break the rules; know that authenticity inspires customers; live your own image; stay true to your roots and your vision; playing it safe gets you nowhere but an open-mindedness can lead you anywhere.

Factory is an exemplary example of the O-form 'kitchen' organization. If your creativity is inspired by a broader purpose than making money, sparked by collaboration and a belief that the collective and its unique connection to a particular place is greater than a singular, universal vision, then Tony Wilson's aesthetic may be what you should aspire to.

RESOURCES

Brookes, I. (2018), 'Lessons in Entrepreneurship from Factory Records', *The Startup Factory*, 15 November: https://thestartupfactory.tech/journal/lessons-in-entrepreneurship-from-factory -records

Movies

Control: www.imdb.com/title/tt0421082/
New Order: Decades: www.sho.com/titles/3473824/new-order-decades

3.5   ADDITIONAL FORMS: ORGANIZATIONAL HYBRIDS, DRAWING YOUR 'WHERE', AND OVERCOMING CREATIVE APPROACH STAGNATION

Creative hybrids

While the kitchen bench categorization of four types of creative organization is a useful way of thinking through the strengths and weaknesses of different configurations, it should not be seen as an exhaustive list of the possibilities. To illustrate, the next two recipes are about hybrid forms. The first is about an attempt to cure social ills through breaking a traditional M-form into a series of local squads. The second is about an organization that seeks to maximize the benefits of scale and diversity across the group, while at once being focused and developing a unique creative approach to address particular problems and develop creative solutions.

While these recipes are combinations of M- and X-forms and M- and O-forms respectively, it would be worth considering whether there are other combinations that you would like to create. The key is to be very clear about which flavours you are seeking to combine, why they might work, and the degree of balance you are seeking.

No matter what form your creative organization takes, and the creative processes you follow, a key challenge is to avoid getting stuck in a rut as processes that were designed to be creative at a particular point in time become habits – habits that become rigid and difficult to change as people become invested in maintaining the status quo.

RECIPE 17. RIVIGO: RELAY TRUCKING VS THE 37TH CASTE (INDIA)

INGREDIENTS:

- One big country
- An unfairly maligned social 'caste'
- 1 seasoned management consultant
- 1 multifaceted master's graduate
- A booming (but stifled) economy

You may know that India has a 'caste' system. This has traditionally pigeonholed people into a social stratum based on their family's status. You may not know that India has 36 caste levels in total, with 36th being the lowest. And if you live outside India, you almost certainly don't know that truck drivers are often referred to as the 37th caste in the village.

This lowly status is because of the life an Indian truck driver must lead. The scale of the country means drivers are often away from home for months at a time, unable to contribute to family or community life in their hometowns, and because of the need to make haste in order to get paid, they take risks with their and other lives. 'Who would marry a truck driver?' is something Indian truck drivers often say with a mixture of humour and regret.

This is obviously a social problem, but recognizing the social problem has led to a massive economic problem. Educating people about the dangers and stigma of truck driving has seen the number of people willing to drive a truck decline sharply. A survey by the Save Life Foundation found that 84% of truck drivers would not recommend the job to a family member, and that far and away the main reason for this was the time they spend away from their families. But now Indian development is choked as delivering goods within an India ready to grow is increasingly slow, risky and unreliable.

Looking at this problem, two entrepreneurs figured out a creative way to solve both the economic and social problem at once: with what they termed 'relay trucking'.

Deepak Garg had been a McKinsey consultant specializing in logistics for ten years. He had been working on an assignment looking at barriers to growth in India. He talked about his findings over coffee one day with a family friend, Gazal Kalra, who had recently graduated with a co-joint master's degree in business and public policy. They decided to investigate the truck driver problem further. 'It all started with a road trip and listening to truck drivers; (with) realizing that they have been marginalized and looked at as outcasts, which needed to change', Gazal says. Also, when they talked to unemployed people in a number of villages, they were surprised to hear how many would rather remain out of work and economically vulnerable than drive a truck. They were choosing social wellbeing over the money.

So, the pair wondered, what if we could develop a system where every truck driver could be back home within a day? They set out to build such a system where the trucks went long distances but the drivers didn't, where they had the scale benefits of an M-form and the close-to-home nature of multiple local X-form squads, and called their venture Rivigo.

With mathematics, some clever algorithms, an easy-to-use app, and a series of depots (which would come to be called 'pit stops', indicating the efficiency of transfer Rivigo was going for), it was possible. Gazal and Deepak borrowed a lot of the logistical know-how from the rail and flight industries, where trains and planes would arrive into hubs and be flown or driven out again by a different crew. It is for that reason that Rivigo calls its drivers 'pilots'. Rivigo logistics managers in control centres would look for the most efficient ways for trucks to arrive and depart into pit stops in a similar way to air traffic controllers.

Social problems, like safety and the status and wellbeing of drivers, have been addressed. Rivigo has published an e-book called *Not the 37th Caste*, which profiles drivers and explores how their lives have been changed, and you can read about how Rivigo seeks to provide their pilots with health, security and financial benefits here: www.rivigo.com/making-logistics-human/

Logistical efficiency and asset utilization have also greatly improved. For example, one driver driving a truck from Delhi to Bangalore would take five days. Rivigo can do it in half that time as the truck keeps moving, with the drivers switching out.

And, the relay trucking structure has seen Rivigo become a huge financial success. With 70 pit stops, 8,000 pilots and 3,000 trucks, it became India's 25th billion-dollar company (or 'unicorn') in 2019, just four years after Deepak and Gazal founded it. But as Gazal reflects:

> Becoming a unicorn was never the objective. We wanted to make the truck driving profession humane. We were not obsessed with valuation; our focus was sending the truck driver back home the same day. If that metric works, it means the driver is happy, the relay model is working well, and customers are happy.

Perhaps you can see a similar way to revolutionize your project, industry or even your region, by questioning some of the logistical conventions that people have adhered to.

RESOURCES

https://thestrategystory.com/2021/04/25/rivigo-relay-business-model/
https://yourstory.com/2019/07/rivigo-unicorn-logistics-startup-gurugram/amp
www.rivigo.com/making-logistics-human/

RECIPE 18. SKUNK WORKS: A NEW MODUS OPERANDI (PALMDALE, USA)

INGREDIENTS:

- 1 large aeronautics company
- 1 necessarily staid culture
- A sprinkling of motivated and talented people
- A stealthy idea to create a separate piece of an organization apart from it

The Cambridge English Dictionary defines a 'Skunk Works' as 'a small department that is allowed to operate outside the normal procedures and systems of a company so that it has the freedom to develop new ideas, products, etc.' But before a Skunk Works was a general concept, it was a particular form of organization designed with a specific goal.

The Skunk Works was first conceived by the team headed by Clarence Leonard 'Kelly' Johnson, at Lockheed Aeronautics in California. Johnson, later described as an 'organizing genius' in the book *The Secrets of Creative Collaboration* by Warren Bennis and Patricia Ward Biederman, was a leading figure at Lockheed and headed up Lockheed's Advanced Development Projects (ADP) from the Second World War until the 1970s. He is not nearly as well known as he should be, but maybe that's the point.

One of the ADP's earliest tasks was the secret development of jet planes to match and surpass German technology toward the end of the war. Much of the Lockheed factory in Burbank on the outskirts of Los Angeles was taken up with the production of the more sturdy and sedate planes like the Hudson bomber, but Johnson and his special projects team erected some makeshift barriers and set about their work.

Eventually, the decision was made that the group should be located away from the main Lockheed site. Johnson was particularly adept at spotting talent, and soon a small but steady stream of innovators found that they were no longer going to work at the place where they had been hired. They'd be reassigned and told to keep quiet about their new assignments. Warren M. Bodie, journalist, historian, and Skunk Works engineer from 1977 to 1984, wrote that from its earliest days, Johnson envisaged that the keys for ADP were: engineering independence, elitism and secrecy.

The first off-site location was an old Bourbon plant, which still smelled of stale casks and sourmash. After a number of site changes, the now expanded ADP works came to be located on a site rendered nearly uninhabitable by the stench from a nearby plastic factory. This was so bad that one of the engineers working there began answering the intra-Lockheed 'house' phone with 'Skonk Works!'

This was a reference to a popular comic of the time called *Li'l Abner*. In the strip, Big Barnsmell's Skonk Works – spelled with an 'o' – is a dilapidated factory located on the remote outskirts of Dogpatch, in the backwoods of Kentucky. Barnsmell, known as the lonely 'inside man' at Skonk Works, ground dead skunks and worn shoes into a smouldering still, for some unknown purpose. According to the strip, scores of locals were overwhelmed by the toxic fumes of the concentrated 'skonk oil'. It's easy to see how the ADP engineers could relate to this place!

When the name leaked out, Lockheed (a massive, and by nature conservative, M-form organization) thought it wisest to change the name to 'Skunk Works' to avoid potential legal trouble over use of a copyrighted term.

Skunk Works stuck, and arguably suited Johnson and his team better. The term rapidly circulated throughout the aerospace community, and the ADP came to be known as Skunk Works and a skunk logo was designed. While it may not have been planned, that the Skunk Works had moved through a number of unattractive and malodorous premises became something of a perverse badge of honour among those chosen to work there.

Johnson's creative leadership style was famously curt and economical. It is claimed that it was he who coined the phrase Keep It Simple Stupid (aka the KISS Principle) that was later adopted by military leaders and became a popular term in management circles, and Johnson's own management style was summed up in the motto he often cited to his recruits: 'Be quick, be quiet, and be on time.' But despite his toughness, Johnson chose his recruits carefully, trusted them explicitly, and then largely got out of their way. A more rounded view of how he approached creativity is captured in what were called Kelly's 14

Rules, the principles by which Skunk Works ran. Some of them are specific to Lockheed and aeronautics, but many may have general appeal, including the following:

- Skunk Works project managers must be delegated practically complete control of their program in all aspects.
- Strong but small project offices must be provided.
- The number of people having any connection with the project must be restricted in an almost vicious manner. Use a small number of good people (10–25 compared with the so-called normal systems).
- There must be a minimum number of reports required, but important work must be recorded thoroughly.
- There must be mutual trust with the contractor, with very close cooperation and liaison on a day-to-day basis. This cuts down misunderstanding and correspondence to an absolute minimum.
- Access by outsiders to the project and its personnel must be strictly controlled by appropriate security measures.

Those chosen for Skunk Works were the quirky, the hard-working and the innovative; those who could bring in a project on budget and ahead of time; and those who were happy to roll up their sleeves and get their hands dirty. Some of the world's most famous aeronautical inventions and ground-breaking planes were developed at Lockheed's Skunk Works: the F-104 Starfighter, the secret reconnaissance plane the U-2, and the SR-71 Blackbird and the beginnings of 'stealth' anti-radar technology. And the simple but clever approach to creativity extended to all aspects of the Skunk Works approach.

Ben Rich, Johnson's successor at Skunk Works, tells the story of how they knew that one key general could not fathom how stealth technology would reduce the radar print of a plane to almost nothing and what the implications of this could be. In presenting the idea to him and his colleagues, the project team working on this technology rolled a ball bearing towards the general and said, 'This is your airplane.' The slow roll gave him time to comprehend just how invisible it would be to foes. The general was compelled to catch the ball as it rolled off his side of the desk. When he caught it, he felt it, and when he felt it, he bought the idea.

Johnson and Rich's creative insight, developed from their sketch benches and applied to the project management experience, came from recognizing that while the large M-form organization of Lockheed had many strengths that should not be dismantled (the finance and the high-tech kit, the reputation, the human resources), a 'safe' space for taking creative risks and doing things differently needed to be found within this. There needed to be an additional special team innovating together, building up and reflecting a particular *terroir*, like many O-form organizations. And it is certainly the case that the particular vibe of the Skunk Works and its grimy locations within the innovative environs of north Los Angeles played a role. Moreover, Skunk Works can be seen to also have something of an X-form about it with its relationship to Johnson's bold, abductive visions, like those of his Burbank neighbour Walt Disney.

To what degree the Skunk Works is an M, an O or an X is not important. These are just useful categories for thinking about things. What this recipe shows is that you can blend aspects of different recipes for organizing creativity and create your own hybrid – so long as there is a logic to what you are trying to do and a resonance with what you are seeking to achieve in your creative enterprise.

RESOURCES

Rich, B. and L. Janos (1994), *Skunk Works: A Personal Memoir of My Years at Lockheed*, Bay Back Books.

Drawing and naming your where

Whether you are inclined to use an M, an X, a Star or an O, or some hybrid form organization, as the place where your creativity is nurtured and developed, it is useful within any of these settings to actually diagram or draw the way what you do is structured. For example, an easy way to make sense of or explain how Skunk Works or Rivigo works is to draw it. Try it, if you haven't already.

It has become popular to refer to and draw an organization's 'business model' in this respect. And the popular business model canvas is a good way of doing it. It's simple really. Just a sheet of paper with nine sections where you can express your 'value proposition', 'key activities', 'key resources', 'key partners', distribution 'channels', 'customer segments', 'customer relationships', 'cost structure', and 'revenue streams', and think about how these aspects link to one another to make the whole process better than the sum of its parts. (Google 'business model canvas' – there are lots of examples.)

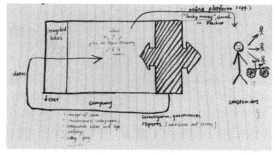

Figure 3.6   Adaptation of Jeff Bezos' original flywheel drawing for Amazon, and a 'value chain' outlining the Ofo Bikes process model when it was conceived

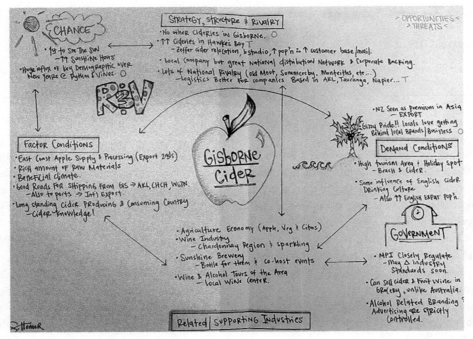

Source: Picture by Sarah Homer

Figure 3.7 Thinking through the creative process of a cidery using the Porter diamond framework

But the beauty of it, as with any approach where you commit thoughts to paper or tablet, is that you, and importantly those you work with, actually get to see what you think and work on editing it. It's an excellent, low-cost/high-reward way of prototyping your creative process. As the motto of FieldNotes, the producers of retro notebooks, states: 'You're not writing it down to remember it tomorrow, you're writing it down to remember it now.'

While the business model canvas has become the most popular tool for this in entrepreneurship and business circles, you can achieve similar effects with other approaches. You can just draw it as you see it – as with Jeff Bezos' original 'flywheel' process on which Amazon was based (see Figure 3.6). Or you can customize popular frameworks, like 'the value chain' that was drawn to depict the Ofo Bikes 'recipe' from Part I of the book, which focus the mind on the things that an organization does to add value and the relationships between these processes.

Another useful approach, particularly if you wish to reflect a specific *terroir*, is the Porter diamond of competitiveness, which encourages the drawer to outline how an organization will draw on particular factors or resource conditions; the nature of local demand; related and supporting industries; strategy, structure and rivalry in the local industry; government involvement; and the chance effects of local geography and culture; as in Figure 3.7. Again, there is lots of information about the Porter diamond online.

Drawing where your creative output will come from is useful, and creatively naming the things you do can be a good way of understanding what you are seeking to do, and also of critiquing and refreshing your approach.

One quite famous example in the art world is Richard Serra's *Verb List*. It is literally a list of verbs, created in the 1960s when Serra was in his late 20s. At the time, he did not consider it a work of art, more a way of figuring out his own direction as a young artist. In a recent interview, Serra said: 'The Verb List gave me a subtext for my experiments with materials.' Verb List is four evenly spaced lists of words written in Serra's hand on two ordinary eight-by-ten-inch sheets of paper. The words selected are active, movement and task-oriented, and are akin to what he had learned from his friends working in music and dance choreography. Regardless of the media, Serra and other vanguard artists of the 1960s were dedicated to the process of making art rather than to the creation of expressive objects or performances, and while we cannot reproduce the whole list here, this selection is a useful set for reflecting on how you might name the steps in your creative organization or process.

- To twist
- To shorten
- To rotate
- To simplify
- To open
- To split
- To mix
- To hook
- To bundle
- To pair
- To complement
- To weave
- To modulate
- To support
- To chip
- To continue…

Oblique strategies for refreshing your Where thinking

Oblique. Adjective 1. Neither parallel nor at right angles to a specified or implied line; slanting. 2. Not expressed or done in a direct way.

A separate but related approach to thinking out the Where of your creativity is Brian Eno and Peter Schmidt's concept of Oblique Strategies. This also encourages you to reflect critically, but constructively, on the Where of your creativity. Eno's focus on the oblique builds on Shakespeare's line from *Hamlet* referred to in our Who chapter: 'By indirections find directions out'. It is a particularly useful way of looking if you or your team are stuck in a rut or lacking in creative process inspiration.

Perhaps there is nobody who has thought more about the creative process than Brian Eno: first as a musician with Roxy Music and then in his own right; and also as a collaborator and producers for artists like David Bowie, U2, Depeche Mode and Grace Jones. He even created the ubiquitous 'Microsoft sound' which signalled the opening-up of a Windows 95 operating system (ironically, Eno created it on a Mac).

In the early 1970s, Eno and his friend, painter Peter Schmidt, had many conversations about the creative process. And finding that they shared many of the same views based on their experiences in the worlds of music and art, they created a series of about 100 cards each with a short message or aphorism about the process written on it. These could be worked through systematically, or selected at random, to help inspire creative thinking about how to create. They called the collection Oblique Strategies, and from 1971 to 1974, before Schmidt's untimely death, updated the set by adding, subtracting or adapting a few cards in the set.

As Eno explained:

'Oblique Strategies' evolved from me being in a number of working situations when the panic of the situation – particularly in studios – tended to make me quickly forget that there were other ways of working and that there were other ways of attacking problems that were in many ways more interesting than the direct head-on approach. If you are in a panic you tend to take the head-on approach because it seems to be the one that's going to yield the best result. Of course, that often isn't the case.

They were never widely publicized and only issued in limited editions, original versions of which sell for hundreds of pounds. They are difficult (but not impossible) to find on the Internet. Eno reflects, however, that many people have told him that they find them useful, and that he still uses them himself.

In our opinion, they are useful for reflecting on any creative process, not just processes for creating music or art. The panic of the situation, which Eno describes as his motivation, is common in any environment in which people are seeking creative outcomes, and can often lead to tunnel vision and the diminution of creativity. So, as you think about the way you are organizing to create, it would be well worth using some of the Oblique Strategies to reflect on and question the assumptions on which your processes are based and perhaps develop other ways of working. We provide some examples below:

Assemble some of the instruments in a group and treat the group
People are atomistic. We like to break things into parts and treat those parts individually. But often group dynamics are what's important: so why don't we view the group as one being and look at it as a whole?

Convert a melodic element into a rhythmic element
We can be quick to categorize: this role is customer facing, this group isn't; this element is not mission critical; this role is better performed by an older person; this role requires industry experience. Reverse those assumptions.

Define an area as 'safe' and use it as an anchor
What's the one thing you like best about how you work/create? Keep that and then seek to build everything else about the way you work around it.

Discover the recipes you are using and abandon them
Over time, everyone develops a modus operandi. But we often forget what it is. Stop and sketch it out. Change it to something better.

How would you have done it?

Stop and ask somebody – an employee; a customer; a friend; the person sitting next to you – how they would organize the process.

Faced with a choice, do both

We often create forks in the road where we think we must go one way or the other: we have to be online or bricks and mortar; we have to grow or stay close to our customers; study or start a business; make or buy; modern or traditional. Outline those forks and look for ways to do both.

Honour thy error as a hidden intention

We are quick to cover over, disown and move past mistakes. But what if those things that look like errors happened for a reason and are trying to teach us something/lead us somewhere else?

Humanize something free of error

Sometimes things are too perfect (i.e., unlikable). How could you give the process and the outcomes a bit more personality?

Make an exhaustive list of everything you might do and do the last thing on the list

Making lists is good. But we tend to put the biggest, most obvious and most difficult things at the top. Then we start the list and lose momentum. Start with the last thing on the list and see what happens from there.

Short circuit (Eno's illustrative metaphor, a man eating peas with the idea that they will improve his virility shovels them straight into his lap)

Figure out what it is about your creativity that the user really likes and design a process that cuts to the chase to deliver it.

Take away the elements in order of apparent non-importance

Over time, details accumulate to complicate things. Strip them away and see if things get better.

Use 'unqualified' people (also abandon normal instruments)

We tend to limit ourselves in creating job descriptions. Find somebody different to do a job and watch what they do.

As Eno has said, these cards should really be starters – they don't need to be adhered to religiously: take what you need and add your own. Build up your own set of cards for prompting you to think laterally and question if your creative processes could be better.

But however you may choose to do it, through thinking about the organization forms and recipes we have described, and/or by drawing or naming or thinking obliquely about your creative Where, if you now have a better idea of where and within what process you would like to see as the ongoing generator of your creative output, then you are ready to move on to the next phase of the book: the Who of creativity.

But before that, to finish Part III, we fill in the Where box of a creativities canvas with an outline of the Skunk Works recipe, with a nod to Kelly Johnson's enacting an oblique strategy: creating a little O-form as a creative anchor within the M-form of Lockheed (see Figure 3.8).

SOURCES AND FURTHER READING FOR PART III

Part III explores different modes of organizing for creativity and different ways of thinking about and developing creative processes. In the first part of the discussion, different organizational forms where creativity can be encouraged are explored. The conventional assumption that creativity comes from individuals acting alone, or in loose chaotic coalitions, is challenged by first exploring how the large 'corporate' forms that we tend to see as the opposite, or killers, of creative processes can in fact be drivers of particular kinds of creativity. We then explore large but 'looser' organizational forms – forms coalesced around magnetic creative individuals; and smaller, more organic coalitions of equals. This part's framework, the bench formation, outlines the choices that should influence thinking about what form of organization could work best for progressing your blend of creativity, or alternatively, how you might best seek to be creative given the organizational form you find yourself operating in.

The later sections of this part examine two techniques for thinking creatively about your creative processes and models: first, sketching out or drawing these processes, thinking critically about what you see, and then seeking to redraw better prototype processes; second, an approach inspired by music producer Brian Eno's 'Oblique Strategy' cards, designed to promote creative and critical questioning that can help people get beyond replicating processes that are no longer inspiring creativity.

Angwin, D., S. Cummings and U. Daellenbach (2019), 'How the Multimedia Communication of Strategy Can Enable More Effective Recall and Learning', *Academy of Management Learning and Education* **18**(4), 527–546.

Benson, N. (2020), 'All Hail Disney: Establishing Corporate Authorship Through Industrial Intertextuality', *Quarterly Review of Film and Video* **37**(1), 25–47.

Cummings, S. and D. Angwin (2015), *Strategy Builder: How to Create and Communicate More Effective Strategies*, London: John Wiley & Sons.

Cummings, S. and D. Wilson (eds) (2003), *Images of Strategy*, Oxford: Blackwell.

Eno, B. (2020), *A Year with Swollen Appendices: Brian Eno's Diary*, London: Faber & Faber.

Eno, B. and P. Schmidt (1979), *Oblique Strategies: Over One Hundred Worthwhile Dilemmas* [cards], London: Brian Eno.

Garland, K. (1994), *Mr Beck's Underground Map*, London: Capital Transport.

Gerstner, L.V. Jr. (2009), *Who Says Elephants Can't Dance?*, New York: Harper Business.

Haigh, G. (2012), *The Office: A Hardworking History*, Melbourne: Melbourne University Press.

Mintzberg, H. and L. Van der Heyden (1999), 'Organigraphs: Drawing How Companies Really Work', *Harvard Business Review* **77**, 87–95.

Osterwalder, A. and Y. Pigneur (2010), *Business Model Generation: A Handbook for Visionaries, Game Changers, and Challengers*, London: John Wiley & Sons.

Peters, T. and R. Waterman (1982), *In Search of Excellence: Lessons from America's Best-run Companies*, New York and London: Harper Row.

Rich, B.R. and L. Janos (1996), *Skunk Works: A Personal Memoir of My Years at Lockheed*, New York: Bay Back Books.

Savage, J. (2019), *This Searing Light, the Sun and Everything Else: Joy Division: The Oral History*, London: Faber & Faber.

Williams, W.M. and L.T. Yang (1999), 'Organisational Creativity' in R.J. Sternberg (ed.), *Handbook of Creativity*, Cambridge: Cambridge University Press.

Worthington, J. (2012), *Reinventing the Workplace*, London: Routledge.

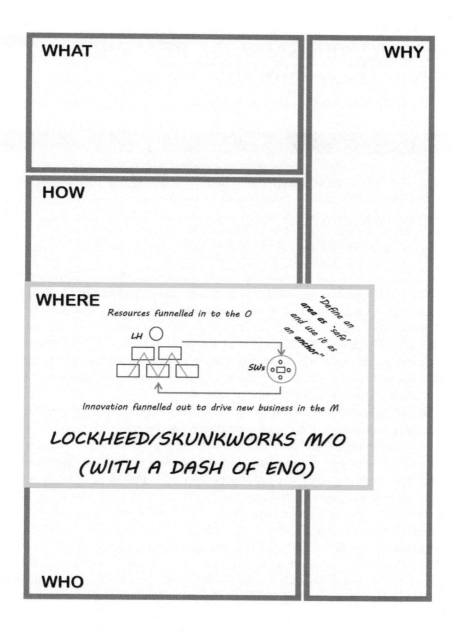

Figure 3.8   Creativities canvas example 3: Skunk Works and the Where of creativity

PART IV
THE WHO – ENGAGING CREATIVE
USERS AND COMMUNITIES

In this part of *Creativities* we move to our fourth question – *who* is the creator? Western models of the creative process present creativity as a self-contained loop and focus on the individuals, teams or organizations at the point of origination. But, just as a meal is not only about the food, so the experience of creativity is not only about the content. Who we are with, where we are, our level of engagement will all add value. Considering the myriad ways in which a creative product is recreated at the point of consumption or user experience, we discover a range of creative inputs, from users and audiences to collaborators and intermediaries (streaming services, social media networks, broadband providers).

This more expansive understanding of creativity takes us past the myth of genius toward a more inclusive appreciation of the 'who' of creativity. The meaning and value of creativity are not self-contained in objects and products, nor in the special talents of artists and inventors. The creative process extends forward and outwards, encompassing wider patterns of complicity and collaboration. Often these patterns of co-creation include what Jay Rosen named 'the people formerly known as the audience'. In Part IV we consider the Who of creativity as a series of expanding circles, with networks of co-creation and collaboration radiating beyond the sole author or genius creator.

The idea of original authorship and individual creative genius is baked into Western culture, especially in the arts. From Renaissance humanism to Romantic idealism to 20th-century copyright law, the idea of an individual creator is hard wired into artistic culture and business models. But that tradition is challenged, not just by attempts to democratize creativity (which we will consider later), but by changing industry structures and new technologies.

In today's cultural and media industries, creative consumption has become a growth area. Today, the most profitable businesses in the creative and media sector focus on the experience of cultural consumption, and monetize the user experience through advertising, harvesting consumer data, cross-subsidizing service contracts and hardware – or some combination of all of these.

Meanwhile content is increasingly 'free', leaving the people who make that content unpaid or underpaid. Copyright law offers some limited protection. But the big technology platforms aggregate content in order to market their services. Copyright creation, ownership and protection are not part of their business model.

Looking at these patterns of co-creation, we can see a wider range of actors contributing *into* the creative process – not just authors and originators but curators, audiences and platforms. We can also see a wider range of businesses and beneficiaries extracting value, especially economic value, *out* of the creative process – brands, advertisers, social media companies and big tech. The creative inputs and outputs are spread unevenly and disproportionately across the network.

In order to survive in this environment, those who create must find new ways of reselling and repackaging their creations. Their consumers become their co-creators – and begin to create new work of their own. This is the world of creativity 2.0 – similar to the network effect of Web 2.0 – in which creativity is directed outwards from the creative core to a wider circle of adapters, influencers, super-users and fans.

The 'Who' framework: four circles of co-creation

In Part IV of *Creativities* we will map this wider network as a series of expanding circles, radiating outwards from the creative core or individual author to encompass ever wider networks of collaboration and co-creation (see Figure 4.1). One circle spills over into the next – creativity is an iterative process, not a single act, and the fruits of one creative idea contain the seeds of another.

JOINING THE CIRCLE: FROM CREATION TO CO-CREATION

The first circle of co-creation recognizes that value – an essential element in standard definitions of creativity – depends upon the recipient as well as the initiator of a creative idea. This involves a complicity between producer and consumer, allowing ideas and products to be customized and co-authored at the point of consumption. The creator plants a seed in the mind's eye of the receiver.

REVERSING THE CIRCLE: FROM ONE-WAY TO TWO-WAY FLOW

The second circle of co-creation takes those diverse reimaginings and repurposings and feeds them back to the point of origin. Here we will consider co-creation as a feedback loop in which the products of collaboration and user experience are reinvested in the core product or idea, generating new forms of cultural and economic value or brand equity.

EXPANDING THE CIRCLE: FROM CORE TO PERIPHERY

The next circle describes a more generous pattern of co-creation, designed not to draw value back into the centre but to open up new opportunities for those on the periphery, building new networks of collaboration and spreading creative possibilities beyond the creative core. The aim here is not just to generate new versions of the product, but new versions of the producer – a second generation of creators who will build a broader creative culture.

BREAKING THE CIRCLE: FROM CHAOS TO COMPLEXITY

As the circles of co-creation continue to expand, it becomes more difficult (and perhaps less important) to distinguish between core and periphery. In this fourth circle of co-creation, we describe a more anarchic pattern with no defined starting point or outcome, instead a viral spreading and sharing of ideas with no obvious purpose or method. Yet out of this apparently random, chaotic process, patterns emerge and value is created; as with complexity theory, an unplanned, chaotic system produces 'order for free'.

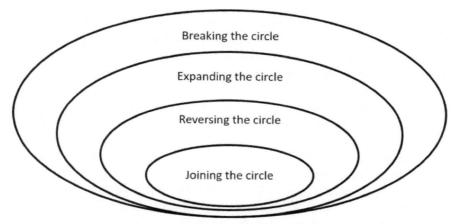

Figure 4.1   Creativities framework 4: four circles of co-creation: joining, reversing, expanding, breaking

These patterns of co-creation or distributed creativity are not unique to the arts, media and entertainment industries, but many of the recipes in Part IV draw on examples from these sectors. There are two reasons for this. First, the core value of cultural products has always depended upon a significant element of 'co-creation' by audiences and users. As the value of content has shrunk due to piracy and 'free' content, that co-creative element has become increasingly important to business models across the creative and media industries.

Second, precisely because value in the creative and media industries is (co-)created in the mind's eye of the consumer, value is unpredictable and the tolerance for risk is high. Most creative and media enterprises accept a failure rate of more than 90% in the products they release; the ratio would be even higher if we factored in products discarded during the development process. In such an environment, transactions and products are risky and short-lived. The key to unlocking long-term value is in customer relationships. In order to enable collaborative relationships with consumers, many creative enterprises are willing to sacrifice ownership and control over their products.

These attitudes and priorities are beginning to spill over into other sectors. Value in service and technology industries is highly dependent on perception. Open-source innovation is the tech sector's version of co-creation. In other service industries, customer co-creation is increasingly accepted as a necessary route to innovation and competitive positioning; the benefits of opening up to customer input outweigh the risks of failure. Some of the 'cultural and creative' recipes in Part IV can accordingly have a wider application. By substituting other co-created values such as brand equity, customer relationships or market valuation, the reader can come up with co-creative recipes of their own.

4.1   JOINING THE CIRCLE: FROM CREATION TO CO-CREATION

'Joining the circle' describes the first and simplest level of consumer co-creation. The possibilities of audiences actively engaging in the co-creation of value and meaning is often associated with new modes of interactive content, especially digital. But this is not a new idea. In 1934, the American philosopher, John Dewey, described the experience of viewing a work of art as analogous to the act of creating it. The viewer, like the artist, goes through processes of deconstruction, synthesis and negotiation between the object and its representation. From this perspective, cultural consumption has never been entirely passive – and even the term 'consumer' may be a misnomer. Better to think of users or – if you can stomach the neologism – 'prosumers' and 'produsers'. And in this Who part of *Creativities*, we will consider some examples of old-school 'analogue' co-creation, alongside the more recent examples of digital interactivity.

If we want to engage users in an act of co-creation, the first stage is to plant a seed in their mind, an idea which can stimulate them to imaginative action. But we must also prepare the ground, providing an environment in which user engagement is encouraged and stimulated. The problem for many artists is that this common ground has become valuable real estate – in today's creative industries, the experience of consumption is a far more lucrative territory for building a business than the production of content. So if artists are to survive financially, they need to find new ways of engaging their fans that bypass the powerful intermediaries which curate (and monetize) the experience economy. As the following recipe indicates, the key to engagement is building a personal sense of connection, taking advantage of the direct human relationships through which an individual artist can outperform a corporate digital platform. For the individual artist, co-creation may accordingly begin as a relatively small-scale affair, drawing on the analogue logic of Kevin Kelly's 'one thousand true fans' rather than a global fan community managed and manipulated by aggregating preferences and patterns using big data.

In the creative and media industries, artists are typically positioned at one end of the value chain, as the originators of content. In terms of the creative process, their work is described as 'ideation', generating raw ideas which are then adapted and exploited by powerful intermediaries. And while artists (musicians, writers, photographers) face a collapse in royalty payments through copyright infringement, hyper-competition and the rise of 'free content', the intermediaries downstream of them, which package and deliver those ideas, are highly profitable. Our first recipe shows what happens when a musician attempts to take control of that valuable terrain, not only as a source of income but as a ground for consumer co-creation, connecting relationships and engagement among fans.

RECIPE 19. JACK WHITE, THIRD MAN RECORDS: CRAFTING CO-CREATION (DETROIT)

INGREDIENTS:

- A rock and blues guitarist who likes to play the drums
- A recording booth
- A slot machine
- A generous serving of wax and vinyl

Jack White is best known as an internationally successful, Grammy award-winning musician, songwriter and producer, founder of the White Stripes, The Raconteurs, The Dead Weather and various other ensembles. He is known as a guitarist and singer, but seems equally comfortable playing drums or keyboards as the mood takes him. His music carries an aura of emotional authenticity and rock and roll credibility; he has preferred analogue to digital recording techniques and is a vibrant and unpredictable live performer. His personal appearance, demeanour and attitude hark back to a more Bohemian age of troubadours and raw musicianship, the antithesis of commercial, mass-produced pop.

The unpolished immediacy of White's performances and recordings reflect his immersion in his craft as a musician. We sometimes forget that musicians are not only 'artists' (originators of ideas), they are also craftspeople, practising long hours to accumulate technical skills, familiarizing themselves with specialist equipment, genres and historical traditions, following a longer pre-industrial tradition of craftsmanship which predates the Romantic elevation of art during the industrial era of the past 200 years. The disconnection of art from craft has been accelerated by the emergence of digital formats which allow artists to transcend their own technical limitations and the limitations of the art object.

Digital formats are spreadable, allowing the raw idea, be it a story, song or movie, to be transformed into a digital artefact which can be shared, liked, streamed and downloaded ad infinitum. Analogue formats are a reminder of the sensual, visceral qualities of craftsmanship – the crackle of needle on vinyl, the lavish artwork on a gatefold album cover. The ubiquity of digital content has led to a revival of interest in the physical materiality of art objects – limited-edition books, 'rare' vinyl albums. These artefacts build a more intimate connection between musician and audience. Their scarcity promises intimacy, uniqueness, connection. The same desire for authentic, unique and tangible experiences underpins the revival in small arthouse cinemas, music festivals and independent bookstores, where fans can connect with each other and with the creators of the work they love.

White's interest in the materiality of music and musical experiences is allied to a shrewd understanding of that audience experience. The music is not just a collection of notes, it is an encompassing sensory experience, from the carefully curated images of the videos and artwork to the look and feel of his records as material objects. By crafting these artefacts, White engages his audience in an experiential world, setting up camp in that terrain of the experience economy which has been colonized so successfully by digital intermediaries. This in turn has led him to become his own manager, record label and recording studio – a one-man experience factory.

White set up his Third Man Records in 2001 at around the same time as the White Stripes released their debut album. In 2009, Third Man established a studio, store and 'novelties lounge' in Nashville; in 2015, a second storefront was opened in White's hometown of Detroit. In 2021, a branch opened in London.

Third Man can claim to be more than a record label. As well as a recording studio and store specializing in limited-edition vinyl by Third Man artists, there is a live performance area, a truck that doubles up as a mobile store and performance stage, and a 'novelties lounge' that includes the world's only operating vinyl recording machine: a 'record booth' containing a restored coin-operated 1947 'voice-o-graph' where customers can make their own bespoke vinyl recording for a mere $15. Other novelties include Third Man 'rattle-snake eggs' and popguns, and a coin-operated 'mold-a-rama', which turns out wax replicas of White's 1964 guitar. The stores host readings, performances and photo shoots; Third Man products include books, film and video as well as music. Everything in the store, including the truck and the uniforms worn by staff, uses the Third Man logo and yellow and black livery to reinforce the label's identity. The branding is reinforced in the retro styling of the building, designed to resemble an old motel frontage, and the coin-operated machines and trinkets.

Whereas merchandising is regularly used by the music industry as an additional revenue stream, Third Man is designed to entertain and engage fans rather than make large profits; the record booth barely covers the cost of the blank vinyl. The restroom includes a toilet attached to the ceiling. The feeling is more like an interactive art installation than a shop. This engagement is extended further on the Third Man website, where fans can enter 'the vault', a subscription service which gives access to live chats and music streaming, limited-edition products and records, a reduced-price subscription to Jay-Z's 'Tidal' streaming service, and a quarterly 'package' comprising limited-edition 12-inch and 7-inch records.

Aside from his musical talents, White has an intuitive understanding of the kind of collectable objects and unique artefacts which excite fans. The storefront and everything it contains represent a site of pilgrimage for fans. And despite offering a '360 degree' package, the emphasis is always on the music. Both vinyl and live performance offer the intimacy and immediacy which is at the heart of the Third Man experience. One of Third Man's strengths is the speed with which it can convert a studio recording into a vinyl disc. Working in lab coats behind a transparent screen visible from the studio, technicians produce a master live recording. White recently claimed the world's fastest 'studio-to-store' time of just three hours. Like the six-day production schedule of *South Park* described in Recipe 8, this speeded-up creative process stimulates the musicians. It's also exciting for the fans. As artist and entrepreneur, White shares and understands the enthusiasms of his audience.

> There's nothing wrong with buying things online, buying digital items, things like that. But the world's a more exciting place when people get out and engage with other people face to face. (Ben Swank, consigliere, Third Man Records)

In our increasingly digitized creative economy, material objects and artefacts have a new scarcity value. Third Man products promise exclusivity and connection, where global intermediaries provide anonymity and universalism. There are other examples of this new material economy of creativity in Dave Eggers' work with McSweeney's, publishing elaborately designed limited-run literary artefacts, Beck's sheet music, Radiohead's packages of limited-edition vinyl and original artwork, Nick Cave's Cave Things ('a shop that sells playful, therapeutic, mysterious, subversive objects' – all either made or curated by the songwriter).

Many independent record labels are headed up by musicians – this gives them a more intuitive understanding of both music and fans, allowing them to double the industry's typical ratio of one hit to ten failures. At the same time, artists like Jack White, Nick Cave or Trent Reznor are reengaging with their craft and rediscovering an older artisanal form of entrepreneurship. Craftsmanship recaptures the sensual connections between artist, artefact and fan from a pre-digital age. It also reminds us that artistic creativity does not have to be limited to coming up with beautiful ideas – manufacturing, packaging and selling these ideas, turning them into objects of desire, building a community of like-minded fans, can be as much a creative process as a commercial one.

How could you build complicity with your customers and allow them to round out the value of your creative projects? And what kind of encounters, objects and spaces would allow that connection to occur?

RESOURCES

Kelly, K. (2008), '1,000 True Fans', *The Technium*: https://kk.org/thetecnium/1000-true-fans/
www.avclub.com/video/we-visit-jack-whites-magic-factory-third-man-recor-99478
www.cavethings.com
www.thirdmanrecords.com

'Joining the circle' describes the first step in co-creation, initiating a relationship between producer and consumer – by engaging fans in co-creation of meaning, the artist draws the audience into the creative circle, initiating a second iteration of the creative process that recreates the first iteration but with a twist. Arthur Koestler describes artistic creativity as presenting an unresolved paradox or juxtaposition that the audience must make sense of. Scientific creativity resolves the 'bi-sociative' juxtaposition into a new paradigm. Artistic creativity, according to Koestler, leaves the problem open or incomplete – it is up to the audience or viewer to round out the creative process.

As the previous recipe indicates, joining the circle depends on a complicity between giver and receiver. In the case of Jack White, there is an intimacy and immediacy in the physical, human contact which is only possible at a relatively small scale. Human contact reinforces the connection – the merchandise fans take away is at least partly 'user generated', albeit using content preloaded or pre-programmed by the artist.

The relatively small-scale, intimate nature of these interactions offers an alternative business model for artists and musicians, allowing them to monetize customer relationships at a time when most of their 'content' is available for free. As Kevin Kelly suggested, it may be that just '1000 true fans' provide a viable basis for a creative career. While intermediaries will continue to take their profits from a bigger pool by aggregating consumer data and consumer attention, artists can still profit from consumer co-creation because consumers value the connection it offers and are prepared to pay for it.

In the next section we consider the next level of the co-creation circle. Joining the circle allows consumers to co-create value, but they do so at one remove from the initiating creator.

What happens when the movement is reversed and the co-created value feeds back into the original product or brand?

4.2   REVERSING THE CIRCLE: FROM ONE-WAY TO TWO-WAY CO-CREATION

J. K. Rowling famously admitted that, far from resenting the many fan sites which have grown up around *Harry Potter* and provide unauthorized explanations and interpretations of her work, she uses them as a source of inspiration and information.

Lego meanwhile has invited customers to submit product designs to its 'Lego Ideas' line. The shortlisted designs are open to a public vote and the winner will see their design go into production – and receive a 1% royalty on sales.

In both cases, we can see consumer co-creation being initiated by the brand owner – but instead of leaving these co-creative ideas in the mind's eye of the individual, they are drawn back into the centre. The fruits of consumer co-creation are then shared with a wider audience, to the benefit of the brand owner and fans who co-created them. If joining the circle is essentially a one-to-one interaction between artist and fan, 'reversing' is a collective two-way process, from one-to-many and back again.

'Reversing the circle' describes this feedback loop, from the originator out to the user and back again. The first step is to hand ownership over to users and allow them to play with the idea. In some cases, this means releasing ownership over intellectual property, or at least allowing others to infringe copyright. As in the next recipe, it also might require some relaxation of corporate control, trusting those outside the inner circle to take your idea in unexpected directions. There is a risk that the brand will be 'hijacked', that intellectual property will be devalued, that profitable opportunities will be lost.

The second step is drawing value back to the centre, a kind of crowdsourcing which pulls together multiple users and interactions. Sharing content with a wider audience opens up multiple opportunities and draws upon the wisdom of the crowd. Open innovation, in particular the open-source software movement, exemplifies this approach. Linux, under Linus Torvalds, pioneered the practice of releasing beta versions of software to users and inviting users to test and debug the program.

Our next recipe shows how co-creation can rescue a failing business, by enabling fans to participate in a joint enterprise, and by granting local employees the freedom to operate the business in their own way. While the original business has collapsed, what was once at the fringes (an overseas subsidiary) has taken centre stage. And the customers have moved into the building.

RECIPE 20. TOWER RECORDS: A TALE OF TWO TOWERS (JAPAN)

INGREDIENTS:

- Bricks and mortar
- A selection of old-media leftovers (CDs, vinyl, magazines)
- Passionate music lovers and collectors (inside and outside the organization)
- Getting somebody else to paint the fence

By the year 2000, Tower Records had become a company earning $1 billion a year. Five years later it was bankrupt. On the surface, the demise of a once iconic record store chain seems easy to explain. The rise of cheaper and faster ways of accessing music through streaming made it impossible for a chain of bricks and mortar retail stores to survive.

Except that this logic does not account for one thing. Whereas the Tower Empire which stretched from the United States to the United Kingdom, from Thailand to Ireland to Israel, folded like a CD case after Tower in the US came down, one Tower survived – and has subsequently thrived: Tower Japan. For each of the last ten years, its 85 Japan stores have brought in close to $500 million per annum.

So what makes Tower Japan different from Tower in the US and its other subsidiaries?

Russ Solomon started Tower in his father's drugstore, which shared a building with the Tower Theatre on Watt Avenue in Sacramento, California, in 1960. Seven years later, Tower Records expanded to San Francisco, opening a store in what was originally a grocery. This was the start of a US-wide growth programme. Arguably the most famous Tower store was purpose built by the company in 1971, on the corner of Sunset Boulevard and Horn Avenue in West Hollywood, with many staff personally contributing their labour to the build. The chain eventually expanded internationally to the United Kingdom, Canada, Japan, Hong Kong, Taiwan, Singapore, South Korea, Thailand, Malaysia, the Philippines, Ireland, Israel, United Arab Emirates, Mexico, Colombia, Ecuador, and Argentina, and Tower stores diversified into selling books, posters, plants, electronic gadgets, video games and toys.

From the beginning, Tower allowed its employees to do it their way. As described in a recent documentary by Colin Hanks which charts Tower's decline (called *All Things Must Pass*), Solomon's whole approach to human resourcing with the Tower 'family' was unique. Every manager in the company started out by working in the store, and Solomon called his managerial style 'the Tom Sawyer method of management'. 'I always got someone else to paint the fence', he explained. 'Everything we ever did was based on ideas from people in the stores.' Many of the decisions in those expansion years seemed to have a 'seat-of-the-pants' character to them.

This led to what the film describes as a period of unprecedented success, decadence and an adolescent feeling of fearlessness and invincibility in the company. Tower became the coolest place in America to be and the coolest place to work, evoking a 'community of outsiders' atmosphere that is captured in films like Nick Hornby's *High Fidelity*. There was, unusually for the time, no dress code. A former employee, rock star Dave Grohl, describes how working at Tower was perfect for him as it allowed him to keep his long hair. Working for the business was a non-stop party, 'so long as you did the work'.

A big part of the community vibe was the free music magazine with reviews and interviews written by staff called *Pulse!*, which Tower began publishing in the early 1980s. Initially, *Pulse!* was given away free in stores, but in the mid-1990s a decision was made to distribute the magazine nationally with a cover price of $2.95.

As the 1990s wore on, Tower started to show signs of growing pains. The rapid expansion had left it heavily indebted, there was greater competition on the high street, and they were slow to respond to changes in the industry. In hindsight, they were overly confident that their cool image would trump changes in technology and new rivals like Napster.

Japan was Tower's first international foray. In 1979, Tower Records Japan (TRJ) started its business as the Japan Branch of the MTS department store. The following year, the first Tower store was opened in Sapporo. TRJ spread the same ethos as their US parent, hiring staff who loved music and promoting a club-like environment where young people could feel in on a music-loving community.

One important advantage that TRJ had relative to the other Towers around the world in the turbulent 2000s was that local management seized on the opportunity for a buyout as the parent experienced its first wobbles in 2002. This gave TRJ management the freedom to chart its own course. It invested heavily in redeveloping its landmark Shibuya store in Tokyo in 2012, making it one of the biggest music retail spaces in the world (it covers 5,000 square metres and nine floors and is regularly listed as one of the world's 'must-see' record stores). This allowed TRJ to capitalize on its other big advantage: the fans.

Similar to the original Tower in America, TRJ publishes three free magazines aimed at specific audiences: *Tower*, *Bounce*, and *Intoxicate*. But in Japan it's not just the employees providing the content, it's the customers and artists too. A broad community of fans, artists and employees are helping to paint the TRJ fence.

TRJ is now the leading CD retailer in Japan, the only country in the world where digital sales are not growing (they are actually in decline, from almost $1 billion in 2009 to just $400 million in 2015). And recognizing that their customers love to collect hard, rather than just digital, copies of products and experiences, TRJ has teamed up with local record companies and artists to develop innovative ways of grouping these things. They were the first in the world to team up with artists to bundle concert tickets and backstage passes with music sales. They sell packages, like those of popular 'J-pop' girl group AKB48, which combine CD purchases with club memberships, stickers, cards, posters, and even rights to vote in AKB48 'elections'. In order to qualify for these benefits, it's not unusual for J-pop fans to buy multiple copies of their idols' CDs.

Like Jack White in our earlier recipe, J-pop idols use merchandise not just to generate revenue but to build engagement with fans. There is a risk that this fan service becomes a distraction – the 'handshake' culture, where fans queue for the chance to touch their favourite idols, places huge demands on the musicians beyond making music. There have been incidents where fans have turned against stars who refuse to acknowledge the 'special' relationships. To be what fans of J-pop and K-pop call an 'idol' requires years of training in the non-musical aspects of stardom – dancing, social media, expected behaviours and personal appearance, etiquette, foreign languages. For some, the strain on mental health becomes too much. In Japan's music industry, for better or worse, the fans are the ones calling the shots.

TRJ has staked its future on this fan-driven music economy. They actively promote in-store concerts, signings and conversations with local acts and labels in a fiercely parochial market (in Japan, acts from overseas make up a paltry 11% of total music revenue).

And they stay open until midnight every day.

TRJ also engaged a much more active diversification programme as the music industry evolved. Whereas Tower in the US carried on as if Napster, the world's first digital music sharing platform, was just a passing fad, TRJ became a majority stakeholder in Napster Japan (although this was wound down in 2010). It has a subsidiary record label, which specializes in what the Japanese call 'idol' performers, and with major corporations NTT DoCoMo and Seven & I Holdings now major shareholders in the company, they are well placed to respond to emerging opportunities and threats in communication technology.

In riding the wave of J-pop fandom, TRJ has allowed its customers to reinvigorate and reinvent the business. Following Solomon's promise to let employees and customers paint the fence, TRJ has opened its doors to the fans, to artists, to its former streaming rivals, to record labels, encouraging them to take centre stage and to build their own Tower.

What are the risks and rewards of getting others to 'paint the fence' of your creative endeavour, in your own industry? Could you get ordinary customers to behave more like music fans, and co-create the value of your products and services?

RESOURCES

All Things Must Pass: The Rise and Fall of Tower Records (Dir. Colin Hanks, 2015): www.youtube .com/watch?v=DrcCAwL01fI

Reversing the circle of co-creation is not without risk. By handing over creative control to fans or staff in a remote branch, the business owners may lose control of their project and see it run on without them. Valuable brands and intellectual property might be compromised or hijacked.

Reversing co-creation activity is a feature of online culture, and a lot of this activity is technically illegal. Copyright holders tolerate copyright infringement by fans because it builds the brand community and extends their market reach. For example, the popular practice of 'fansubbing' (*zimuzu*) in China involves communities or 'clubs' of mostly young enthusiasts providing a free translation service for Western media content, usually without the copyright holder's permission. When we interviewed a BBC executive about Chinese fansubbing of the popular BBC show *Sherlock*, she confirmed that the BBC sees Chinese fan culture in terms of marketing opportunity rather than competitive threat or copyright infringement. Zimuzu translators add their own creative twist to the text (for example, substituting 'I swear to Chairman Mao' as a translation for 'I swear to God'). And despite government crackdowns, zimuzu versions are more popular than official translations, helping to spread the popularity of everything from Japanese anime to Harvard online courses and Western TV series like *The Big Bang Theory*.

Games developers use a similar collaborative approach. When players started modifying ('modding') games illegally 20 years ago, games publishers started to sell them developer kits to do the same thing legally – and this in turn laid the foundations for today's 'free-to-play' games, where a paying minority subsidize a freeloading majority through their in-game purchases of various accessories and costumes ('skins'). Here, too, there is an element of risk and trust – just as the originator risked handing over their content to the crowd, now the crowd risk having their contributions stolen back again. Trust and goodwill are important. Aggressive commercialization risks destroying that mutual exchange.

Rather than taking a legalistic approach to block fan co-creation, many businesses recognize that the benefits of bringing in creative ideas from the outside outweigh the risks of losing ownership. For example, K-pop fans use 'fan fiction' to spin elaborate fantasies about their idols, inventing speculative homoerotic relationships between band members and sharing these artefacts on fan forums and communities. These stories threaten the carefully constructed image of the idol system, yet they are tolerated and even encouraged by K-pop artist management companies.

Our next recipe illustrates both the risks and rewards of handing over a valuable franchise to outsiders. Licensing a business's most valuable assets to what looks like a competitor allows them to mess with the product and risks diluting the purity of the sport. But by reversing the circle of co-creation, the creative contributions of these 'outsiders' feed back into the core, bringing huge popularity back to the brand.

RECIPE 21. BOOMSHAKALAKA!: HOW *NBA JAM* REINVENTED BASKETBALL (USA)

INGREDIENTS:

- A comedian with a catchphrase
- A flame-grilled burger
- A sports franchise aiming for the big time
- A family-friendly video arcade

Co-productions between videogames and sports organizations are common now. But this was not always the case. Following the logic of competitive strategy, video games and sports were competitors, and sports organizations were very conservative and protective of their brands. Back in 1993, the NBA turned this logic around, seeing the threat of substitution as an opportunity to collaborate. This change of perspective eventually led to the development of the first collaboration between a major sporting league and a video game manufacturer: *NBA Jam*.

NBA Jam, designed by now defunct but once famous gaming company Midway, depicted the league's actual stars – minus one contractually excluded player (Michael Jordan had a clause in his contract that enabled him to exempt himself from any NBA promotion). Gamers could peruse the stats and select real players who shoved and slammed their way through a cartoonish version of two-on-two basketball. Dunkers launched and rose to superhuman heights. Hot shooters actually caught fire.

Released in early 1993, the game shattered revenue records. By some accounts it earned $1 billion in quarters alone and made $2 billion in total revenue. It became part of popular culture too, launching new catch phrases like '*Boomshakalaka!*' and '*He's on fire!*' into the lexicon. Organized sports, the gaming industry, and popular culture have not been the same since.

Midway lead developer Mark Turmell was a basketball fan. Part way through the process of developing mock-ups, Turmell and his team decided to take the gameplay to new heights – literally. Players would be able to jump to the height of the backboard (about 13 feet / 4.3 metres). Inspired by flame-grilled burgers, developers introduced a 'fire mode' with flames shooting out when a player was 'on fire'. Instead of hiring a high-profile announcer, they chose a friend of one of the production team, an aspiring comic named Tim Kitzrow. Kitzrow's over-the-top voiceover became an integral part of the game's success. His most famous phrase came from the funk music the developers were listening to at the time. Sly and the Family Stone had a song, appropriately titled 'I Want To Take You Higher'. In it they say 'boo-laka-laka-laka'. This was twisted slightly and the word 'boomshakalaka' was inserted into Kitzrow's early scripts.

However, fellow developer Jonathan Hey was worried that the craziness might be taking *Jam* a little too far. 'It was [getting] too ridiculous, too gaudy. I wanted to maintain the purity of the sport. [To] tone it down to where it was acceptable.'

Another member of the team, John Canted, wanted to build greater links to reality too:

> I was down on the monster dunks, I have to admit. [But] I loved the NBA for what it was; I didn't want to turn this into a clown show… we can't have John Stockton taking off from the top of the key and jamming it over [Dikembe] Mutombo. Nobody's going to want to play that. How about each player gets certain specialties – if it's Stockton, he never gets the ball stolen from him, and so on. I really wanted to protect the individual players' [actual] identities.

Ultimately, though, a balance was achieved where the fun factor was retained. Josh Tsui, another developer, reflected that, 'A lot of sports games back then were just trying to mimic the sport. This felt like the sport, but it also felt like a crazy arcade game.' Turmell was elated with the results. 'It was so clear that we had lightning in a bottle.' Yet conventional strategic thinking nearly blocked *NBA Jam* before it even got off the ground.

'We put together a demo, a video tape, and we sent it to the NBA and said, "hey we're making this cool game"', explained Turmell, 'And they immediately shot it down and said, "no, we don't want the NBA logo in the arcades".'

According to NBA licensing director Michele Brown, 'Arcade games were primarily in bars at the time, and that's not the image we wanted. Midway had a long haul to convince us this would not discredit our brand.' Turmell and his team responded by shooting footage of family-friendly entertainment areas, malls and bowling alleys in Chicago where arcade games were actually being played. They sent this new tape to the NBA and said, 'Look, your logo would be here.'

The NBA executives were eventually persuaded. The contract included a proviso that *NBA Jam* should not be situated in any unsavoury areas. The result was perhaps the most successful arcade game in history.

Jam's initial success surprised everybody. As Midway President Neil Nicastro recalls, 'We heard reports that operators said the game was broken. That got us all upset. "Why don't we know what's happening? Well, get out there and check it out, goddammit!" It turns out the cash boxes were stuffed [full]. The coin mechanisms couldn't take any more quarters.' Operators wanted Midway to make the consoles' coin boxes bigger because they had to clear them so frequently.

Anything over $1,000 a week was considered a good result for an arcade game console. At around this time, *Mortal Kombat* consoles were making about $1,200 to $1,400. By *NBA Jam*'s second week, consoles were making over $2,000. And whereas 2,000 console units was breakeven point for a new game, Midway shipped around 20,000 *Jam* consoles in its first year. The next biggest game of 1993, *The Terminator*, only sold half of that number. Turmell remembers that, 'One arcade in Chicago set a Guinness world record [for a single console]: $2,468 in one week. I still have that earnings report. You'd see *NBA Jam* at the top, making four times what the No. 2 game was making.'

But the development team kept tweaking the game. When it was first introduced there were no stats that differentiated the players. So as Turmell explained, people just assumed 'that Shaq was a bad 3-point shooter or that Stockton could steal the ball... we realized pretty quickly that we had to up our game [with better statistics] to match the real world'. So more and more detailed stats were introduced for gamers to think about, strategize with, and discuss among their friends.

The success of *NBA Jam* grew and grew. Midway developer John Carlton describes how he and a colleague 'went to see what the hell was going on out there. We walk into the arcade and there are like 20 guys standing around while four players play. They were watching it like they're watching an actual basketball game, cheering every basket.'

NBA Jam had become a social phenomenon. It wasn't that people were choosing between playing *NBA Jam*, playing basketball or following the NBA. *Jam* was inspiring them to do all of these things. For example, on the 25th anniversary of *NBA Jam*, Tim Kitzrow told ESPN that one of the amazing things about the game was how it bred supporters. Many people he spoke to told him about how the love of certain players in the game, and the virtual relationships they developed with them, encouraged them to support the particular teams they played for in reality. (Back in 1993, there were fewer NBA franchises and most were located on the East or West coasts, so many people found it hard to find a team to barrack for.)

NBA TV host Trey Kerby believes that Midway just 'cracked the code. It was just a simple, superfun version of basketball... If you could dream up the way a kid wants to play basketball, that's exactly what *NBA Jam* was. It got rid of all the boring stuff: free throws, backcourt violations... You were just left with the goods.'

But it wasn't just popular among kids. Everyone up to the NBA pros loved it too. Miami Heat forward Glen Rice relates how he would 'go to the mall arcade and there'd be lines out the door. But they'd let me cut. They'd be like: "Oh my god, it's Glen. Let's play with the Heat. You be Rony Seikaly and I'll be you." And I'd be like, "Oh no. I love Rony, but I need to be me."' Utah Jazz player Stephen Howard described how he and his teammates would spend their per diems in the arcade on *NBA Jam* and *Mortal Kombat*. And Shaquille O'Neal installed a couple of machines in his house and asked a friend from the arcade industry to install machines in his hotel room when he was on the road.

That the greatest players in basketball played *NBA Jam* gave the game even greater kudos. More than that, *NBA Jam* helped grow the popularity of basketball and the NBA at a crucial time – just as new media organizations like ESPN were becoming a force in the marketplace, looking for new content and prepared to pay big dollars for it.

In the late 1980s, basketball was a minor sport. Only around 5% of Americans claimed it as their favourite sport, about the same who named hockey or motor racing ([American] football and baseball were way ahead on about 25% each). In one year, 1993, thanks to *NBA Jam* and high-profile players like Shaq and Michael Jordan, the number claiming basketball as their favourite sport spiked 50% from 8% to 12%. By the end of the 1990s, America had three sports clearly out in front. Football on 27%, baseball on 17% and basketball on 13%.

Eventually, inspired by the NBA, other sports organizations recognized the value of seeing video games as complementors rather than substitutes, the value of getting fans interested in relating the personalities of the players to interesting statistics, and *NBA Jam*-inspired games like *NFL Blitz* and *MLB Slugfest* emerged. But at a key moment, an arcade game that turned on a generation with some cool catchphrases and stats that really got people involved gave basketball a huge boost. And it may be that *NBA Jam* has something to do with why the average salary of an NBA player is higher than for any other sporting organization on earth.

This recipe might make you think about how you turn your potential competitors into collaborators. How might you persuade your team that handing over your creation to those outside the circle, allowing them to mess with the brand and reinvent your values, might lead to an implausible creative slam dunk? Boomshakalaka!

RESOURCES

The True Story Behind 'NBA Jam': www.youtube.com/watch?v=L9GeUDNmPag

4.3   EXPANDING THE CIRCLE: FROM CORE TO PERIPHERY

Our next stage of co-creation widens the circle, moving from the commercial logic of 'added value', towards a more generous, altruistic spirit of gifting. Expanding the circle opens up creative possibilities for those who were previously excluded. There is no expectation of added value or return on investment to an original product or core business. Instead, the focus is on the periphery, stimulating creativity in others rather than building value at the centre.

Lewis Hyde describes the true nature of art as a gift – something given to another with no expectation of benefit or reward, other than a shared reciprocity between giver and receiver. In his influential anthropological study of creativity, *The Gift*, Hyde explained how primitive societies used gifts to establish community and connection; when colonial empire-builders arrived in the New World, they did not understand this gift economy, and introduced instead their own model of commercial trade, where the outcome was not reciprocity and connection but exploitation and profit.

Today, that gift economy characterizes many online creative endeavours. As David Gauntlett has observed, the sharing of user-generated content online, together with the techniques and processes behind them, has become a feature of online culture, building new forms of online community, dependency and mutuality. As with the 'cognitive surplus' described by Clay Shirky, individual acts of generosity accumulate into shared assets, exemplified by Wikipedia or by 'how to...' videos on YouTube and TikTok. This generosity is characteristic of the early years of internet culture, shaped equally by the Californian idealism of early virtual communities and by the enlightened self-interest of the open-source software movement. It also characterized many of the free online classes offered by artists and makers during the 2020 lockdown.

As noted above, reversing the roles of producer and consumer in online consumer creativity challenges the conventions of copyright and ownership which have turned creativity into a marketable asset for the past two centuries. Instead of seeing creativity as the work of an identifiable author resulting in a completed product, the hi-tech gift economy encourages a free exchange of prototypes and beta versions, inviting others to share and improve them.

Whereas 'reversing the circle' aims for a return on this investment by drawing value back into the centre, expanding the circle focuses on the act of giving. To allow others to co-create rather than attempting to control the process oneself requires a self-effacing attitude. In education and community development, teachers, participatory arts workers and social entrepreneurs attempt to empower rather than to control, allowing others to speak rather than forcing them to listen. At the same time, to initiate the outward movement of spreading depends upon making resources available to participants and 'scaffolding' their learning and development.

Compared with the earlier recipes in Part IV, expanding the circle of co-creation is more geared to social outcomes than commercial ones – the ultimate goal is towards cultural democracy, a more connected, participatory society. And while the primary goal of expanding the circle is more likely social than economic development, building creative capacity across a wider social network also lays the foundations for new forms of creativity which may eventually contribute to economic as well as social change.

RECIPE 22. NORWAY'S CULTURAL RUCKSACK: A NATIONAL EXPERIMENT IN EVERYDAY CREATIVITY (NORWAY)

INGREDIENTS:

- A country of 5.5 million people
- Approximately 840,000 school students
- An audience of 3 million people
- Dancing Queens, Lush Life and a Killing

The Cultural Rucksack (Den Kulturelle Skolesekken – DKS) is an arts education programme in Norway, providing access to professional theatre and music performances, museum visits and arts workshops in Norwegian schools for children aged 6 to 18. While there are similar programmes in many other countries, the Norwegian scheme is unusual in that it is nationwide, covering every student in every school (97% of Norwegians attend state schools). And while it is a national programme, it is delivered locally, allowing local administrators the autonomy to choose what to programme.

The Cultural Rucksack was established in 2002 as a joint venture between Norway's Ministry of Culture and Ministry of Education, designed to complement (but not substitute for) the school curriculum. Yet the emphasis of the programme is tilted towards artists rather than teachers – indeed some teachers have complained at feeling excluded, while arts organizations have complained that some teachers can appear disengaged or indifferent.

At the core of the programme is the idea of an 'encounter' between student and artist or artwork – an experience which is empowering and transformative. This experience might be educational, but in the broad sense of personal development and life-long learning rather than school-based learning outcomes. The Cultural Rucksack is informed by the German concept of *bildung*, a 19th-century Enlightenment ideal of personal growth and moral education through experience, encapsulated in those novels by Goethe or James Joyce which chart the formative experience of an artist or writer (the *bildungsroman* or character-building novel).

The programme is not without controversy. First, there is an assumption that culture is intrinsically good, and that art has the power to transform us. According to its critics, the Cultural Rucksack has its roots in the 19th-century civilizing mission – a paternalistic belief that exposure to certain (predominantly 19th-century) art forms will 'civilize' the uneducated masses. Other more popular or demotic art forms are left out of this mission, and elitist cultural hierarchies are preserved. More recently, the Cultural Rucksack has been seen to favour the professional artists and arts organizations over the experience of students – more watching, less doing. Meanwhile the school curriculum has become more focused on measurable learning outcomes, further reinforcing the division between school education and cultural *bildung*.

What has this got to do with creativity? By providing resources (material and cultural), the Cultural Rucksack provides a platform for individual creativity. The Nordic cultural policy tradition is driven by a desire to democratize culture, opening out elite culture to popular participation. Democratization of culture, often at a local level, feeds cultural democracy, in which a diversity of talents can forge their own cultural expression. The aim of cultural democracy is to foster everyday creativity, maintaining 'the right freely to participate in the cultural life of the community', according to Article 27 of the Universal Declaration of Human Rights. There are comparable cultural democracy programmes around the world – for example the 'Fun Palaces' project in the UK, initiated by the writer Stella Duffy, opening up cultural institutions and activities for an intensive weekend of popular participation. The Cultural Rucksack is notable mainly because of its scale and its pervasiveness in the cultural life of the country, touching *every* school student (and their families).

Of course, this social and cultural investment can also have economic outcomes. In neighbouring Sweden, the country's musical superstars include the likes of Avicii, Robyn, Zara Larsson, Basshunter, Ace of Base – and, of course, Abba. Swedish performers, producers and songwriters are among the most successful in the world, after the US and the UK. Latterly, Sweden has emerged as a leader in music tech; Spotify started life as a Swedish start-up, Soundcloud and Beats (later absorbed into Apple Music) also originated in Sweden. And behind this economic success story is another government investing in everyday cultural participation.

As with the Cultural Rucksack, Sweden's government has invested in schools and local cultural infrastructure to make music accessible to all. Around a third of Sweden's children benefit from municipal after-school music education ('Kommunala musikskolan'). The Swedish government provides what it calls 'the social welfare behind the Swedish music miracle', subsidizing municipal recording studios, free music instrument hire and individual artist grants, allowing musicians to start their careers somewhat protected from economic uncertainty. These localized safe havens have made possible risk, experiment and diversification.

This expansion of creative opportunities across the population in Norway and Sweden is driven by social and cultural idealism, not by industrial or economic policies. It would be naïve to say that Swedish electronic dance music, Spotify and the emergence of Scandi noir in film and television, are all the products of a deliberate cultural policy. They might be more like a happy but unintended consequence. Scandinavian countries have not pursued the same aggressive combination of internal investment, market opening and cultural export which characterized Korean creative industries policy through the 1990s and the subsequent Korean Wave ('Hallyu'). Nordic cultural policy is still mainly premised on social inclusion, participation and equal opportunity. The Cultural Rucksack must be seen in the context of Nordic traditions of high taxation and government investment, of a state education system which places Scandinavian schools at the top of the international PISA tables, and a generous universal welfare system.

As the example of Sweden suggests, such a system can help to launch the careers of global superstars. But it also makes possible thousands of smaller, less visible transformations among children, amateurs and participants – spreading creativity through the nation. We can admire the spectacular fireworks of the Swedish House Mafia or the darkness of Nordic noir – but the real miracle of Scandinavian culture may be the tiny sparks igniting the imaginations of the thousands of children taking part in Cultural Rucksack and Swedish music schools.

Could an unplanned creative 'encounter' with other previously unrecognized stakeholders spark creativities outside your own circle of workers, partners and stakeholders? And by encouraging those outside the circle to be creative, could you ignite new creativities back inside the circle as well?

RESOURCES

Bjornsen, E. (2009), 'Norwegian Cultural Policy: A Civilising Mission?' https://core.ac.uk/download/pdf/46907.pdf

The Cultural Rucksack: A National Programme for Arts and Culture in Norwegian Schools (Arts Council Norway, 2015): www.kulturradet.no/documents/10157/a7464045–2cb6–4988–9948-ffd834508a5d

While the previous recipe illustrates how expanding the circle operates in the context of education, development and non-profits, spreading creativity can also be applied to the commercial media and entertainment industry. Everybody knows that showbiz is a 'know-who' business, where mere 'know-how' is not going to be enough to build a successful career. This, in turn, has made it much harder for those who don't have the right combination of gender, ethnicity, class and social connections to crack the code. In the last few years, the exclusive character of our creative and media industries has become glaringly apparent. The following recipe is not a perfect solution to these problems – there are still plenty of injustices and inequalities remaining to be tackled. But it does show the possibility of new networks and new sources of social capital and connection emerging, and of extending the possible answers to the question of 'who' gets to be creative.

RECIPE 23. FROM OPRAH TO SHONDALAND: BREAKING THE NETWORK'S CREATIVE CODE (USA)

INGREDIENTS:

- A sofa
- A rags-to-riches tale
- A primetime medical drama
- #BLM

Oprah Winfrey is one of the most powerful and influential figures in the US media system – and, by extension, in the world. According to *Forbes*, Oprah's net worth was $2.7 billion as of March 2021. Growing up as the daughter of an unmarried teenage mother in rural Mississippi, she experienced poverty and sexual abuse in her childhood, and became pregnant at the age of 14. In 1975, while still at college, she began working for a local black radio station as a newsreader, and moved from there into local television.

In 1983, Oprah moved to Chicago, where she fronted a struggling TV talk show. After turning the ratings around and becoming the number one rated show on the network, she launched the *Oprah Winfrey Show* on ABC in 1986. Oprah's combination of empathy, curiosity and social conscience helped to create a new genre of popular confessional television, covering complex, controversial topics by focusing on personal, emotional stories. Oprah's appeal lay in her ability to make her guests trust her with their stories. She became a popular choice for celebrities seeking a sympathetic (mostly uncritical) listener – Michael Jackson, Lance Armstrong and Prince Harry with his wife Meghan Markle all used Oprah to tell 'their side of the story'.

Oprah's success as a broadcaster allowed her to launch a parallel career as a media entrepreneur. She bought the *Oprah Winfrey Show* from ABC and set up her own production company, Harpo (Oprah spelt backwards), becoming the first black woman (and only the third American woman) to own her own studio and production company. She invested in Oxygen, a cable TV network for women in 1999, and launched a magazine, *O: The Oprah Magazine*. She created Oprah's Angel Network in 1998, a charity supporting some of the causes she covered on her show, and continued to donate around 10% of her earnings to a variety of charities. The Oprah Winfrey Book Club, beginning as a segment on the TV show from 1996, became an influential tastemaker in the world of books, lifting the chosen authors up the *New York Times* bestseller lists.

Oprah had also begun to explore new possibilities as a producer and an actress. In 1985, she appeared in the film of Alice Walker's book, *The Color Purple*, starring Whoopi Goldberg and directed by Steven Spielberg. In 1989, she was executive producer for a TV miniseries, *The Women of Brewster Place*, and in 1998, she produced and starred in a film adaptation of Toni Morrison's *Beloved*.

While at first these productions were extensions of Oprah's own personal brand, often featuring herself on screen, they also showed Oprah using her power and influence to open doors for others, promoting books by black female authors she admired and backing black filmmaking talent. In 2009, she executive-produced *Precious*, taking the film from the festival circuit to the Academy Awards, where it received six Oscar nominations including a Best Picture and Best Director nomination for Lee Daniels. More recently, she executive-produced two influential projects by Ava Du Vernay, exploring themes of racial justice. *Selma*, a 2014 film, told the story of Martin Luther King's Alabama protest march in 1964, while *When They See Us* was a 2019 Netflix miniseries about the wrongful arrest and imprisonment of five black teenagers accused of raping a white female jogger in Central Park in 1989.

Without Oprah's involvement, it is highly unlikely these projects could have been realized. Not only did she help to finance the productions, her influence raised additional funding and publicity as well as guaranteeing coverage through Oprah's media network (and her newsworthy social profile). Just as her sofa had been the platform for celebrity guests and authors to tell their stories, her position as America's most powerful black woman now provided a platform for a new generation of storytellers.

Shonda Rhimes is another influential black woman in American television. Seventeen years younger than Oprah, and from a middle-class academic background, Rhimes benefited from some of the educational and career opportunities that Oprah's generation had lacked. After a false start in advertising, she went back to college at USC to study film and began to pursue a career in film in LA. Her first job as a script reader helped her understand what the industry was looking for, and she began pitching script ideas of her own. It was when she switched her attention to TV that she scored her first career-defining success. Noticing the demand for medical dramas on TV, she began developing *Grey's Anatomy*.

Not being familiar with the conventions of television, Rhimes decided to pursue a 'colour-blind' approach to casting the show. In the scripts she did not give her characters surnames, and this helped to avoid preconceptions during casting. The effect was to open up parts to black actors. The diversity of the cast became one of the most notable features of the show, and a calling card for Rhimes as its creator.

Rhimes too set up her own production company, establishing Shondaland in 2005 as one of the production companies for *Grey's Anatomy*. Shondaland became the production vehicle for all of Rhimes' future work, including *Scandal* (2012) and *How To Get Away With Murder* (2014). In 2014, the ABC network filled its entire Thursday primetime slot with Shondaland-produced content. In 2020, Shondaland made *Bridgerton* for Netflix. Released on 25 December, *Bridgerton* became the most watched original series on the platform, reaching number one in 76 different countries. Netflix announced the show had been streamed by 82 million households during its first month. Reinventing British costume drama for a contemporary, younger, global audience, Shondaland's trademark 'colour-blind' casting helped to make the show not only popular but also one of the most talked-about television shows during lockdown.

Like Harpo, Shondaland is an extension of its founder's personality, and can be seen as an astute piece of self-branding. But like Oprah, Rhimes has used her success to create opportunities for others, both in front of and behind the camera. Shondaland provides master classes, mentorships and competitions for female directors, producers and screenwriters.

Television and film are notoriously difficult to break into, with an oversupply of talent and ideas kept at bay by tightly-knit networks of industry insiders. It is perhaps no surprise that Oprah Winfrey and Shonda Rhimes built their careers in television rather than film. The starting budgets for television are smaller (especially at local level) and the appetite for content (especially now through streaming services like Netflix and Apple+) is bigger. It is also perhaps more important for television to reflect the lived reality of different audiences than it is for the Hollywood dream factory. Certainly, many black British actors, directors and producers have been given a first break in American television, while American film continues to be criticized for its lack of diversity, from #OscarsSoWhite in 2015 to the row over Golden Globes nominations in 2021.

Connections and contacts are still the best way into television. Outsiders, especially women, people of colour or those from working-class backgrounds, are less likely to have the necessary social networks (or the social confidence needed to negotiate those networks). Oprah is unusual in having made it through apparently on her own, although she has cultivated many powerful friends on the way up (including the Obamas). Rhimes was mentored by the producer Debra Martin Chase, who in turn was helped in her career by Denzel Washington; indeed, Rhimes' first internship in the film industry was with Washington's production company Muddy Lane Entertainment, under Chase's supervision. Chase (a contemporary of Oprah, with a background in law) continued to support Rhimes as her career progressed, and that early career mentoring may signal a generational step forward from Oprah's lonely achievement to Rhimes' ability to access and build support networks. Now it seems that Shondaland might be providing a similar foothold to the next generation of black producers, directors and screenwriters.

Apart from investing in talent (Oprah) and creating opportunities through colour-blind casting (Rhimes), both Oprah Winfrey and Shonda Rhimes are visible as successful black women in a mostly male, mostly white industry. By setting up their own production companies, they have demonstrated the importance of taking up powerful positions in the industry, not just in front of the camera. If even a few are persuaded to follow their examples, they will have spread the creative possibilities a little wider and made it a little easier for other black women to build their own media careers, establish their own businesses and tell their own stories.

How can leaders like Oprah and Shonda prompt you to widen your own creative circle? Could a greater diversity of people lead to greater diversity of thought? What can those inside the circle do to open up creative opportunities to those on the outside?

RESOURCES

2021 Hollywood Diversity Report: https://newsroom.ucla.edu/releases/2021-hollywood-diversity -report
Women in Film and TV Reports: www.wftv.org.uk/reports
Workforce Diversity in the UK Screen Sector – Evidence Review (CAMEo, Leicester): www2.bfi .org.uk/sites/bfi.org.uk/files/downloads/bfi-workforce-diversity-in-uk-screen-sector-evidence -review-2018–03.pdf

4.4   BREAKING THE CIRCLE: FROM CHAOS TO COMPLEXITY

The fourth layer of co-creation takes us still further from the deliberate, authoritative voice of the single creator. 'Breaking the circle' describes the apparently unplanned transmission and reproduction of creative ideas, especially in the world of online fandom. Instead of following a pattern of rational planning and commercial logic from the centre, fandom is driven by random, sometimes anonymous figures on the margins sharing memes, copying and pasting, throwing in unexpected extras. This 'who' of creativity is not only marginal; it is also multiple, with several apparently unconnected events and individuals triggering a creative outcome.

As well as challenging the idea that creative outcomes are driven by a core cluster of creative ideas and personnel, breaking the circle challenges the commercial logic of inputs and outputs. The behaviours of both producers and consumers in fan cultures appear to go beyond what is needed. Fandom is a word closely related to fanaticism, and there is something excessive about the devotion of many fans. This excessive investment in the loved object, as noted earlier, creates a surplus – an overspill of ideas, emotions and creativity – which is not designed to produce a return on investment, simply to demonstrate membership in the tribe or a shared passion. Breaking the circle, like expanding the circle, is thus part of the gift economy, motivated by generosity rather than gain. Fans are looking for reciprocity and connection among their peers rather than seeking to produce valuable products. Yet out of this random, viral spread of ideas, new patterns emerge and new commercial opportunities become available. In complexity theory, the emergence of new patterns from chaos is described as 'order for free'. In this case, the viral culture of memes, fandom and sharing feeds a corporate culture of big data and platform capitalism.

Expanding the circle of creativity radiates outwards from a focal point. The originator initiates the movement and provides the resources and opportunities for consumer creativity on the margins. Breaking the circle is open to all comers, making it hard to determine where the movement begins and ends, or who was responsible for starting it. The diffusion of ideas is explosive, following a geometric progression, not an incremental curve. It expands rapidly, then disappears almost as quickly. Yet while it is still in process, it results in an overflow of ideas and initiatives as others jump onto the bandwagon. This results in the 'cognitive surplus' alluded to earlier. And while the viral spread of ideas online is temporary, they leave behind a residue of creative content – collateral information which may in turn be picked over and reshared or exploited in the future.

Alongside this cognitive surplus, online activity generates what Shoshana Zuboff calls a 'behavioural surplus' – a bank of information about consumer behaviour which is the basis for what Zuboff describes as 'surveillance capitalism'. Each time we click on a photo or like a post, we leave a data trail. Collateral streams of behavioural data flow from our apparently random online interactions and are then monetized by tech companies like Facebook and Google as 'prediction products'. These products are then sold to advertisers, or used in-house to produce or sell products, in the case of Netflix/Amazon Prime and Amazon respectively.

Zuboff raises the possibility that apparently random interactions may be harnessed to a darker purpose. For example, she traces the success of Pokémon Go to a massive contagion experiment initiated by Niantic (a commercial partner of Google), designed not just to track consumer behaviour but to drive it, using geo-mapping to increase footfall around participating businesses. In other words, 'breaking the circle' might be part of a more deliberate strategy – the spreading of random memes and GIFs on social media used to harvest data on consumer behaviour or even to influence it.

There is a risk, then, that what is broken up by fan cultures and viral flows of information is simply aggregated by big business. Surveillance capitalists are the big game hunters in this ecosystem, tracking down apparently random ideas and products, and absorbing them into their private menageries. Random, anarchic ideas are unwittingly co-opted as cogs in the machinery of surveillance capitalism, viral content used to generate marketable consumer data. Or, the break-up of the circle is later found to have been deliberately orchestrated – like corporate graffiti sprayed onto urban pavements.

The #shantytok craze of January 2021 saw millions of people sharing and liking videos of bearded men singing sea shanties on TikTok. These videos were shared and co-created many times over, with professional and amateur musicians adding layers of instrumentation and harmony. Sea shanties seemed to strike a chord during the dark days of lockdown – tapping into a nostalgia for authenticity, connection, and simple, honest endeavour at a time when many were isolated, disconnected and inactive.

It all started when a Scottish postman, Nathan Evans, uploaded to TikTok his version of a 19th-century sea shanty, 'Soon May the Wellerman Come', in December 2020. Over the next days and weeks, his version was re-recorded, shared, duetted and remixed. The song began trending on TikTok and Spotify. Celebrities and musicians recorded their own versions. Electro shanty remixes dubbed in electronic dance music beats. Memes featured people singing along in cars. The simple melody, driving rhythm and the call-and-response structure of the shanty was an open invitation to join in the chorus, and multiple users added their own voices, harmonies, videos and captions. Evans himself appeared on TV shows in Britain and America, won himself a recording contract and began planning a post-Covid tour of the UK and Europe.

A few months later, #shantytok was no longer trending. Apart from Evans' record deal, some traditional shanty singers, for example The Longest Johns (who had recorded 'Wellerman' in 2018), enjoyed a brief surge in popularity. Viewers and listeners had been entertained. But perhaps the biggest beneficiary was TikTok itself, consolidating its status as the world's most popular video-sharing app and adding to its over 1 billion monthly active users. TikTok's owners, ByteDance, are reputed to possess some of the most advanced artificial intelligence technology designed to measure and track user behaviours on the platform. As the random connections proliferate and the attention of users is fragmented into a thousand 30-second clips, the AI quietly consolidates the underlying user data. By indirections, the platforms find direction out. They find us out.

There are other platforms emerging, some on the 'dark web' or 'dark forest' of online culture, where new connections are being made. Some of these are distinctly sinister – the new counterculture encompasses extremist politics, violence, criminality, sexual exploitation. In the creative field, new platforms attempt to provide opportunities for users to generate or share creative content among emerging artists and their fans, operating on the fringes of commercial media and using advertising or subscriptions to generate revenue.

Wattpad ('the world's most loved social storytelling platform') is typical of this hybrid between community and commerce. Wattpad provides an online self-publishing platform for writers to publish and share their work using a variety of Creative Commons licences. A key feature of the platform is enabling and encouraging creators of fan fiction to make derivative works from pre-existing stories and characters – and to license their own work for other co-creators.

The Creative Commons licences used by Wattpad and other co-creative platforms allow writers to be credited as originators without restricting others from reusing or remixing their work. This depends upon a degree of mutual trust and tolerance – and the platform still has to abide by copyright law when users are borrowing material from outside the Wattpad community. In cases of infringement, Wattpad will issue takedown notices. The platform also attempts to maintain some community standards on content.

Perhaps it is inevitable that these 'alternative' platforms for co-creation struggle to survive in our copyright culture of individual authorship and corporate ownership of intellectual property. Some like PledgeMusic have eventually gone out of business. Many like MySpace have been acquired and domesticated by corporate media. Google bought YouTube, Facebook acquired WhatsApp – and in January 2021, Wattpad was acquired by South Korean media conglomerate Naver.

Still, sometimes the sheer randomness of online viral media flows defies commercial logic. Generous and random acts of creativity produce commercially valuable outcomes. Some of this value is no doubt extracted by corporations like Google and Facebook, which specialize in mining data from every click, like and share in our online lives. But they can also benefit artists, brands and independent businesses. 'Breaking the circle' is not commercially driven, and the rewards seldom circle back to the originator. But these unplanned exchanges still generate what economists refer to as 'positive externalities' or 'cognitive surpluses'. Some of these benefits are commercial, but others are less tangible – a feeling of community and connection, perhaps. The fact that the benefits are uncharted and unevenly distributed reflects the intrinsic unpredictability of these patterns of co-creation. Our final recipe shows how breaking the circle can implicate both commercial and altruistic purposes, and how users can co-create meaning, not because they want to get rich, but just for the joy of it.

RECIPE 24. THE HARLEM SHAKE: WHO STARTED THE VIRUS? (NEW YORK – OR NOWHERE)

INGREDIENTS:

- A guy in a crash helmet
- An Australian longboarding crew
- A legion of tweeters, YouTubers, brands and platforms
- A man dancing, alone

In February 2013, a video of young people dancing 'went viral'. The 'original' video (itself inspired by an American comedy video posted a few days earlier) was posted on YouTube on 2 February 2013 by a group of Australian teenagers collectively known as Sunny Coast Skate. One member of the group wearing a crash helmet is dancing to an electronic dance track, 'Harlem Shake' by Baauer. The others studiously ignore him until a beat drops and they all begin gyrating wildly.

The next day, another group of teenagers in Florida posted their version of the dance. At this stage, the video was in the 'pre-viral' stage, with views in the tens of thousands. Over the next few days, Baauer's record label and others began tweeting links to the videos, and a production company and branding consultancy 'Maker Studios' produced a version (Harlem Shake v3 Office Edition) that attracted 7.4 million views. By the end of February, the video had been viewed by 700 million people, with over 100,000 imitations, including versions by the Norwegian Army, various sports franchises, protesters in Egypt and *The Simpsons*. And almost as quickly, by the end of the month the number of views and Google searches began plummeting back towards zero.

According to Kevin Ashton in *Quartz*, the viral spread 'had nothing to do with community and everything to do with commerce'. Over a period of roughly two to three weeks, various marketing agencies, online influencers, record labels and DJs (including Bauuer's own Twitter account and that of his record label, Mad Decent) recognized the viral potential of the video and used it to promote their own brands. They were joined by established internet companies like BuzzFeed and brands like Pepsi, together with politicians. By the end of the month, the video had become so widely imitated by increasingly mainstream users that the trend was declared 'dead'.

'Harlem Shake' provided a template for 'viral' promotion. Unlike previous music videos, such as Beyoncé's 'Single Ladies' or PSY's 'Gangnam Style', the content was made by amateurs. The dance itself was said to have originated with Al Boyce (aka Al B), a basketball fan who performed a drunken dance during half-time at games in New York. Boyce received no financial benefit from the dance he had originated (his mother later claimed she advised him to 'patent' his moves, though it's not clear whether this would have been legally enforceable). Baauer, having failed to obtain copyright for two vocal samples he used in the track, also faced legal difficulties in 'owning' the musical content (although he undoubtedly benefited from YouTube advertising revenues as well as brand awareness). The teenagers who posted the first video could not claim copyright. From a legal perspective, the amateur/unprofessional origins of the track opened up the video for unconstrained commercial use.

The other key to viral spread was the involvement of ordinary users. Harlem Shake spread through social media influencers and their followers, primarily on Twitter. Some of the influencers, for example prominent YouTubers or tweeters, gained social capital among their followers (which in turn could be cashed into commercial revenues by promoting other brands now or in the future). But the followers responsible for many of the 'shares' and 'likes' had no commercial interest at stake. Unlike a professional production where views might have been funnelled through a single 'official' YouTube channel, the views were dispersed across many versions and platforms, allowing consumer attention to be corralled in multiple directions by diverse commercial brands.

And while the craze was briefly popular, it was not co-opted by any single 'owner'. Baauer (aka Brooklyn music producer Harry Gonzales) did not become a global brand. There was no 'official' remix. Compare this with other 'community' movements in popular culture, from music and dance to street fashion, which are eventually claimed by the mainstream. For example, the 2016 Luis Fonzi hit song 'Despacito' achieved some of its global exposure as a result of being adopted by South American football fans, notably the Buenos Aires 'Escuela do Bandones' (School of the Terraces), who take pride in adapting and recording songs which then spread 'virally' among football fans. Yet Fonzi remained the accredited author and prime beneficiary (graciously acknowledging his gratitude), up to and including the inevitable Justin Bieber remix.

Where is the 'who' of creativity in the Harlem Shake story? Western culture privileges origination as the core of the creative process. Yet in this story the originators are uncredited, underpaid and all but forgotten – Al Boyce, who came up with the original 'Harlem

Shake' dance, the forgotten hip hop artists who adopted it, the vocalist whose signature call of 'con los terroristas' was sampled by Baauer. The comedian George Miller, who originated the first dance, and the crew of teenagers who popularized it a day later, adding in new elements including the mysterious man in a crash helmet, likewise remained on the periphery of Harlem Shake's popular and commercial success. Unlike other internet 'memes', there was no obvious singular source for subsequent variants.

Western theories of creativity also assume that imitation is the antithesis of creativity. Yet an internet 'meme' depends upon repetition; indeed, ease of repetition was one reason for Harlem Shake's rapid viral spread. The internet meme is itself a 'memetic' adaptation of Richard Dawkins' use of the term 'meme' to describe a cultural idea transmitted across space and time in the manner of genetic information. 'Meme' evokes the French word '*même*' (same); though like genes, memes are never quite the same, they are always mutations – repetitions with a twist.

'Creativity' in Harlem Shake is only loosely based on 'originality'. Rather, creativity is manifest through recognition and adaptation. First of all, commercial brands recognized the potential of the first iteration of Harlem Shake as a vehicle for their brands. One of the producers at Maker Studios, responsible for the highly successful 'v3 (Office Edition)' recognized the video's 'pre-viral' potential (citing its popularity on Reddit, one of the internet's 'edgier' social media sites) and used this to promote the company's own brand. Knowing which trend to follow and when to adopt it is an underrated creative aptitude. The second creative ingredient was adaptation. No two versions of 'Do the Harlem Shake' were alike and the adaptations became increasingly bizarre and improbable. The popularity of Harlem Shake on Google and YouTube searches was prompted by the possibility of discovering yet another new variant. The simplicity of the basic elements – the music, the dance, the sudden change in pace and participation – allowed for apparently limitless variations, the quintessential requirement for a successful internet meme.

Finally, perhaps Harlem Shake captured the imagination precisely because it seemed to lack purpose or 'value' – one of the key components in any classic definition of creativity ('creativity = novelty plus value'). Many apparently spontaneous internet memes turn out to have been orchestrated by advertisers towards a specific commercial goal, often starting with a professionally produced video (for example, the Cadbury Dairy Milk gorilla campaign, the Cadbury 'eyebrows' campaign) or a concerted campaign (the 'ice bucket challenge' designed to raise awareness of ALS/motor neurone disease). By contrast, 'Harlem Shake' encapsulates a mood of aimlessness. The initial stage of each video is a scene of passivity and ennui, a room full of people united by apathy; the second part is all energy, a joyful release of flailing limbs and non-choreography, directed not towards anything 'useful', only perhaps to celebrating its own existence.

'Do the Harlem Shake' does not conform to a classical model of the creative process. There is no obvious starting point of 'ideation' or creative breakthrough. Instead, there is a sampling of various pre-existing elements thrown together without any avowed purpose (other than having fun, perhaps). Creativity is realized through a process of recognition and adaptation. Kevin Ashton is surely right to point to the commercial manipulation of internet memes and the role of advertisers and intermediaries in promoting them. User-generated content may have benefited commercial interests here and in countless other cases, but its adaptability and continuity depend on popular culture, specifically on the creativity of users, not originators. The Harlem Shake did not in the end belong to a single brand, nor to a single author, but to a global community of internet users who searched, liked, shared and recreated it.

Where is the cognitive surplus in your team or organization? Who is behind them, and who is spreading them? How and why does an idea 'go viral'? Are there unplanned ideas spreading virally which could spill over and transform your own creative projects?

RESOURCES

Ashton, K. (2013), 'You Didn't Make the Harlem Shake Go Viral – Corporations Did', *Quartz*, 13 May: https://qz.com/67991/you-didnt-make-the-harlem-shake-go-viral-corporations-did/
Richard Dawkins on Memes – Cannes Lions 2013: www.youtube.com/watch?v=xCzb6SuyriU
Clay Shirky Ted Talk – How Cognitive Surplus Will Change The World: www.ted.com/talks/clay _shirky_how_cognitive_surplus_will_change_the_world?language=en

Much has been written on the ethical, cultural and legal implications of the shift towards 'platform capitalism' in the cultural sector. In Part IV we have instead looked at the implications for creativity, where adaptation and user experience take over from origination and product innovation. These new forms of Creativity 2.0 may be exploitative, especially in relation to intellectual property. But they also open up more collective, democratic ways of working. They challenge the 'who' of creativity, inviting users and audiences to take centre stage, recreating and co-creating beyond the 'original' idea and its individual author. This, in turn, encourages us to see creativity not as a completed project but as a continuing process, not as genius but as culture, not as a commodity but as a gift.

Consumer co-creation and the gift economy challenge the conventions of copyright and ownership. For this reason, co-creation has often been harnessed by big tech companies to undermine the status of creators while at the same time monetizing the attention of consumers. At the same time, co-creation enriches the public domain. In a Darwinian theory of creativity, ideas or 'memes' are transmitted and reproduced within an ecosystem, following a cycle of blind variation and selective retention to gradually improve their value and resilience as part of an evolutionary process. The behaviours outlined in Part IV make possible the 'blind variations' in the Darwinian model. Ideas are transmitted memetically, shared, modified and shared again across multiple users and co-creators. It is up to us to decide which of these variations to select and retain and what to do with them.

We have described the Who of creativity as a series of expanding circles, rippling out from the individual act of creation. Creativity is not self-contained; it seeds secondary acts of creation among audiences and collaborators. In many cases these second acts are more influential or more profitable than the first. And while the movement outwards from core to periphery can threaten creative professionals and benefit intermediaries at the expense of originators, it also democratizes the creative process. No doubt platform capitalism is the big beneficiary of this democratization, with companies like Facebook and Google exploiting a 'behavioural surplus' as more of us share and participate in a wider circle of creative exchange. But the recipes and examples in Part IV also illustrate benefits to artists (Jack White, Nick Cave, Nathan Evans aka the singing postman), to alternative platforms (Wattpad, Chinese *zimuzu* clubs), legacy businesses gaining a second life (Tower, NBA) – and ordinary citizens (Norwegian children, Swedish musicians, everyday creativity). Above all, the Who of creativity, like the other questions posed in this book, allows for many answers and many forms of creativity.

The idea of creativity as a gift, as something random or untamed, capable of generating different forms of value (social, economic, aesthetic) for different types of user leads us to Part V. The non-profit community project can seed commercial returns; commercial businesses can trigger social and cultural acts of creation. There are many second acts involving different actors and different credits. A gap opens up between non-commercial intention and commercial outcome. If creativity can mean so many things to so many different people, if it can be appropriated or misdirected, recycled, extended or set free, what is its purpose? In the final analysis, do we care about the motivation or intention of the 'original' creator (whoever that was)? The Who of creativity inevitably invites us to question its purpose as well. This leads on to our final question, the Why of creativity.

We finish Part IV with a creativity canvas showing the Who elements of the Harlem Shake recipe.

SOURCES AND FURTHER READING FOR PART IV

Part IV considers how the 'genius' model of creativity (Weisberg 1993) has been superseded by a growing recognition of patterns of co-creation, with fans and 'the people formerly known as the audience' (Rosen 2006) increasingly calling the shots when it comes to value creation. The sources below include a range of readings on fandom and co-creation (Jenkins et al. 2013, Hills 2002). Much of this research is in response to new forms of consumption online (Ritzer and Jurgenson 2010, Booth 2010, Gauntlett 2011), especially via social media, and to hacks and 'mods' of cultural products like video games (Lee 2011). The Papi Jiang recipe in the next section, Part V, links to a sub-set of this digital economy, the emergence of 'self-media' (Marwick 2015). We have also highlighted that the idea of consumers co-creating meaning is not new, with John Dewey having described 'an aesthetic experience' in the 1930s as one in which the viewer reproduces the imaginative work of the artist, Lewis Hyde arguing in the 1960s that artists offer their work as a 'gift' to the audience which creates community and reciprocity, not a transactional exchange, and Stuart Hall's influential work on active and resistant audiences in the 1980s, which signalled an interest in audiences as co-creators of meaning in media studies. From a business perspective, co-creation informs the idea of learning organizations, crowdsourcing and the 'wisdom of crowds' (Surowiecki 2005, Howe 2008), as well as business models of 'open innovation' or 'open source' where consumers are co-opted as co-workers (Chesbrough et al. 2008). Finally, we have included some recent critiques of 'platform capitalism' by Nick Srnicek (2016) and Shoshana Zuboff (2019), describing the rise of big tech companies which commodify and exploit the 'behavioural surplus' of creative consumption for their own ends.

Booth, P. (2010), *Digital Fandom: New Media Studies*, New York: Peter Lang.
Chesbrough, H., W. Vanhaverbeke and J. West (eds) (2008), *Open Innovation: Researching a New Paradigm*, Oxford: Oxford University Press.
Conor, B., R. Gill and S. Taylor (eds) (2015), *Gender and Creative Labour*, Chichester: Wiley/The Sociological Review.
Dewey, J. (2005), *Art as Experience*, New York: Perigee Books.
Gauntlett, D. (2011), *Making is Connecting: The Social Meaning of Creativity, from DIY and Knitting to YouTube and Web 2.0*, Cambridge: Polity Press.

Hall, S. (1980), 'Encoding/Decoding' in S. Hall, D. Hobson, A. Love and P. Willis (eds), *Culture, Media Language: Working Papers in Cultural Studies 1972–1979*, London: Hutchinson, 128–138.

Hesmondhalgh, D. and A. Saha (2013), 'Race, Ethnicity, and Cultural Production', *Popular Communication* **11**(3), 179–195.

Hills, M. (2002), *Fan Cultures*, London: Routledge.

Howe, J. (2008), *Crowdsourcing: How the Power of the Crowd is Driving the Future of Business*, London: Random House Business Books.

Hyde, L. (2006), *The Gift: How the Creative Spirit Transforms the World*, Edinburgh: Canongate.

Jenkins, H., S. Ford and J. Green (2013), *Spreadable Media: Creating Value and Meaning in a Networked Culture*, New York: New York University Press.

Kelly, K. (2008), '1,000 True Fans', *The Technium*, http://kk.org/thetechnium/1000-true-fans/

Lee, H-K. (2011), 'Participatory Media Fandom: A Case Study of Anime Fansubbing', *Media, Culture and Society* **33**(8), 1131–1147.

Lessig, L. (2008), *Remix: Making Art and Commerce Thrive in the Hybrid Economy*, London: Bloomsbury.

Marwick, A. (2015), *Status Update: Celebrity, Publicity and Branding in the Social Media Age*, New Haven, CT: Yale University Press.

Prahalad, C. and V. Ramaswamy (2004), 'Co-creation Experiences: The Next Practice in Value Creation', *Journal of Interactive Marketing* **18**(3), 5–14.

Ritzer, G. and N. Jurgenson (2010), 'Production, Consumption, Prosumption: The Nature of Capitalism in the Age of the Digital "Prosumer"', *Journal of Consumer Culture* **10**(1), 13–36.

Rosen, J. (2006), 'The People Formerly Known as the Audience', *PressThink*, 27 June: http://archive.pressthink.org/2006/06/27/ppl_frmr.html

Srnicek, N. (2016), *Platform Capitalism*, London: Polity.

Surowiecki, J. (2005), *The Wisdom of Crowds*, New York: Anchor Books.

Weisberg, R. (1993), *Creativity: Beyond the Myth of Genius*, New York: Freeman.

Zuboff, S. (2019), *The Age of Surveillance Capitalism*, London: Profile Books.

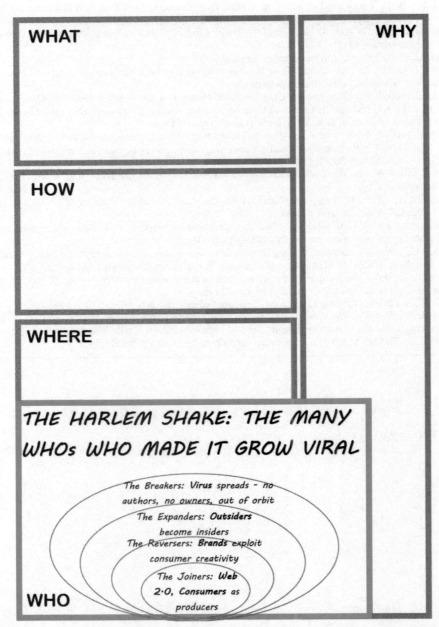

WHAT

WHY

HOW

WHERE

THE HARLEM SHAKE: THE MANY
WHOs WHO MADE IT GROW VIRAL

The Breakers: *Virus spreads* - *no
authors, no owners, out of orbit*
The Expanders: **Outsiders**
become insiders
The Reversers: **Brands** *exploit
consumer creativity*
The Joiners: **Web
2·0, Consumers** *as
producers*

WHO

Figure 4.2   Creativities canvas example 4: Harlem Shake and the Who of creativity

PART V
THE WHY – CREATIVE PURPOSES

'But from a "business" point of view, you're a failure, right?'

This is the question posed by the narrator/interviewer in the film *An Impossible Project* to Florian Caps, the man who bought the world's last Polaroid film factory in the Netherlands. Caps saved the factory but found it hard to gather the money and expertise necessary to make viable products. A young intern hired by Caps told his venture capitalist father about the project, he came in with big money, and Caps was ousted. Not long after that, in 2017, they (the father and son, not Caps) sold the factory back to Polaroid, who had subsequently seen the instant camera market as an interesting niche, and made a tidy profit.

Caps does concede, 'My wife thinks I am the World's biggest loser', but balances this by countering, 'But I think I'm one of the World's biggest winners, who maybe had a bad year when that happened.'

After thinking further about the question, though, Caps says, 'Anyway, a business?… What *is* a "business"?'

That all of these people can be right about the creativity it takes to resurrect or build a product is a function of the fact that people can have different 'whys'. That the conventional 'why' of a business is to achieve some kind of financial gain can lead one to see Caps as a failure (and for his wife's jest to be bittersweet). But Caps' why is different, his why – his 'reason for doing' (or raison de faire) – is to save analogue technology, and if it wasn't for him and the chain of events he set off, Polaroid instant cameras would have vanished from Planet Earth. He won at that – which to him is good business – and he's launched from that on to other impossible resurrections: vinyl, notebooks, old hotels, advising Facebook as they seek to become more analogue. If he had dug his heels in and tried to tough it out to make money from the factory, he and everyone else would have lost. It's why he bears no ill-will to the subsequent owners of Polaroid – they were important Whos (see Part IV) in the creative process.

Simon Sinek has famously argued that finding and being clear about 'your why', like Florian Caps, should be the starting point in the entrepreneurial or creative journey. In highlighting the importance of meaning and purpose, Sinek echoes one of the fundamental assumptions about creativity – that creativity is driven by an intrinsic sense of purpose and fulfilment.

Other 'extrinsic' motivators (material rewards, professional structures) might occasionally be 'synergistic' but all too often they will distract from or fatally undermine our inner drive. And by extension, creativity is an inherently fulfilling and meaningful experience, linked to the positive psychology of 'flow', and 'higher' needs and motivations.

In this book we have argued that there is no single recipe for creativity. Just as there are many answers to the What, How, Where and Who of creativity, so too there are many motivations which drive creativity – not always pointing in the same direction.

The 'Why' framework: the creative pathways matrix

In this final part of *Creativities*, we make a distinction between two types of Why. The first of these fits with the imaginary identity of the artist or entrepreneur, as described by Sinek, providing a foundational purpose behind the creative enterprise or creative career. Creativity is inevitably uncertain with a high risk of failure, making a strong sense of purpose especially salient. Because value and purpose connect to values and ethics, we call this 'the personal why'. For example, creativity might be driven by 'dark' purposes (the creativity of terrorist acts, the creative discoveries behind nuclear weapons or climate destruction). It might be inspired by idealism or by greed and self-interest. It will be personal to the individual and it forms the starting point for all that follows.

If the personal why is the start of the journey, the next set of questions comes later, as the product of our creativity (outcome, enterprise, career) evolves in sometimes unexpected ways. At this point we find ourselves asking, 'Why are we still doing this? What is this for? Why should we change?' These questions are not only personal; they must take account of how the product we created has changed, changed us and changed the world around us. Over time our personal why is challenged and reframed by the Why of our process or product.

For example, the personal why for a painter may be to develop a new hobby, but as the product of the painter evolves, that Why could become building a new form of the craft, or using it as a therapy, or something else. You may accept a management position – the personal why being because you want to move into something different or you feel it is your turn or duty. But then you may be very good at it, and enjoy it, so your why might evolve into something different. You may start out wanting to be an actor in order to make this a profession, but come to see it more fulfilling as a social enterprise.

Confronting this new reality, our sense of purpose and value must adapt to the purposes and values of others as well as to the consequences of our product's evolution and reception. We might have to concede some control, or accept a change in direction. Our 'personal why' has to adapt to a new set of purposes and possibilities unleashed by the product, enterprise or career we have set in train. Because these questions revolve around the products or outcomes of our creative act (and where it's taking us), we call this 'the productional why'.

5.1   THE PERSONAL WHY

The Why of creativity is built into the definition of creativity as 'novelty + value'. Much of the creativity research agenda, especially in organizations and business, assumes that creativity is built on a solid foundation of purpose and value, and that individual creative processes are driven by intrinsic motivation or a sense of satisfaction in a job well done ('task fulfilment'). In turn, creative work is often expected to be 'good work' – autonomous, fulfilling, ethical.

We will argue that these motivations might be more complicated and compromised than these assumptions allow. Certainly our motivations to create remain highly personal and individualized, based on our beliefs, values and needs. But intrinsic motivation is not necessarily intrinsically positive. Nor can our inner 'personal' why be entirely divorced from external realities (resources, rewards, opportunities) – even at the beginning of the journey, these extrinsic motivations may have become internalized to the point where it's hard to tell the difference.

Creativity is iterative – as we search for novel solutions and ideas, our personal why provides both a sounding board (values or criteria for success) and a continuity of purpose (motivation and self-belief). We can visualize the 'why' of creativity as the opposable thumb against which our other questions (the What, How, Where and Who) are fingers, allowing them to grasp the problem in hand.

Just as the Why of value and purpose helps to direct and evaluate the products, processes and people of creativity, so too the changing patterns of What, How, Where, Who inevitably challenge the value and purpose of creativity. In other words, the Why of creativity is not set in stone – it moves against the other questions, it grips, releases, stretches. Our values, and the value we produce, are relative and contextual to our changing experiences, outcomes and associations.

Our first recipe considers how purpose can be redefined or refined among a group. As Sinek has emphasized, a sense of purpose is an essential starting point – not least in the unpredictable environment of creativity, where outcomes are by definition uncertain or unknown. Having an inner purpose, our 'personal why', allows us to navigate this uncertainty, giving us a reservoir of self-belief and a sense of direction. But that inner compass will periodically need to be reoriented, and the reservoir refilled – and in a group, the personal beliefs and values will not always be aligned.

RECIPE 25. THE BEATLES: SEPARATE WHYS (UK)

INGREDIENTS:

- A chance meeting between two lads who liked writing songs more than football
- One unrecognized song-writing talent
- One charismatic, heavy-sounding, drummer
- The most prolific song-writing team since Mozart and Bach

Perhaps one of the most traumatic times in modern cultural history was The Beatles break-up. How could this band, whom so many had taken to heart and were perhaps the first celebrities that people felt they 'knew' (and whose creative volume was probably only matched by Mozart or Schubert) fall apart? In 1969 and 1970, many fans and observers were consumed by the world's most famous 'divorce' – as John Lennon called it.

Even now, the four characters that made up the group exert a strong pull on people's emotions, and there are many online surveys that you can take to determine 'which Beatle – John, Paul, George or Ringo – you are most like' So their demise, then and now, seems sad and bewildering.

The chronological debris of their break-up has been well picked over:

In 1966, Beatlemania got to the point where it was becoming too difficult and too dangerous to continue to tour and play live. The group, famously democratic, took a vote as to whether they should continue. Lennon, Harrison and Starr had had enough, only McCartney wasn't adamant that their touring days were over, but it was a clear majority. The treadmill of touring that kept them together as a family of friends taking on the world stopped abruptly, and the four were free to pursue their own creative interests.

John, feeling depressed and guilty about his (actual rather than metaphorical) failing marriage, isolated himself and 'experimented' further with drugs. His relationship with Yoko Ono, whom he met late in 1966, became something of a lifeline in this context.

Paul, by contrast, lived the life of a single cultural dilettante in London, wrote prolifically and more on his own rather than in close collaboration with Lennon as he had done previously. John (whose relationship with Paul was fruitfully collaborative *and* competitive) would complain that he simply couldn't match Paul's creative output in this period.

George explored spirituality and became deeply engaged in Indian culture and musicianship. He also emerged as a songwriter with a distinctive creative identity, a development that nobody had foreseen in the shyest and youngest Beatle.

Ringo, whom Peter Asher described as having two great strengths – being an incredible and unique drummer and being naturally charming on camera – got more interested in acting in movies. Ringo also began writing music that reflected his own distinctive identity.

When they came back together to record, the group dynamic had changed too. The unofficial leader of the 'one-person one-vote democracy' had always been John. He was a couple of years older than George and Paul and was the most extrovert of the four. To begin with, Lennon was also the main song-writing protagonist. But *Sgt. Pepper's Lonely Hearts Club Band* was Paul's concept, and in 1967, he led the group in rehearsing and recording most of the material on what many regard as the finest Beatles album. In 2003, *Rolling Stone* magazine ranked it as the number 1 album of all time.

But this new creative dynamic, which took them to another level musically, was also sowing the seeds of The Beatles' demise.

The Beatles output was previously powered by the close-knit Lennon–McCartney song-writing unit and their shared love of American rock and roll. Their individual creative development meant that their collective output was increasingly varied, and beyond the conceit of *SPLHCB* (where The Beatles assumed the personality of a fictional band), it became difficult to fit all of their emerging material into one coherent album.

The Beatles worked around the widening individual tangents and creative riches in the next 'proper' album that followed (*Magical Mystery Tour* was more of a multimedia project even more driven by another of McCartney's ideas containing only a few new songs). This was called *The Beatles*, but is known as *The White Album* on account of the fact the cover is a blank white canvas, as if to signify that the songs on it were not joined by a unifying vision as *SPLHCB* had been. *The White Album* was a rambling and disparate double LP.

At its core was a collection of songs that a rejuvenated Lennon–McCartney had penned while on a spiritual retreat that Harrison had arranged in India, early in 1968. (Harrison was apparently annoyed that the two had spent more energy writing songs than meditating.) But beyond this were songs written individually by Harrison, twee as well as heavier pieces that McCartney had written independently, some experimental material that Lennon had developed with Yoko Ono, and even the first Ringo-penned song on a Beatles album. A total of 30 songs of varying quality added up to a collection often referred to as 'sprawling'.

That the best song on *The White Album* was considered by many to be Harrison's 'While my Guitar Gently Weeps' further questioned whether The Beatles was John and Paul's band. And other cracks in the status quo started to widen over the next year.

Ringo was the first to leave, albeit temporarily, claiming that his musical efforts weren't respected enough by the others (although his departure was kept quiet and he returned to the fold a few weeks later).

John put increasing energy into a variety of projects with Yoko. And as they became inseparable, or 'one person', in John's words, when the group came back to the studio there were five creative presences, a factor that led to tension among the original 'fab four' (although the other three appreciated that Yoko was a positive force for John). John also later admitted that he was finding it difficult to come to terms with the fact that The Beatles might not be 'his' band anymore.

George, reflecting on the positive response to his songs on *The White Album*, increasingly began to wonder why his 'allocation' of songs per Beatles LP was so low. He mused that his 'output of songs [wa]s too much to just sit around waiting to put two songs out on an album – I've got to get 'em out', explaining his decision to prepare a solo album.

Paul had started a serious relationship with Linda Eastman and was becoming more of a 'home-body' as a result, but as the other three continued to withdraw their creative energy (or at least gave McCartney the impression they were withdrawing it), it was McCartney who took on the responsibility to pull the group together. However, as he became more and more directive, the other three stepped back or further away.

A further complicating factor was the financial problems The Beatles now faced. Brian Epstein – the manager who had shaped The Beatles – had died in late 1967. Epstein was a much-needed professional when it came to image management, and as he was only a few years older than The Beatles, he became something of an older/wiser brother figure that the four all respected and listened to. They felt the loss of his stewardship deeply. But Epstein's strengths were more marketing and human relations than financial management, and by 1968, The Beatles' fiduciary affairs were a mess, and tax and other unpaid bills were mounting.

The band's attempts, led by McCartney, to right the ship by creating a company called Apple to manage their affairs only partly stopped the rot, and soon that company, described as a new kind of hippy-capitalist enterprise, was bleeding more money than it was consolidating. Professional management was required fast, and McCartney thought he had a solution: his new in-laws the Eastmans had a company that could step in.

The other three Beatles, fearing that this was tilting the ship too far toward McCartney's new family, met with the Rolling Stones' manager Allan Klein, who was more than happy to become an alternative. McCartney didn't trust Klein, so it came to a vote. McCartney lost 3–1, and while The Beatles could work around their creative tangents in the studio, the financial differences were more intractable, particularly as lawyers became involved, and the press subsequently prodded John and Paul for comment on legal proceedings.

Despite this, The Beatles regrouped for their final LP, *Abbey Road*, in 1969, another album that regularly tops the best-of-all-time lists. And despite the gnashing of teeth and the mourning that took place as The Beatles split, beyond a difficult few years where the gloves came off between Lennon and McCartney, the four either stayed in contact and collaborated with each other, or at least reconciled.

Creatively too, the break-up was fruitful. Who could have foreseen that Harrison would have so much good solo material stored up that it would fill the world's first triple LP: the acclaimed *All Things Must Pass* was released in 1970. Or that Starr would have a run of hit singles ('It Don't Come Easy', 'You're Sixteen', 'Photograph').

While McCartney's output was deemed too middle-of-the-road by many, he was the one who went on to fill the stadiums The Beatles once played to with his band Wings. And John's partnership with Yoko produced work far more interesting and challenging than what would have been possible within The Beatles, and in addition gave us perhaps the most-loved pop song of all time: 'Imagine'.

So, on balance, The Beatles break-up was sad – in the sense that it brought to a close the run of the world's most creative popular group, one that the Baby Boomer generation had, quite literally according to Malcolm Gladwell, 'grown up with' – but it was also a good and inevitable thing if the forces involved were to continue to grow creatively. So, that having been said, what did cause the break-up, and what can we learn from it?

Yoko Ono became the glib shorthand answer to the 'what caused the break-up?' question (and a convenient scapegoat for those who mourned The Beatles). But as she explained, 'I don't think you could have broken up four very strong people like them even if you tried. So there must have been something that happened with them – not an outside force at all.'

While all of the external elements described above (including Yoko) played some role in the split, perhaps the biggest force was internal. Simply put, it was that The Beatles' Whys diverged.

As Paul McCartney noted in a recent podcast, when they started out, they were just four working-class lads from Liverpool and their motivations were the same. They all wanted to play rock'n'roll, they all wanted to make some money, and they all dreamed of maybe buying a car, or even a house! This point was consistently reinforced by John Lennon in a variety of interviews in the 1960s when asked about what his aim for the group was, 'We're just trying to enjoy ourselves, having a laugh', he said. But that stock answer became increasingly strained as the pressure mounted and years went by.

What brought McCartney and Lennon together, via a chance meeting, was their being different from other young working-class lads in Liverpool. As McCartney reflected in the *Eight Days a Week* film by Ron Howard, 'When I talked to other people who asked what I was into and I said "writing songs," they looked blank and changed the subject to football or something... When I met John, he said, "Really? So do I!" That's how The Beatles started.'

As fellow musician Ian Hunter put it, 'It's amazing those two wound up in a band. It was only a matter of time before they got fed up, because they weren't the same. Paul was always middle, John was very left.'

So, while in their youth all four were united in their love of the fun of writing and playing American-inspired rock'n'roll and touring, they operated as a kind of O-form organization (see Part III), an all-for-one democracy. As their Whys grew, and those four personalities each had the strength of character to strive to stay true to them, they had to continue their creative ways as four separate Star-forms. And while people were (and are) sad they split, in this way we were spared the sight of The Beatles as another nostalgia act regrouping each decade to churn out 'all their best-loved hits, one last time' in paler stadium tours around the world. We should probably be grateful the four Beatles had the strength to follow their Whys.

What holds together the personal whys in your own creative group? Is there a tipping point when your own and others' personal whys might drift out of alignment – either now or in the future? And if you did have to 'break up the band', however painful this might be, what new creativities might emerge from the wreckage?

RESOURCES

'All You Need is John... The 30 Greatest Lennon Songs', *Uncut Magazine*, January 2008.
Davies, H. (2017), *The Beatles Lyrics: The Unseen Story Behind Their Music*, Weidenfeld & Nicolson.
'Interview with Paul McCartney', *Adam Buxton Podcast*, 11 December 2020.
Kahn, A. (ed.) (2020), *George Harrison on George Harrison*, Chicago Review Press.
'Why the Beatles Broke Up', *Rolling Stone Magazine*, 3 September 2009.

5.2   THE PRODUCTIONAL WHY (OR HOW CREATIVE PRODUCTS TAKE ON A LIFE OF THEIR OWN)

In the first section of Part V, we considered the personal motivations which drive individuals and groups in the creative act, especially in the early, formative stages of a creative career. The focus was on the creative act or the creative individual. In this second part, we turn our attention outwards to the extended possibilities and repercussions beyond that singular act of creation. The project, products and processes described in this book have a life beyond the moment of conception, and extend beyond the person or people who originated them. In deciding what happens next, where to take our idea, our product, our market, we encounter a new set of questions: why are our purposes and values changing? Have our original intentions been distorted or betrayed? Has a new intention or possibility emerged and how can we adapt to it?

Whereas the 'personal why' came from within, the 'productional why' is inflected by what is happening outside – markets, reactions, audience behaviours, competitors. As the outcome or product opens up new possibilities, we may need to rethink our choices and make changes. Our inner sense of purpose must adapt to external circumstances which cause us to reorient our internal sense of ourselves, our beliefs and values. That 'personal why' which was so clear and purposeful at the beginning gives way to a more complicated, messier 'productional why'. The product has moved beyond our original intention and may even boomerang back onto its creator, challenging the singular purpose we began with and forcing us to compromise, rethink, redirect.

We believe this process can be approached from two angles. First, do we continue to follow the same path, or do we try something different? Along this pathway, the productional why becomes stronger, either reinforcing our current direction or pulling us onto a different course. Second, do we try to retain control, or do we accept a looser, more adaptive mindset? Do we let go, like Florian Caps, for our own good and perhaps for the good of the product too? On this pathway, the personal why becomes less dominant, and more flexible.

We have summarized this in the creative pathways matrix in Figure 5.1, with the 'same or different' options mapped on the vertical axis and the 'tight or loose' options mapped horizontally. Appropriately enough, this model is itself a repurposing of an earlier model, and readers may notice that the figure is inspired by Ansoff's innovation matrix.

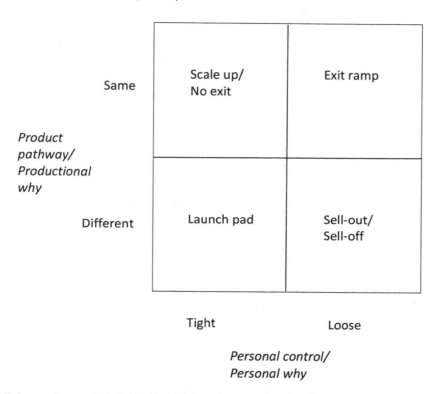

Figure 5.1   Creativities framework 5: the creative pathways matrix

As with Ansoff's matrix, the model is less concerned with discrete either/or choices between the four positions, hard and fast, than with the dynamic processes of movement across them and reflecting on the different pathways that could and should be taken to satisfy your (and your collaborators') Why. And the last recipe in Part V, and in the *Creativities* book – the operational hijab – will demonstrate how a venture can be developed across the matrix to enable different Whys to be satisfied at once.

In the creative pathways matrix, this movement comes from a combination or tension between the 'productional' and 'personal' why; sometimes the product and its components lead us to do something different, sometimes our personalities pull us in the opposite direction. If we are unable to reconcile these forces, we are likely to become frustrated or blocked, both at a personal level and in the business process. By evolving a new Why, we can start to map a pathway into a new stage for the creative product and for the creative personality behind it.

The starting point for all of these pathways is at the top left of the matrix – our initial venture starts from our personal why (our motivation or purpose) directed into a product or enterprise which fulfils that purpose. That product or enterprise combines all the other elements described in this book – the What, the How, the Where, the Who.

Over time, these other elements evolve as the business grows – and we change with it, finding new interests or directions (or in some cases, we fail to adapt – a problem we will return to later). We will begin by describing the more gradual, incremental of these evolutionary pathways – 'exit ramp' and 'launch pad' – before describing the more radical and transformative pathway – 'sell-out/sell-off'. We will then go back to the beginning to look at two possible outcomes if we decide to 'stick to the knitting'. First of all, what happens when the person or the product becomes locked into the original purpose and identity with no possibility of evolutionary change ('no exit')? Second, what happens when the personal and productional whys are dynamically aligned, and it is possible to grow and change from within the same product/person ('scale up')?

5.3   STEPPING OFF: TAKING THE EXIT RAMP

Some of the greatest creative innovations were not driven by a clear purpose but emerged unexpectedly from a more random process. From that moment of discovery, a more purposeful approach may take over. We describe this emergent purpose as 'the productional why'. The 'exit ramp' describes the point at which these two pathways diverge and the creative individual steps away from what they created. From here, creator and creation pursue their separate journeys. On the creative pathways matrix, the combination of a strong productional why and a loose personal why means that the entrepreneur is happy to 'let go' of the enterprise, while the enterprise takes on a life of its own and continues to progress independent of its founder.

In this scenario, it is not necessary for the creative individual to have a strong sense of purpose or direction. The 'personal why' is more like curiosity (what happens if I do this?) than purpose (what do I need to do to make this happen?). In management studies, this mindset would be described as 'emergent strategy' – businesses like Honda or Lego have been celebrated for adapting to emerging consumer behaviours rather than attempting to predict or predetermine a 'deliberate' strategy. In creativity studies, we might describe such thinking as 'intuitive' or 'spontaneous'. In terms of our model, the personal why is loose or even absent – the creator doesn't really know what they are doing or why, but out of this apparently random process a gathering purpose takes shape.

As the venture takes off, the other four elements of creativity – the What, the How, the Where, the Who – combine to map out a path. This 'productional why' drives the venture forward. The personal beliefs and values of the inventor or founder may happily coincide with this direction, or they may gradually diverge. At this point, the personal why is secondary to the productional why – the creator or entrepreneur finds purpose in the active process of doing, not in the creative process of envisioning.

How this works out will depend on a range of external factors, but above all on an internal attitude. Somebody who likes to be in control will very likely find such a random, incremental path frustrating. Somebody who is happy to 'go with the flow' will adapt to unexpected changes and growth relatively easily. This becomes especially apparent when the productional why and the personal why start to diverge.

When Robert Oppenheimer saw in the aftermath of Hiroshima the implications of the atomic weapons he had helped to create, his 'personal why' sharply diverged from the 'productional why' of a nuclear arms race. In the post-war period, he used his position on the Atomic Energy Council to argue against the proliferation of more powerful thermonuclear weapons. Oppenheimer's arguments were controversial as the Cold War intensified. He was accused of harbouring communist and pro-Soviet sympathies (the first charge partially true, the second demonstrably false). Oppenheimer was a complex, contradictory figure – there was no easy 'exit ramp' for him. He was able to continue his academic work, notably his research into black holes, and he was partially rehabilitated by Presidents Kennedy and Johnson a few years before his death in 1967. But his pioneering role bridging between the worlds of scientific creativity and political power was no longer tenable. Oppenheimer cared too much about the politics of war to live comfortably with his own legacy (the productional why) and cared too much about science to walk away from it quietly (his personal why). His creative abilities as a scientist were never able to take flight and his career remained unfulfilled while others pursuing different priorities and visions were promoted above him.

Our next recipe offers a very different outcome. In the case of Ben & Jerry's ice cream, the personal why was secondary to the productional why. To begin with at least, neither Ben Cohen nor Jerry Greenfield had a strong sense of purpose or mission. This is not to say that they were unprincipled or unmotivated. They put long hours into setting up the business and making it work. But this was never their 'raison de faire'. Consequently, when 'Ben & Jerry's' became something bigger than 'Ben' and 'Jerry', they were able to walk away in relative equanimity, in a way that Oppenheimer could not. Fans of Ben & Jerry's have been far more vocal in criticizing the corporate takeover by Unilever than the founders.

The exit ramp is the first of our pathways, showing how a 'productional why' can drive the business forward without the direct involvement of the founders. The essential purpose remains the same, but the direction is set by the creative enterprise, not by the creative entrepreneur. This allows the creative individual to step back and the thing they have created to thrive. As the following recipe illustrates, in this creative journey the 'personal why' is not always what really matters.

RECIPE 26. BEN & JERRY'S: THE ACCIDENTAL ENTREPRENEURS (VERMONT)

INGREDIENTS:

- Two childhood friends who like food
- Some simple rules for running a business (most of which you ignore)
- Second-hand equipment and the search for 'big chunks'
- A generous scoop of hard work and a sprinkle of happy accidents

Ben Cohen and Jerry Greenfield always seemed like unlikely entrepreneurs. Ben had dropped out of college, and when he moved to New York he was pursuing the idea of becoming a potter. His childhood friend Jerry had dropped out of medical school and moved into the apartment. They decided to open a shop together. Their first idea was to sell bagels, but the bagel-making equipment was too expensive. So they decided to make ice cream instead. This set a pattern of happy accidents driving the business forward. Asked whether they had ever planned on running a successful business on the 'How We Built This' podcast, both men laughed. They imagined doing ice cream for a couple of years before taking up something else. Maybe long-distance truck driving.

Their next decision was to open an ice cream parlour in Saratoga Springs. But when they got there, they found another ice cream parlour had just opened, so they decided to set up shop somewhere else. Eventually they settled on Burlington, Vermont, chosen because it met their two criteria – a population of college students, and no other competitors. The absence of ice cream shops may also have reflected the fact that Vermont gets extremely cold in winter.

Neither had any experience in business – they relied on leaflets mailed out by the Small Business Administration in New York to learn about budgets and cash flow. Nor had they any experience in making ice cream. They sent off for a correspondence course and taught themselves the basics. Jerry, with his medical training, was in charge of production. Ben was chief taster but suffered from a condition which meant he had no sense of smell, so instead of tasting the ice cream, he relied on 'mouth feel'.

One of Ben's preferences was for 'big chunks' in the ice cream. This was easier to achieve with the home-style equipment in their first shop – it would prove much harder when the business expanded and they began to use larger, industrial-style machines. But Ben insisted it was better to have the possibility of 'one big chunk' than trying to achieve a uniform distribution of smaller pieces.

They opened their shop in 1978 in a former gas station on the edge of town. In the summer, groups of college kids would queue up for a scoop, and to enjoy the laid-back vibe of the shop where Ben and Jerry were genial hosts. In winter, business was slow. The pair were making just about enough money to get by, but the business didn't seem to have much future. The Small Business Administration came to the rescue. They got hold of a business plan from a pizza parlour which they copied, substituting 'scoop' for 'slice' in the sales forecasts. The cash flow projections showed that the business was going to go bust. Like many entrepreneurs, Ben and Jerry responded by making up some new numbers (and asking the bank to defer repayments on their loan).

One of the reasons they didn't make much of a profit in the shop was portion control – they liked to make their customers happy, and trying to control the size of the scoop would upset people. So in 1980, they hit on another idea – if they sold the ice cream in one pint containers, there would be de facto portion control.

So they began selling ice cream in pint-size cartons, featuring the soon-to-be-iconic dairy cows which were designed by a local artist. At around this time, they also had their first stroke of luck when a 1981 *Time* magazine feature on local ice cream parlours described Ben & Jerry's as 'the best ice cream in the world'.

The business continued to grow. Ben and Jerry found themselves responsible for managing staff, finance and strategy – none of which they much enjoyed. At the same time, they seemed to have a talent for it. Ben in particular had an intuitive gift for marketing. Yet they continued to behave as if this was not a real business, just something they had drifted into.

That idea of not being a real business, or at least not 'business as usual', became part of the Ben & Jerry's brand. In 1984, Häagen-Dazs tried to prevent distributors from shipping Ben & Jerry's. Ben and Jerry ran a successful campaign against Pillsbury, Häagen-Dazs' parent company, asking, 'What's the Doughboy afraid of?' (the Pillsbury Doughboy being the beloved icon of the Pillsbury brand, a pudgy cartoon baker). It was a classic David and Goliath stand-off, and even if they could not afford to challenge Pillsbury in the courts, Ben and Jerry won the PR battle.

At around the same time, both Ben and Jerry became disillusioned with the daily grind of managing the business and decided to sell up. They had never intended to be a corporate organization and did not want to be a capitalist enterprise. It felt like the business had taken on a life of its own and they were no longer in charge of their own destiny.

A friend persuaded them to stay on. If they didn't like big business, why not try to run the business in a different way? So Ben and Jerry introduced benefits for their workers and placed a salary cap on senior managers. They set up a charitable foundation funded out of pre-tax projects to support community projects. They began campaigning on progressive issues. They partnered with a social enterprise employing ex-offenders to make the chocolate brownies in their ice cream.

This anti-corporate, progressive approach only served to make the brand even more successful. Having never really intended to run a business in the first place, Ben and Jerry were now heading up a global brand. Their association with progressive politics, their maverick, outsider status, and their image as hippy dropouts all drove the brand forward; the launch of the 'Cherry Garcia' flavour ice cream in 1987, dedicated to Grateful Dead singer and leader Jerry Garcia, perfectly encapsulated their identity as hippy capitalists. In 1988, they received the title of 'US Small Business Persons of the Year', awarded by President Ronald Reagan.

The foundation of Ben & Jerry's was not inspired by a burning sense of purpose. Their entrepreneurial drive, like their creative innovations in the ice cream business, seemed to result from a series of happy accidents. Even their progressive political beliefs, which became integral to the brand through the 1990s, seemed to have been gradually added as the business grew; indeed, their 'progressive' attitudes probably seemed more like common sense for people from their background and lifestyle.

Without ever planning to, they not only became successful, they were innovators in their field. They invented new flavours. Cookie dough ice cream, one of the most popular flavours today, was a Ben & Jerry's invention. Their jokey, informal approach to branding and marketing has influenced other 'progressive' businesses, from Innocent Smoothies to Oatly oat milk.

In 2000, Ben & Jerry's was acquired by Unilever. Ben and Jerry opposed the sale but were overruled by the board. They withdrew from the business. Despite the change of ownership, Unilever allowed Ben & Jerry's to support a range of progressive movements, from Occupy Wall Street to Black Lives Matter. In politics, the company campaigned against Trump and for the left-wing Democrat Bernie Sanders. Even without Ben and Jerry, Ben & Jerry's appears to have evolved its own Why in a progressive, liberal corporate culture. With many activists serving on an independent advisory board, Ben & Jerry's support for social justice still carries greater credibility and conviction than comparable corporate social responsibility efforts by other brands, which often come across as opportunistic posturing.

Creativity theory makes a distinction between 'creation' and 'discovery'. Ben Cohen and Jerry Greenfield can be said to have discovered their identity and purpose as innovators and entrepreneurs. They found their Why through a process of trial and error – the classic 'ready, fire, aim' mantra of entrepreneurship theory. Their creativity was not something they set out to realize; it just seemed to happen as they worked.

This is perhaps the missing piece in the puzzle – for all their bonhomie and apparent disinterest in management, Ben and Jerry describe themselves as both having a very strong 'worker mentality'. The early days of working long hours just to make their loan payments informed their approach to business – which Jerry explains they perceived simply as 'busy-ness', or in a less controlled metaphor, like falling down a cliff and grabbing hold of whatever they could to survive.

There is an echo here of Picasso's famous quote about creative inspiration – none of us knows when the muses will come, but when they do, 'let them find me working'. In other words, passion, purpose and intrinsic motivation are not always the starting point – you might find your Why, when you least expect it, at the bottom of the tub, in a chunk of cookie dough.

When you start working on a creative project, do you know where you are going or do you just see where the journey takes you? Do you need to feel personally invested in a creative purpose for that purpose to be effective? What is your version of 'busy-ness' and has this resulted in unexpected creative outcomes? And if you walked away from your business or project tomorrow, would it continue its journey without you? How does the answer make you feel?

RESOURCES

Alvarez, S. and J. Barney (2007), 'Discovery and Creation: Alternative Theories of Entrepreneurial Action', *Strategic Entrepreneurship Journal* **1**(1), 11–26.

Ben & Jerry's, *How I Built This* podcast: https://podcasts.apple.com/gb/podcast/ben-jerrys-ben
-cohen-and-jerry-greenfield/id1150510297?i=1000395020996

Sarasvathy, S. (2007), 'What Makes Entrepreneurs Entrepreneurial': www.effectuation.org/sites/
default/files/research_papers/what-makes-entrepreneurs-entrepreneurial-sarasvathy_0.pdf

5.4   HOPPING ON: THE CREATIVE PRODUCT AS A LAUNCH PAD

Our second pathway is like the first, a case of 'letting go'. But this time the 'personal why' takes precedence. The personality and energy of the creative individual outgrow the 'productional why' and seek a fresh outlet. From the outside, it can look a lot like the 'exit ramp' – but in this case the journey continues with the individual creator, not with the business they left behind. This is the mentality of the serial entrepreneur or inventor, somebody who can jump from one opportunity to the next, relying on their own 'personal why' to drive them forwards.

This is not to say that 'letting go' is easy. Unlike the relaxed, easy-going personality of the 'exit ramp', the launch-pad personality has a strong inner sense of purpose. This internal drive can become entangled in the productional why of the enterprise or creation, making it difficult to detach oneself. Precisely because the enterprise or creation is so strongly dependent on its creator, it is likely that the original venture will collapse as soon as the founder leaves. So switching loyalties to launch a new product might be a painful process, albeit a necessary one.

Jack Conte, the co-founder of the crowdfunding platform Patreon, never intended to become a platform entrepreneur. He began his career as a musician, enjoying financial and artistic success as one half of the band Pomplamoose, together with his wife Natalie. He got the idea for setting up Patreon when he saw a friend successfully raise money from a crowdfunding appeal on the Kickstarter platform. At the time, Conte was struggling with the economics of music streaming, where thousands of plays result in a trickle of revenues, compared with the steady income he had enjoyed from downloads on iTunes. If he was to survive as a musician, he would need to find another source of income. Patreon was designed for artists like Pomplamoose, with a moderate level of success and a community of supportive fans, fans who would be happy to contribute a regular donation to support the artists they loved. Together with his business partner, Conte set out to build the platform, raise capital, attract artists and their fans.

As Patreon became more successful, it was no longer a side project. Conte realized that if he wanted Patreon to fulfil its potential, he was going to have to choose between this new venture and the band. In effect he had to adapt to a new 'productional why' which demanded more of his time and energy than he could spare as a budding musician. At this point, according to his interview with Guy Raz on the 'How I Built This' podcast, Conte became what he had always promised himself he would not – that guy who used to be an artist in their 20s and becomes a business entrepreneur in their 30s. Painful as it may have been to give up on his musical career (at the same time forcing his wife to move on from Pomplamoose), Conte had a clear enough sense of his own strengths and direction to make that difficult decision and commit to the new venture. It is also possible that, despite his early success, Conte was not wedded to the dream of musicianship. He enjoyed it, but it was an eclectic lifestyle – crafting music videos, playing with different genres, performing live, running a YouTube channel – perhaps this diversity reflected a certain restlessness.

The switch from one project to another is what characterizes the 'launch pad' pathway. This requires a strong sense of self and inner confidence. The personal why is strong enough to override the pull of the productional why and move forward to a new challenge. The productional why is also important because the external changes and opportunities of the production process offer new directions and pathways. Unlike the 'exit ramp' walking away from the old venture, the 'launch pad' leaps onto the next one. The productional why provides a framework for self-actualizing the 'personal why'.

Steve Jobs exemplifies some of the traits associated with 'launch pad' – a very confident sense of personal destiny which imposes itself on others in the business, and a dominant personality which moulds the business in its own image. At Apple, Jobs' attention to detail led to accusations of bullying and control-freakery – his personal why shaped the productional why of whichever business he was in. His personal charisma was at the core of Apple's innovative model. In 1985, Jobs was forced out of the company by former Pepsi CEO John Scully (whom Jobs had personally persuaded to join the company two years earlier). Jobs went on to launch NeXT Computers and then co-founded Pixar. While NeXT was not commercially successful, its technological innovations would eventually feed back into Apple. Pixar, meanwhile, transformed film animation much as Apple had transformed personal computing. Jobs' personal why continued undiminished, launching new products and businesses. Apple's productional why was meanwhile floundering. Apple's customers behave more like fans than rational con-sumers, and it became clear that part of that fandom was tied into the mythology Jobs had built around himself, the visionary entrepreneur and CEO, the polo-necked impresario presiding over product launches and keynotes.

The productional why of Apple was built from the personal why of Steve Jobs and the two turned out to be inseparable. While Steve Jobs proved he could survive without Apple, Apple could not thrive without Steve Jobs. Brought back to Apple in 1997, Jobs' 'second coming' confirmed that his personal identity and mission were written into the company's DNA. With the launch of the iPod, iTunes and the iPhone, Jobs continued to introduce new products even after being diagnosed with terminal cancer. It was only after his death that a new CEO, Tim Cook, could take the company forward. Through successive product launches and design innovations, the productional why of Apple was continually evolving and changing, yet the personal why of Jobs remained stubbornly immovable. Like his uniform of Issey Miyake polo-neck and Levi's 501s, the personal brand was constant and so was the inexorable pursuit of the next innovation – the product consumers didn't yet know they wanted. According to at least one of his several biographers, this driving will undoubtedly made Jobs difficult to work with. But his personal why was responsible for launching a steady stream of innovations, creating a legacy his successors will always struggle to live up to.

Launch pad describes a combination of strong personal motivation and a pursuit of novelty, alongside a dismissive attitude to 'business as usual'. This combination is especially evident in 'self-media', where young 'entrepreneurs of the self' use their personality as the online launch pad for a range of products and brands across social media. In order to sustain a successful career as an online micro-celebrity or influencer, it is necessary to maintain a consistent, 'authentic' self-image, even while playing multiple roles and launching different ventures. Unlike Steve Jobs, the new generation of YouTubers and TikTokers do not obsess over the products they either create or promote, nor do they need to be especially charismatic. The construction of a commercially viable 'ordinary' persona, adaptable to different purposes but recognizably consistent and relatable, becomes the primary goal. Our next recipe illustrates this paradoxical authenticity, in which a recognizable and accessible everyday personality becomes the launch pad for multiple brands and business ventures.

RECIPE 27. PAPI JIANG: HYPER-ORDINARY CREATIVITY (CHINA)

INGREDIENTS:

- 'A woman possessing beauty and talent'
- An appetite for the ordinary
- 44 million followers
- Everyday authenticity

China has seen a rising tide of online 'micro-celebrities' on popular platforms like Weibo, WeChat and Douyin (TikTok). The phenomenon of 'self-media' describes ordinary people projecting their everyday lives and experiences to their followers. The more successful among them are able to earn a living through product endorsements or sponsorships; if the brands are well chosen, they will further enhance the celebrity's reach and reputation.

This is not a uniquely Chinese phenomenon. Online KOLs (key opinion leaders) are common across the world, often providing advice on make-up and cosmetics, or (like PewDiePie) live-streaming videogames. But this content is especially popular in China, providing a more authentic, intimate form of communication than traditional broadcast media. Even though China's online media have become more heavily regulated, platforms like Bilibili, Youkou and Weibo still offer a more diverse, irreverent alternative to traditional programming.

Papi Jiang (real name Yilei Jiang, a mature student at the Central School of Drama in Beijing) emerged in 2016 as one of China's biggest online celebrities. She had previously dabbled in acting, directing and fashion blogging before launching her comic videos in September 2015. Within a year she had 28 million followers on Weibo alone, with 44 million followers across all platforms. By 2018, she had acquired around 120 million fans across all platforms. Some of her videos had racked up 100 million views.

Like many Chinese micro-celebrities, Papi was not tackling overtly political subjects. Her videos describe the everyday experiences of urban living, topics with which her audience of mostly urban educated young women could readily identify. She pokes fun at regional accents, pretentious use of English words to signal sophistication, public displays of affection, the obsession with appearance among her contemporaries, male inability to understand female conversation. What makes her videos stand out is their style. Papi uses her experience and training as an actress to play different characters, and uses jump cutting, speeded up footage and a digitally rendered, cartoonish high-pitched voice to provide an exaggerated, satirical commentary on everyday life for a young, educated woman in China.

In Part IV we noted the term 'everyday creativity' to refer to the democratizing of creativity to encompass ordinary users and everyday activities. During lockdown, broadcasters noticed a trend in 'comfort viewing' towards programmes which show somebody engaging in everyday tasks. For example, in the UK, a surprise hit was the BBC show *Repair Shop*, where skilled craftspeople repair loved objects, using traditional skills such as upholstery, carpentry and metalwork. The stories attached to these objects and their owners seem ordinary and familiar. The programme showed craftspeople working, handling everyday objects, using their hands. This ordinary, everyday quality carried a powerful emotional charge at a time when everyday life was so disrupted.

Self-media can be seen as an extension of this trend. From the perspective of the viewer, the ordinary, everyday aspect of creativity is part of the appeal. Papi Jiang makes much of her ordinariness and 'girl next door' persona. While the videos are artfully constructed, Papi herself does not project any special abilities or celebrity persona. Viewers like to spend time with her. They also like the fact that she is working hard. There are echoes here of Jerry Greenfield of Ben & Jerry's, and his definition of business as 'busy-ness'. Papi always seemed busy – like so many of her viewers, a young woman living an energetic, fast-paced life in the buzz of a big city.

Self-media places an emphasis on authenticity – intimacy, self-expression, honesty. In some respects, Papi's videos deliver on this promise – the videos are not highly produced (she used widely available apps to shoot and edit the material herself), they are filmed in her messy apartment, not in a studio, she appears with little or no make-up (many of her contemporaries project an idealized feminine appearance, often using cosmetics provided by their sponsors, a style Papi gleefully mocks in her videos). At the age of 29 in 2016, she was older than many of the fashion influencers who dominated Chinese social media at the time, and she sometimes referred to herself self-deprecatingly as a 'leftover woman'. When she signs off each video with the words 'I am Papi Jiang, a woman possessing beauty and talent', there is something defiant and mocking in her tone. Of course, there is beauty and talent here, but it is also ordinary and unforced.

Another key to Papi's success may be the impression she gives of not trying too hard. Unlike many influencers, Papi makes little effort to engage with her many fans in conversation during or after the video. While this is 'self-media', there is no confessional or personal revelation.

What was Papi Jiang's Why? She certainly made a great deal of money, but this does not appear to have been her primary motivation. On 22 April 2016, she auctioned an advertising slot to precede her next video, receiving the unprecedented sum of approximately $3.15 million from a Shanghai cosmetics firm. She promptly donated the money to her old drama college. In March 2016, she secured the equivalent of a $1.8 million investment. But her sarcastic, satirical style was not an obvious choice for celebrity endorsements, and one of the investors withdrew funding later that year. At around the same time, she was warned by the state regulator for using offensive language and had most of her content taken down. Undeterred, she continued to produce videos and, despite her spiky reputation, to attract advertising from brands including Jaeger-LeCoultre watches and Max Factor lipsticks. Her personal why as a storyteller took precedence before the productional why of the media brand.

The paradox of social media is that an ambition to succeed may precipitate failure. Fans are alert to any signs of inauthenticity or 'selling out' – Papi Jiang managed to attract sponsors and investors while remaining resolutely grounded in her everyday experience of urban living. As with Ben & Jerry's ice cream, what appeared to be an anti-commercial, subversive attitude became a valuable asset. The sponsors and fans who stayed with her recognized this quality of ordinariness. Papi's winning quality was to reflect a 'normal' existence, not to project star quality.

In 2016, Papi established PapiTube – a platform for others wanting to upload online videos. The popularity of self-media has led to increasing numbers of bloggers and online influencers. The platforms which host them are sometimes referred to as micro-celebrity networks (MCN). PapiTube stood out by providing support and advice to users on promotion and commercialization as well as access to Papi's network and reputation. By 2018, she had a staff of 70 and had transmuted from online celebrity to online entrepreneur. Yet, repeating the pattern of her earlier career, Papi did not attempt to grow the business (for example by branching out into live-streaming or by imposing her personal brand on other users on the platform). This was just another creative outlet, not a media empire.

At the same time as heading up PapiTube, Papi has reverted to her original vocation as an actress, appearing in roles which build upon her Papi Jiang persona (a failed screenwriter, a quirky internet star). In April 2021, she starred in *Tomorrow Will be Fine*, a romantic comedy which took $3.5 million in its opening weekend at the Chinese box office. Without appearing to commit to a career or compromising her own identity and values, Papi Jiang has been able to bridge between different roles and systems. Her seeming 'ordinariness' and work ethic endear her to fans and affiliated vloggers, as well as appealing to brands and investors. And she has been able to transition professionally without (apparently) changing or compromising personally.

Papi Jiang remains something of a dilettante. While not falling into the category of Florian Caps at the start of Part V ('From a business perspective, you're a failure, right?'), Papi Jiang was (according to most Chinese observers) only moderately and briefly successful. Ever the actress, she seems to have enjoyed trying out multiple roles. Similar to Caps, her personal why (her own self-fulfilment) took precedence over the productional why of the business. This allowed her to launch multiple careers and enterprises without compromising her own integrity and autonomy.

'Self-media' attracts those hungry for fame, jostling for that scarcest of commodities on the internet, attention. Here, perhaps Papi's apparent insouciance was her biggest advantage. She seems not to have cared who watched her, how much money she made, what people thought of her, what constituted her personal brand. She gave no press interviews. She was simply amusing herself. Like YouTube's biggest star, PewDiePie, she gives the appearance of performing for herself rather than for an audience. And as with PewDiePie, we have the impression of being secret observers of a young person who is simply having fun. Her fans saw somebody like themselves – an ordinary young woman from Shanghai, making her way in the world and expressing her opinions. And that's why they love her.

Is your personal fulfilment more important to you than the material success of a project? And might 'not caring' (or not appearing to care) about business success be the key to a successful creative business? Could you apply your personal creativity to a new or unfamiliar field? And could moving out of the comfort zone of your productional why help you to satisfy your personal creative why?

RESOURCES

Qin, A. (2016), 'China's Viral Idol: Papi Jiang, a Girl Next Door with Attitude', *New York Times*, 24 August: www.nytimes.com/2016/08/25/arts/international/chinas-viral-idol-papi-jiang-a-girl-next-door-with-attitude.html

World Economic Forum – An Insight, An Idea with Papi Jiang: www.youtube.com/watch?v=jI7dU-9EHRQ

5.5 SELLING OUT: CREATIVE NEW DIRECTIONS

Thus far we have considered incremental changes in the purpose and direction of a creative person or product. Exit ramp described the productional why taking the enterprise forward while the personal why drops away – the creator withdraws and the creation takes centre stage. There is a change of personnel but there is a continuity in product and production. From the outside it looks as if nothing has changed – but inside the enterprise, different people with different motivations have replaced the originator (or originators in the case of Ben & Jerry's).

Launch pad described the personal why taking the lead and abandoning one product in order to launch the next one. This is the path of the serial entrepreneur. It is also the path most travelled in the media and entertainment industries, where project-based enterprise is the dominant mode of production; a series of prototypes are launched, but the creator is already moving on to the next idea. Here, continuity comes from the personal brand or charisma of the creator. Even if the products are different and must stand as self-contained projects, there is continuity in the vision and personality of the founder of each of these enterprises.

We now move to a more radical transformation in the direction and purpose of a creative idea, where both the personal and the productional whys are open to change. The personal why is not fixed – the creator is not locked into a particular purpose or vision. The productional why is similarly open to new possibilities, not attempting to preserve or repeat a successful formula or model. This allows the creative process to evolve in unexpected ways – not without purpose, but with many purposes.

One of the most mythologized versions of this radical transformation might be an artist like David Bowie, who reinvented himself with the launch of each album and tour. But actually, there is a continuity across all of these iterations. Despite the many identities and roles he played, Bowie remained Bowie – he could recreate his old personae and still play his greatest hits. In the following recipe, the transformation is more extreme – both the person and the product seem to have been discarded and reinvented several times over in ways that seem unrecognizable.

The sell-out is often considered to be a dilettante or even a failure – somebody who is not sufficiently committed or serious to continue down one path. Their personal motivation appears weak, their ideas and products not substantial enough to sustain attention or impetus. Selling out implies a lack of integrity or authenticity. This is the antithesis of Sinek's 'find your why' – instead the sell-out is interested in finding a new What or a new How, continually experimenting with novel ideas and identities. The subject of our sell-out recipe does not enjoy the reputation of a Bowie or a Madonna or a Gaga – all considered to be serious artists with a clear sense of direction, in control of themselves and their work, despite their bold artistic changes. By contrast, MC Hammer is dismissed by most music journalists as a minor figure, somebody more concerned with short-term commercial success than the art form. Hammer's cultural identity is also problematic – like the protagonist in Paul Beatty's novel *The Sellout*, Hammer subverts our expectations of what black artists should look like and how they should behave. Yet Hammer was undeniably a very creative person, pioneering many innovations in his industry. He also seems to have managed the rollercoaster of success and fame better than many of his more 'credible' contemporaries, perhaps because he learned early in life to roll with the punches and ride his luck rather than committing to a singular vision.

RECIPE 28. STANLEY KIRK BURRELL: HAMMER TIME AFTER TIME (OAKLAND, CA)

INGREDIENTS:

- One youthfully eclectic entrepreneurial spirit
- One odd-ball mentor
- An acute understanding of the market
- A desire not to be pigeonholed
- A curiosity about new technology and trends

MC Hammer divided opinion at the height of his powers. In 1990, when his song 'Can't Touch This' and the album *Please Hammer, Don't Hurt 'Em* were released, he quickly became one of the world's most recognizable celebrities. Some toasted him for becoming 'the first mainstream rapper'. Others roasted him for being a 'gimmicky sell-out'.

But dismissing him as a musical sell-out is less easy to do if you take account of the backstory. Music was in many respects a vehicle for Hammer for taking his creative why and two first creative loves (dance and entrepreneurship) to the next level.

MC Hammer (real name Stanley Kirk Burrell) describes himself as being a dancer from the age of three, and an entrepreneur from the age of nine. These two creative impulses first came together at a shrine to his third love: sports – in his hometown of Oakland, CA.

Stanley's two older brothers worked for the Oakland Athletics (As) baseball club as bat boys gathering up the players' discarded bats, and they would bring their younger sibling with them at the weekends. The Burrell boys would mingle with the players before games, and the great Reggie Jackson gave Stanley the name Hammer because he thought he looked like Hank 'The Hammer' Aaron – one of baseball's biggest hitters.

The players were given allocations of tickets, which they often sought to sell to make some extra cash, and they began to give them to Stanley to peddle outside the stadium for a share of the profits. Because Stanley loved to dance, and because he had an entrepreneurial eye for a business opportunity, he worked his dancing into his sales shtick, drawing particularly on his dance heroes like James Brown.

Stanley's act/business was incredibly successful and, a few years later, he came to the attention of the As owner and one of professional sports' great entrepreneurial oddballs, Charles O Finley – known affectionately as Charlie-O.

Finley had owned the club since it was based in Kansas City, moving the team to Oakland in 1968. He is most famous for having talked Brian Epstein into getting The Beatles to add an unscheduled date during a US tour and playing Kansas during what was supposed to be a day off, and for being the only owner in professional sports to have developed a mascot based on himself: Charlie-O the Mule.

The quirky Finley spotted the talent and told Stanley that he'd rather have him working inside the tent with him than outside the stadium, and offered him a back-office position. According to Burrell, as a teenager he became the world's youngest sports executive. His 'job' was to mix with the team and be Finley's eyes, and keep the owner informed of any interesting developments. Gradually, Hammer became a more integral part of the club's operations and would often speak to the team, particularly when they travelled, which is how the MC (Master of Ceremonies) came to be added to his name by the players.

After a stint in the army, another integral piece of Hammer's development, Burrell returned to Oakland and started to involve himself in the fledgling hip-hop scene. As the documentary series *Hip-Hop Evolution* explains, the Oakland culture was a different breeding ground than the rest of the US. Oakland was a dance town. Even the Black Panthers, founded in Oakland, had a street dance troupe that was deployed to attract kids to community events. So, as Hammer began to embrace and develop his music, dance was not a gimmick added on, it was integral to the act, and his act – as he saw it – was to entertain as many people as possible.

Burrell was not young (in hip-hop terms) when this happened. He did not start to rap until his early 20s, and when his act started to gel he was mature enough to see the dangers and the possibilities, so he was relatively well placed to deal with the fame when it hit.

And when it did, it scaled up fast. 'Can't Touch This' was not only Best Rap Solo Performance at the Grammys in 1991, it won Best R&B Song and was the first hip-hop song to be nominated for Record of the Year. It and the album went to number 1 in multiple countries and became probably the most ubiquitous song of the early 1990s.

Rather than being overwhelmed by this success or rest on his laurels, Hammer just raised the bar. He wasn't limited by the boundaries of hip-hop. He claimed that his idols were entertainers like James Brown and The Jacksons. And while he was comfortable hanging out with Tupac, Snoop and other rappers, he saw himself as competing with the likes of Prince, Madonna, Cindy Lauper and Michael Jackson. And that led him into further entrepreneurial avenues.

He sought sponsorship from big companies, not just from shoe makers, but from brands like Pepsi, figuring that if the sports stars he used to work with were profiting in this way, why shouldn't musicians too? Having won Best Rap Video and Best Dance Video against his rivals at the newly established MTV Music Awards, he wanted to be the best multimedia musician. A cartoon for kids called Hammerman had been developed, and he could see that video was the future, but also that the technology needed to evolve to enable the data necessary to be streamed effectively. So he entered partnerships in the tech world of Silicon Valley to see if he could be the first to solve the problem and exploit the resulting opportunities.

Hammer's pathway since has been rocky, a lot of successes but also many failures. But it has always been varied and interesting and he has emerged as a senior sage in music, in business and in culture, particularly as a supporter of young musicians and entrepreneurs in his hometown of Oakland. He is now at once a preacher, a business/music mentor, town-booster, and Twitter sensation and influencer, where his statements about philosophy and science are followed widely.

Hammer's Why? As the son of a professional card player, he claims he's always understood and been about the hustle. But he says that he could see the dangers of being sucked in to believing that the hustle is the point. The hustle should only be a means to other ends: to entertain, to share the wealth, help one's community, to share the knowledge or the consciousness. And so for MC Hammer, the point of perfecting a particular hustle or game is to use that as a platform for launching into the next thing and sharing the results.

Hammer helped make hip-hop mainstream and connected it to other elements of culture and business that it was once cut off from. In so doing, his creative journey trod a path to be followed by the kind of artists who may have once sneered at his pop sensibilities. 50 Cent, Queen Latifah, LL Cool J, Jay-Z and Ice-T, among others, have been able to continue to expand their creative personas, rather than being trapped by them, by following Stanley Burrell's creative model.

Is your creativity bound by rules and expectations of what is 'authentic' and what is 'mainstream'? What would happen if you tried to cross those boundaries? Do you have a mentor figure like Charlie-O encouraging you to 'work inside the tent' instead of on the outside? Would selling out to commercial partnerships and opportunities break your creative spirit? Or could it ignite opportunities and set it free?

RESOURCES

Hip-Hop Evolution, HBO Canada/Netflix 2016–2020.

Interview with MC Hammer, Revolt TV, 9 September 2017: www.youtube.com/watch?v=iEGAq 4igCzE

'MC Hammer's Philosophical Tweet Goes Viral and Sparks Memes', *The Independent*, 23 February 2021.

5.6 NO EXIT: CREATIVITY TRAPPED

Previous recipes in Part V have shown how motivations, both intrinsic and extrinsic, can change over time. The personal why and the productional why evolve and lead the individual and their products down a new path. But what happens if both the personal why and the productional why remain constant? The personal why is strong, and so is the productional why.

On the surface this looks like an ideal situation. The creative individual is committed to a product which resonates with their personal motivation. The individual is fulfilled, the product is consistent.

But this kind of alignment is usually short-lived. The other pathways we have described all started here, but over time they evolved. The perfect alignment of the personal why and the productional why starts to pull apart. These changes might be painful (like the break-up of The Beatles), but the alternative is standing still, which carries its own risks. When personal why and productional why are locked together, where does change come from?

There are two possibilities here. On one hand, the productional why and the personal why continue to be mutually reinforcing and mutually fulfilling. Rather than changing, the enterprise can expand or extend within these parameters. The core purpose of the enterprise and of the entrepreneur remain the same, just operating at a different scale. We call this 'scaling up'.

The other possibility is that the personal why and productional why remain constant, but they fall out of alignment. The personal motivation remains strong, but without some external change in the productional model the creative individual becomes trapped in a repetitive cycle, attempting to relive a golden moment of fulfilment and achievement which cannot be repeated.

This is a common problem in media and entertainment industries. The star personality becomes a trap, the person behind the personality is locked into repeating the same roles, aligning with a productional why over which they have little control. This can lead to self-destruction as the creative energies turn inwards, unable to move forward. The personal price of success plays out as tragedy – a story charted in the experience of Amy Winehouse, a talented singer and songwriter from north London who found it impossible to escape from her celebrity persona as Amy. Her decline into alcoholism, drug abuse and early death followed a similar pattern to that of Billie Holiday, one of Amy's influences and idols. The difference was that Holiday's death at 44 was not quite as early as that of Winehouse, aged just 27.

Amy's story is the subject of an award-winning documentary by the film-maker Asif Kapadia. Kapadia would make a later documentary about another doomed genius, Diego Maradona. Like Amy, Maradona's personal why was beguilingly simple; she was a girl who wanted to sing, he was a boy who wanted to play football. And while it seemed that the personal dream and the professional career were perfectly aligned, it proved impossible for Amy or Diego to grow and evolve in the ways possible for the other subjects in this part of *Creativities*. The productional why of professional success enforced repetition rather than growth, squeezing out the personal why. No longer in control of their own careers, Diego and Amy were expected to perform the same part, in a role that no longer fulfilled them. For those watching, the performance remains beguiling – but for the performer, the journey becomes increasingly meaningless. And perhaps the memory of a strong intrinsic motivation, a personal why, makes the disappointment, alienation and frustration even harder to bear – a reminder of what could have been, now thwarted by processes the individual can no longer control: no exit.

RECIPE 29. DIEGO MARADONA: CREATIVITY CORNERED (BUENOS AIRES AND NAPLES)

INGREDIENTS:

- One irresistible talent on the rise
- An underdog club
- An 'us against the world' mentality
- A dark web of selfish interests

Like The Beatles, Diego Maradona's journey is a rags-to-riches story of creativity, but Maradona came up from lower – quite literally the ghetto – and he, unlike each of The Beatles, lost his way and fell hard. Film of him in his prime compared with the state he was in by the 2000s is difficult to watch.

Diego was born and grew up in Villa Fiorito, a shantytown on the outskirts of Buenos Aires. When his talent was spotted by Argentinos Juniors in 1975, their contract provided him with an apartment that became his family's first proper home. Maradona's Why when he started out was similar to many who grow up in poor circumstances: he wanted to buy a house for his parents.

Maradona became a staple of the club's youth team *Los Cebollitas* (The Little Onions), and the charismatic and hugely talented junior was already nicknamed 'The Golden Boy' when he was transferred to Boca Juniors (one of Latin America's biggest clubs) in 1980. In 1982, his transfer from Boca to Barcelona was for a then world record fee of £5 million ($7.6 million).

Diego never settled in Barcelona. He didn't feel wanted, believed the Spanish looked down on people like him from Latin America, was scrappy with and hassled by the Spanish media, got into fights on the field, was suspended, then got injured and then struggled to get back into the top team. Talk that Barca would look to sell Maradona on and recoup their losses began after his first season, but none of the top-flight international clubs were interested.

Then a surprise buyer emerged – one of Europe's poorest top division football clubs: Napoli in southern Italy. The move caused many to speculate that both the world's best footballer and one of the world's most indebted football teams had lost their marbles. But, over the next five years, Maradona would lead the club on an unprecedented and unrepeatable run, taking the perennial cellar-dwellers to their only La Liga titles in the 1986–87 and 1989–90 seasons and making them the best team in Italy and one of the best in Europe.

A mainland southern Italian team had never enjoyed such success before, and as Maradona rallied his new home to believe that they could take on and be better than their richer northern countrymen, the football champion became a cultural, social and quasi-religious icon for the region too. Just how much the team's success and Maradona's leadership meant to the people of Napoli can be best grasped by understanding how the rest of Italy goaded them: fans of wealthy clubs like Juventus and Inter Milan would humiliate them by chanting of Napoli as the scum/filth/sewer of Italy and sing that the team's 'cholera infested' supporters were unclean, calling upon 'Vesuvius to wash them with fire'.

In hindsight, perhaps Napoli's move to acquire Diego, and the success that subsequently ensued for the club and for Maradona, was not so irrational. Film-maker Asif Kapadia, whose previous films included *Amy* and *Senna*, completed a documentary on the footballer in 2019. He reflected that 'Diego didn't fit in at Barcelona [and he wouldn't have fitted in at other] old-school, respected clubs... their players had to act and train a certain way. He would never have felt comfortable there, but he felt comfortable in Naples because it was built like him.'

Like the retreat to the studio after the chaos of touring for The Beatles, Diego's retreat from Barcelona seemed to offer an opportunity for rejuvenation and a relaunch. When asked in 1984 what he wanted from the people of Napoli, Diego said he wanted 'respect for his football and peace'.

The respect came, particularly as the team improved beyond anyone's wildest imagination. But Maradona worked hard to earn it. He found the initial transition to the Italian game tough. The football was harder and faster than what he was accustomed to in Argentina or Spain, and the defenders were bigger and rougher and they targeted him. So he took his creative 'ingredients' and sought to blend them in a different way.

Maradona formed a tight-knit team within the Napoli organization of himself and the one thing he had wanted to bring with him from his days at Barca: personal trainer Fernando Signorini. After team training, Diego and Signorini would work separately. Signorini did not want to lose what made Maradona great: his explosive speed, his footwork, his ball control; but he sought to improve his fitness (so that he could outrun opponents for longer) and his strength (so that his small frame could hold its own and he could stay on his feet when jostled). In this way, Signorini and the environment in Napoli, where Maradona was free to train independently, took his creativity to another level.

However, the peace that Diego sought was harder to manage. The energy in Naples was exuberant and chaotic, something captured well in Kapadia's film. 65,000 fans crammed Napoli's stadium just to witness Maradona's arrival from Spain. The ensuing press conference descended into farce as the first question implied that The Camorra (mafia) may have played a role in bringing Maradona to the club. President Corrado Ferlaino called the journalist a disgrace and sought to have him expelled amid much pushing, shoving and name-calling.

But initially, Maradona responded to a culture that energized him. He became inspired by a sense he and his team were fighting against the richer, more privileged teams and cities who looked down on him and 'his people'.

Perhaps this context helps us comprehend Maradona's response to his most infamous act. Argentina defeated England 2–1 in a World Cup quarterfinal in 1986. Maradona scored both of Argentina's goals. One was probably the most sublime ever scored (where Maradona took the ball 70 yards out from goal and ran through what seemed to be the entire English side), the other the most ridiculous (where the 5-foot, 5-inch Maradona rose above the 6-foot England goalkeeper to tap the ball in with his fist). The referee awarded the goal and Maradona said nothing. But, as with Napoli, part of Maradona's creative mix was a sense of fighting against injustice. He, like many Argentinians, felt embarrassed as the Argentinian army was easily dismissed as British forces re-took the Falkland Islands a few years previous. In his mind, the goal from his fist was scored by the 'hand of God'. God's will was acting through him. So be it.

However, after Diego returned from the World Cup and Napoli won their first championship, the city that rejuvenated him developed into a trap. As Napoli became more and more successful, more and more Neapolitans wanted a piece of Diego. They crowded the fences around his house to get signatures and photos, cheered and sang his name whenever they saw him around town, and sought to kiss and hug a man who was fearful of being touched. Diego felt increasingly claustrophobic, but there was nothing anybody in Naples could do about that. Except The Camorra.

Members of the criminal Giuliano family offered to protect Maradona and his family. Over time the Giulianos and Diego became closer and they were able to provide him with whatever he wanted. Under the family's protection, Maradona was able to go out and be left alone. He stayed out later and later and lived an increasingly unhealthy lifestyle. For a time, his natural talents and willpower enabled him to party from Sunday night to Thursday and then train hard to be ready for the next Sunday match.

By 1989, however, things were catching up with him. His increased body weight was more obvious, his fitness was poor as he was visibly puffed on the pitch, and he was addicted to cocaine. But remarkably, he was able to lead Napoli to a second championship.

Unfortunately, the controversy that followed the championship, in the 1990 World Cup in Italy, hastened Maradona's demise. A combination of bad luck and bad management led to Italy playing Argentina in a semi-final in Naples. Diego, thinking that because he was for Napoli then they would be for him, urged fans to support Argentina. Encouraging Italians to go against their own country worked out badly, particularly after Maradona ran around the stadium celebrating Argentina's victory on penalties.

And so Maradona got stuck. He begged to be released from his contract and traded to another club, but Ferlaino wouldn't budge. Maradona was the goose laying the golden eggs that made Ferlaino the most successful club president in Napoli's history. Unable to leave, Maradona sought solace in drugs supplied by The Camorra and became beholden to them for the drugs to feed his addiction. The fans began to hate him because they believed that he sought to turn them against their national team and because he had the temerity to beat their team in 1991. Maradona went from being feted to haunted and hunted. That Napoli wasn't winning so often didn't help matters either. All the while, Maradona's football prowess declined and his value plummeted.

The final straw was being set up in a drug sting by the Italian authorities and banned from the game for six months. By the time he emerged again, he was broken. Not unlike the tale of one of his heroes, George Best (whose alcoholism blocked the development of creative exit ramps), for the equally mercurial Maradona his passion and addictions eventually made him vulnerable to forces that he could not control and they destroyed his creative potential.

Diego Maradona's story is a lesson in how even the brightest creative force can self-destruct unless there is a development pathway, or a way to exit the arena with dignity. Despite all their conflicts, each of The Beatles – the greatest popular musicians of the 20th century – were able to do that; probably the greatest footballer of the 20th century was not.

What are the traps which could lock down your creativity and how might you avoid them? Thinking about these, can you plan an escape route through one of the other pathways described in this part of the book (an exit ramp, a launch pad, a sell-out)? Who are the coaches helping you grow your creativity, and who are the gangsters dragging you back down – and how do you spot the difference?

RESOURCES

Diego Maradona, film by Asif Kapadia (2019).
Five Things You Never Knew About Diego Maradona: www.shortlist.com/lists/5-things-you-never
-knew-about-diego-maradona-400298

5.7   SCALING UP: DOUBLING DOWN AND GOING FOR GROWTH

It doesn't have to be any of the ways we've outlined. You don't have to step away from your creative enterprise, hop on to something else, sell out or feel trapped by your creative output. Instead, your creative Why might lead you to double down and ride the product of your creativity as far as you can. Despite the Whys we've already covered, it's possible for the founders or originators to remain closely involved and strongly motivated. It's possible to reiterate the same essential business idea and take the scale to another level. The key difference is that this time, as opposed to the earlier Why combinations in the creative pathway matrix, the productional why and the personal why remain tightly aligned (as they were for The Beatles, until around 1967). And actually, taking this path does not preclude stepping on to one of the other pathways should the personal and productional diverge at a later stage.

In fact, the 'double down and scale up' is the move most commonly associated with an entrepreneurial spirit at this stage in the creative process. Hence, there are literally hundreds of books written on how to scale a business and be a successful entrepreneur. And rather than seek to reinvent the wheel in this regard, we thought we'd cut to the chase and provide you with four useful and well-regarded lists of scale-up steps in Figure 5.2.

As you'll see, there are many commonalities, from the importance of being focused and clear about your commitment and goals at the start, to planning and preparing for growth, learning from others and building your team and networks, and having clear processes for proceeding while being prepared to innovate and adapt these as you travel. The real choice is whether you prefer a shorter list or a longer one. Or you may want to create your own through blending the ideas to suit you, so long as you have a plan, determine your endgame, and are flexible with regard to how you get there as things unfold. As for recipes, you'll find many in any entrepreneurship or business magazine, or just by searching 'successful start-ups'.

If doubling down on your creativity and scaling up is the only thing that's going to scratch the itch of your Why, then armed with a clear approach, some inspiration from others who have travelled that road before, and the support that almost every regional government will provide entrepreneurs (as was the case with Ben & Jerry's, just search 'entrepreneur help advice'), you need to go for it.

The final recipe that we focus on is a little different, though. It could have been a scale-up, but that didn't really fit the Whys of the two protagonists, so thinking through what they really wanted to get from their and their community's creative endeavours led them in a different, hybrid direction: part local scale-up and launch pad on to other creative projects locally; part sell-off – or at least lease-out – and exit internationally. As such, it is a good place to end Part V. And, as it allows us to express their thinking on the creativity canvas, it's a good place to end the book and hand it on to you to reflect on your creative endeavours. We've included a few empty canvases for you to use to record your creative Whys, Whats, Hows, Wheres and Whos.

Tim Ferris in Entrepreneur.com 3 steps	Forbes 6 steps	StartUpDonut.uk 10 steps	Tony Robbins 11 steps
1. Get clear on your endgame.	1. Commit to grow.	1. Focus on what you want to be – not what you are.	1. Know your purpose.
2. Learn from others about how to grow, e.g., by bootstrapping, hiring advisors, or building relationships.	2. Build broad management skillset.	2. Make sure you're ready and prepared for growth.	2. Develop a business map.
3. Get creative with financing to raise cash.	3. Build collaborations.	3. Learn from competitors who've successfully grown.	3. Perfect your product or service.
	4. Establish standardized processes.	4. Protect your business values.	4. Create thoughtful processes and operations.
	5. Identify core competence.	5. Build a great team of employees.	5. Establish your team.
	6. Articulate competitive strengths.	6. Have rules for your staff to follow.	6. Learn when to delegate.
		7. Access outside expertise when required.	7. Build your brand.
		8. Never compromise on quality or consistency.	8. Connect with your customer.
		9. Identify your barriers to growth.	9. Work on your networking skills.
		10. Try to predict the future.	10. Prioritize sustainability.
			11. Continue adapting and innovating.

Figure 5.2   Three, six, ten and eleven steps to scale up

RECIPE 30. A CREATIVE GOOD: THE OPERATIONAL HIJAB (NEW ZEALAND/ THE WORLD)

INGREDIENTS:

- A community need
- A barrier for Muslim women
- Substantial desire to make a difference through creativity × 2
- Embracing the concept of user- and co-design
- An understanding of sportswear fabrics blended with pattern-making skills in functional performance apparel

In 2019, a new community design project brief put forward by the New Zealand Police crossed the desks of Deb Cumming and Nina Weaver. They were intrigued. In an effort to seek recruits that better represented the country's ethnic and cultural diversity, a barrier had been identified that was making it difficult for many Muslim women to join the police. Officers could not wear a hijab as part of their uniform: the uniform was standard issue, and that standard issue catalogue did not include a hijab. The wearing and visual identification of the hijab was considered important to reflect inclusivity and community diversity while providing a safe operational piece of uniform. This issue was brought into sharper focus after the Mosque attacks on the Muslim community in Christchurch, New Zealand on 15 March 2019.

The police had sought to find a solution by contacting other forces around the world, only to find that they also did not have an operational hijab that fitted all their safety requirements as part of their uniform. So, they brought the problem to Massey University's School of Fashion and Design, New Zealand's leading fashion school, and Deb, who was developing an interdisciplinary course in Accessible and Inclusive Fashion Design, saw 'the operational hijab' as a perfect case study to highlight user-led accessible design to her students. Accessible design was part of an initiative to broaden views of fashion, to see how design skills could be applied to create innovative clothing for people that the fashion market generally overlooked or undervalued.

The operational hijab was the kind of creative challenge that excited Deb. Her academic specialization was cutting and draping one-piece one-dimensional patterns that could be sewn into complex three-dimensional products. Using creative approaches to fashion to break down barriers, achieve social goods, and make a positive difference in the world was something that inspired her and, she believed, could explain the concept of accessible design and inspire her students in the new course.

Deb started to explore the idea with Nina, and they both became more engaged in thinking about what might be possible. Nina's expertise in contoured knit apparel and previous background working for a world-leading swimwear company was also uniquely well suited to the problem, and her experience complemented Deb's perfectly. Their combination of skills met and went beyond what the police had initially thought might be useful to meet the brief.

But the NZ Police brief added further complexity to what, on the surface, may have seemed a simple garment. It would require 'twisting' the traditional look and cultural significance of the hijab to meet the police's operational and technical requirements.

The prototype design by Deb and Nina, with help from NZ Police and members of the broader Muslim community, combined modern technology and material with the operational needs of the police uniform alongside the cultural needs of the Muslim community. It was robust and stable, yet contoured to enable maximum head movement, optimal vision and minimal grab, and shaped to allow tucking into a shirt collar without interference with body armour and outer garments. It was made from a hi-tech material enabling long-wear comfort, robust stability, moisture wicking and temperature control. It was easy-care and it could be worn under regulation cap and other operational headwear. It integrated seamlessly into the existing uniform with facility for operational communication devices, and the design incorporated quick-release fastening for greater safety. Plus, and importantly, despite all this, it looked like a hijab.

As Deb recalled, 'The Police were great to collaborate with: they had clear expectations and user requirements, thorough ethical processes, wear and safety testing, and were serious about developing something that would make a positive change.' Also a key part of the community mix designing the operational hijab was Constable Zeena Ali, who was to become New Zealand's first hijab-wearing policewoman. Constable Ali would also become a key advocate in the community promoting the project. 'It felt great to be able to go out and show the New Zealand Police uniform hijab,' she explained, 'because I was able to take part in the design process.'

Source: Photo by Jillian Reid, New Zealand Police. Reproduced with permission from NZ Police Media

Figure 5.3   Constable Zeena Ali (centre) wearing the Operational Hijab with her graduating class

The finished prototype (and now product) has been well received and has proven extremely popular. It is being manufactured for New Zealand and international organizations. Local New Zealand orders are sewn by a small local Wellington firm run by an alumnus of the Massey fashion programme. And the New Zealand Police and the Massey University team are also sending the solution abroad, with the UK Police force having sought out the design and many other interested agencies around the world making inquiries as to how they can incorporate the hijab into their uniforms.

The model adopted for enabling the spread of the operational hijab is to lease the design to users, who can then arrange for the product to be manufactured locally. Explaining why they were happy to lease out the intellectual property (IP) rather than expand their own manufacturing from New Zealand, Deb says they never set out to grow a business. 'I know it sounds corny, but we were in it to make a difference. And this way the idea can spread to create the maximum good. And we can continue to focus on what's really important to us.'

With regard to that, the earnings from leasing the design now feed back in to fund further accessible and inclusive design projects for students and faculty at Massey. And as that good floats back in, the impact of the operational hijab continues to ripple out. Nina explains that 'the operational hijab is not just a solution for the police. Because it's a great product it can be applied in other areas, breaking down barriers in a whole range of occupations for Muslim women and opening up new career pathways.'

'A further circular thing the police hijab project has done', Deb explained, 'is that it proved the Why that drove us to create the Accessible and Inclusive Design course in the first place. It was a proof of concept in the best possible way. Now when we teach the course, we start with this as a real example of what's possible, to explain that creativity in fashion can be aimed toward social as well as economic and environmental goods.'

Indeed, one of the most important things that New Zealand Prime Minister Jacinda Ardern did when visiting and mourning with those affected after the Christchurch Mosque attacks, and a clear signal that the rest of the community stood in solidarity with those targeted, was to wear a hijab.

Has a brief to create something new helped to invigorate or vindicate your creative purpose? Could pursuing a wider 'creative good' (making a difference) inspire your personal creative Why? Could leasing or giving away IP allow creativities to spread out from your initial idea (like the 'expanding circles' in Part IV), sparking a new set of creative enterprises beyond your own?

This recipe was written by Deb Cumming, Nina Weaver, Chris Bilton and Stephen Cummings.

RESOURCES

'Massey Helps Design NZ Police Uniform Hijab' (Massey University College of Creative Arts): https://creative.massey.ac.nz/stories/research/massey-helps-design-nz-police-uniform-hijab/
'UK Trialling NZ Police Hijab Design', *New Zealand Herald*, 28 January 2021: www.nzherald.co .nz/nz/uk-trialling-nz-police-hijab-design/OKPJY6YLP4STXIRK4SPXPDRH7E/

5.8 WHY NEXT?

As with many of the other questions relating to creativities in this book, there is no single Why to creativity. In Part V we have outlined different pathways to a creative purpose. It's up to you which recipe you will choose to follow (or whether to combine insights from them or make up your own).

For most of us, purpose and direction are not set in stone. What we wanted to do, how we wanted to go about it, where we positioned ourselves, who we wanted to become and why we wanted to achieve it, will inevitably draw out different answers as we grow older and as the world turns. Rather than seeking out a singular why, it may make more sense for some creatives to understand how their motivations and goals change over time – to look forward to the next Why rather than persist with their original goal.

Strong intrinsic motivation is often assumed to be the key to unlock creativity – but as illustrated by some of the earlier recipes, single-minded pursuit of a goal can be destructive of the individual (Diego Maradona) or of those around them (Steve Jobs). If we are not able to rethink our purpose and change direction, we risk trapping ourselves in a shrinking circle of possibilities. Finding a new Why allows us to find new answers to the other creative questions as well.

Like the business model canvas, the creativities canvas invites you to answer some funda-mental questions about your own creative practice – whether as an artist, an entrepreneur, a leader, or as an everyday creative person. The answer to one question will inflect the others – the What, the How, the Where, the Who, the Why. Changing the Why, as Simon Sinek intimated, will change all the other questions as well – and will be changed by them in turn. By understanding our own creativities (and how they are changing, changing the products of our creativity, and changing us), we are more likely to align them – to produce a recipe for our own creativity, rather than a 'dog's breakfast' (no offence to any dogs) of incompatible ingredients.

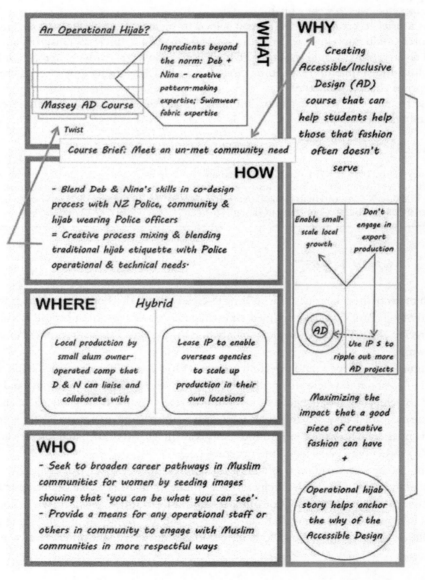

Figure 5.4   Creativities canvas example 5: the police hijab and the Why, What, How, Where and Who of Creativity

We have concluded previous parts of *Creativities* by addressing one of four questions – the What, the How, the Where and the Who of the creative process – and shown one set of possible answers to these questions on the creativities canvas. The Why of creativity is the bridge or link-road that connects these parts together and provides a way to check that you are on track and in sync with why you are seeking to create. In Figure 5.4, we have taken the final recipe in the book, the operational hijab, and filled in all five boxes of the canvas in consultation with the people engaged in that creative project, to illustrate how you can think through a creative process in terms of the What, How, Where, Who and Why of creativity.

The final pages of this book are blank creativities canvases. We invite you and the people you create with to fill them with questions and answers relating to your own creative ventures. And we encourage you to repeat the process periodically, as often as you need to – to change your recipes and change direction, to respond to changes and to make change happen. Like those old family recipe books passed down the generations, the best recipe is the one that you, having been inspired, have scribbled out yourself at the back of the book.

SOURCES AND FURTHER READING FOR PART V

In the final part of the book we consider creative purpose and motivation. Motivation is placed at the core of entrepreneurship, where Simon Sinek's advice to start with the Why (before proceeding to the What and the How) is the starting point for this chapter. In creativity theory, 'intrinsic motivation' is recognized as the necessary basis for creative thinking – in this field Teresa Amabile's influential work has drawn on both experimental research and organizational settings. While the primacy of intrinsic motivation remains a dominant assumption in creativity research, many (including Amabile herself) have questioned this, noting that variations in motivation might be necessary according to different stages in the creative process, different people or different settings (Dew 2009). A further complication is that extrinsic motivations are themselves sometimes internalized, making it harder to distinguish between internal drive and external rewards and endorsements (Kasof et al. 2007, Gagné and Deci 2005). This latter point leads to our discussion of 'the productional why' in which inner purpose is inflected by external events and opportunities.

A selection of the literature on motivation and creativity follows below. We have also included references to some theories of entrepreneurial action (Sarasvathy 2001, Alvarez and Barney 2007), and the influential idea of 'good work' in the creative industries as an idealized form of self-fulfilled, autonomous labour (Oakley 2014). This ideal connects to the idea of being in the zone or 'flow', pioneered by Csikszentmihalyi (1997) – something which we have criticized as an oversimplification of the lived experience of many artists (Bilton et al. 2021) and criticize again in this part of the book.

Alvarez, S. and J. Barney (2007), 'Discovery and Creation: Alternative Theories of Entrepreneurial Action', *Strategic Entrepreneurship Journal* **1**(1), 11–26.

Amabile, T.M. (1997), 'Motivating Creativity in Organisations: On Doing What You Love and Loving What You Do', *California Management Review* **40**(1), Fall, 39–58.

Amabile, T.M. (1998), 'How to Kill Creativity', *Harvard Business Review*, **76**(5), **77**(12). Also available in *Harvard Business Review on Breakthrough Thinking*.

Bilton, C., D.R. Eikhof and C. Gilmore (2021), 'Balancing Act: Motivation and Creative Work in the Lived Experience of Writers and Musicians', *International Journal of Cultural Policy* **27**(6), 738–752.

Csikszentmihalyi, M. (1997), *Creativity: Flow and the Psychology of Discovery and Invention*, New York: Harper Perennial.

Dew, R. (2009), 'Creative Resolve Response: How Changes in Creative Motivation Relate to Cognitive Style', *Journal of Management Development* **28**(10), 945–966.

Fabian, F. and d. ogilvie (2005), 'Strategy as Art: Using a Creative Action-Based Model for Strategy Formulation' in S. W. Floyd, J. Roos, C. D. Jacobs, and F. W. Kellermanns (eds), *Innovating Strategy Processes*, Malden, MA: Blackwell Publishing, 57–71.

Gabora, L. and N. Holmes (2010), 'Dangling from a Tassel on the Fabric of Socially Constructed Reality: Reflections on the Creative Writing Process' in D. Cropley, A. Cropley, J. Kaufman and M. Runco (eds), *The Dark Side of Creativity*, Cambridge: Cambridge University Press, 277–296.

Gagné, M. and E. Deci (2005), 'Self-determination Theory and Work Motivation', *Journal of Organizational Behavior* **26**(4), 331–362.

Kasof, J., C. Chen, A. Himsel and E. Greenberger (2007), 'Values and Creativity', *Creativity Research Journal* **19**(2–3), 105–122.

Oakley, K. (2014), 'Good Work? Rethinking Cultural Entrepreneurship' in C. Bilton and S. Cummings (eds), *Handbook of Management and Creativity*, Cheltenham: Edward Elgar Publishing, 145–159.

Sarasvathy, S. (2001), 'Causation and Effectuation: Towards a Theoretical Shift from Economic Inevitability to Entrepreneurial Contingency', *Academy of Management Review* **26**(2), 243–263.

Sinek, S. (2011), *Start with Why: How Great Leaders Inspire Everyone to Take Action*, London: Portfolio Penguin.

Yoon, H.J., S.Y. Sung, J.N. Choi, K. Lee and S. Kim (2015), 'Tangible and Intangible Rewards and Employee Creativity: The Mediating Role of Situational Extrinsic Motivation', *Creativity Research Journal* **27**(4), 383–393.

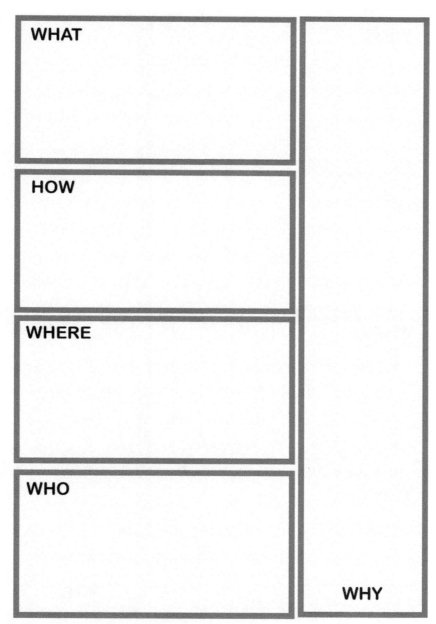

Figure 5.5   Your blank (creativities) canvas

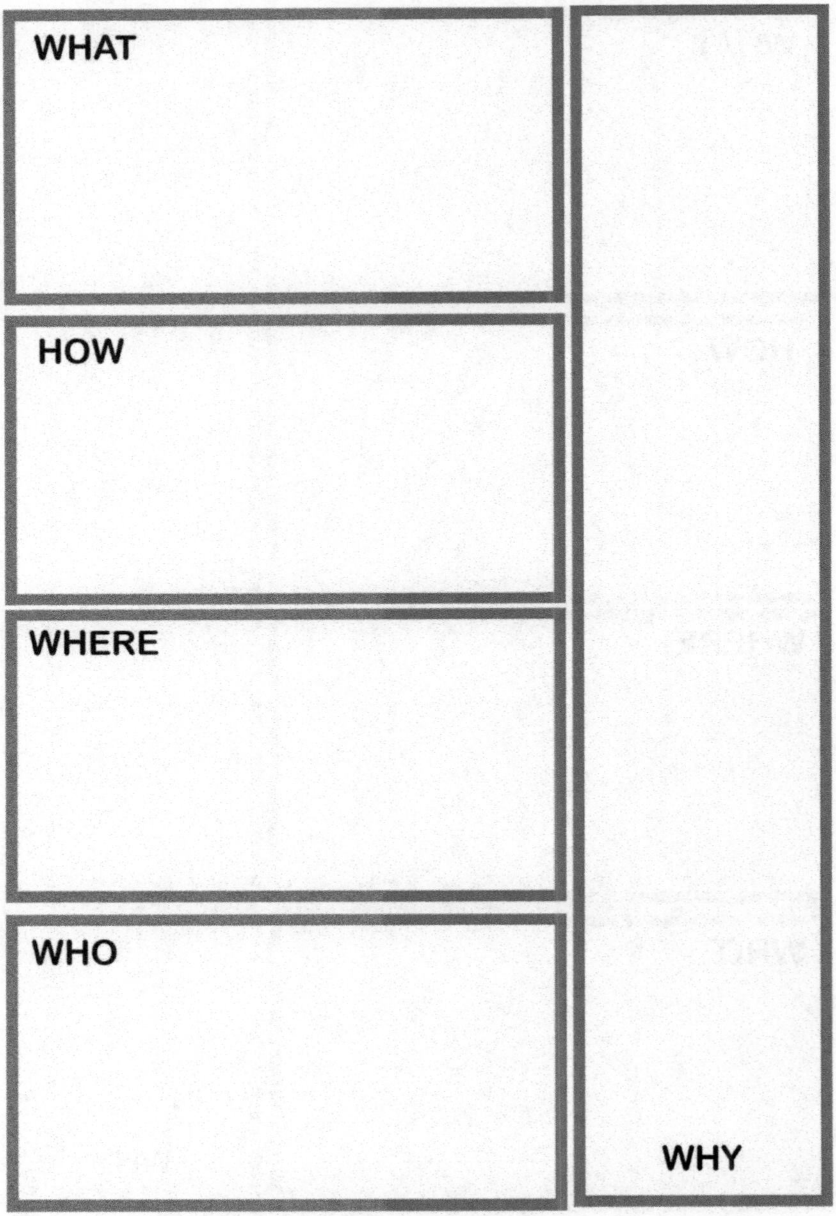

WHAT

HOW

WHERE

WHO

WHY

Figure 5.5   Your blank (creativities) canvas

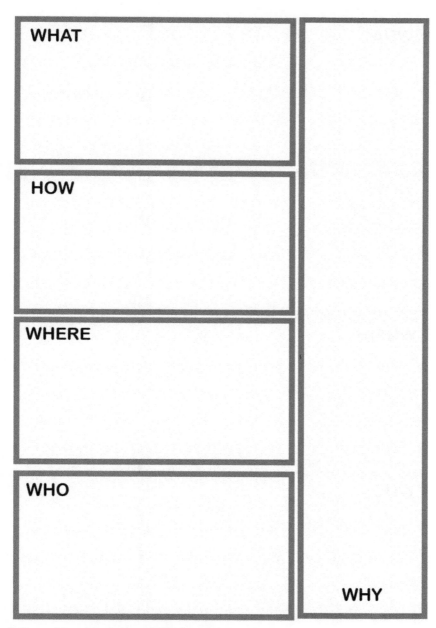

Figure 5.5   Your blank (creativities) canvas

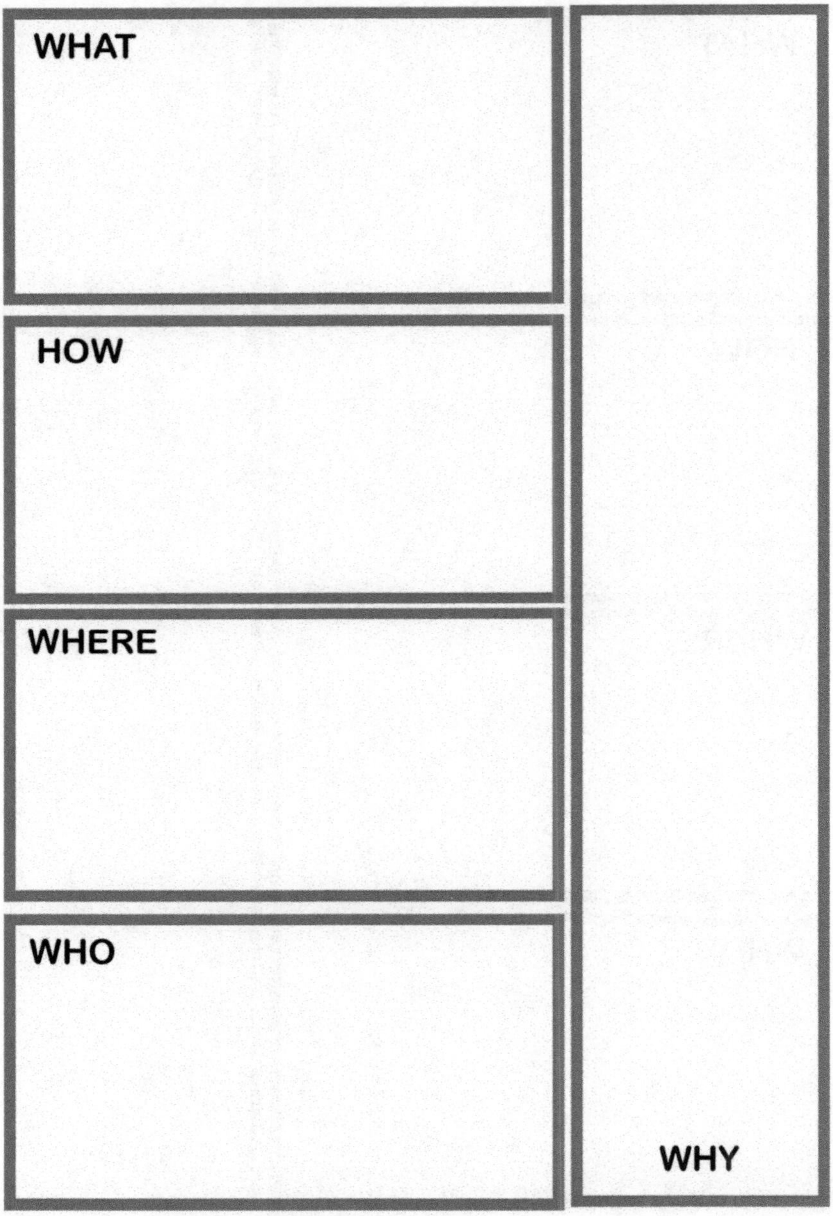

WHAT

HOW

WHERE

WHO

WHY

Figure 5.5   Your blank (creativities) canvas

INDEX